WOMEN in WARTIME

THE ROLE OF WOMEN'S MAGAZINES   1939-1945

ACKNOWLEDGEMENTS

Permission to reproduce is acknowledged:

To IPC for *Woman's Own, Woman and Beauty, Mother and Home, My Home, Woman's Home Companion, Modern Home, Modern Woman, Woman, Woman's Journal, Woman's Weekly, Woman's Sphere, Weldon's Lady's Journal, Everywoman, Britannia and Eve, Woman's Pictorial, Woman and Home, Ideal Home* and *The Farmer's Home* (supplement to *The Farmer and Stockbreeder*).

To the Lutterworth Press for *Woman's Magazine.*

To *The Lady* magazine.

And to *Home and Country* magazine.

Grateful thanks to all editors past and present.

WOMEN in WARTIME

Play YOUR PART !

By joining the W. A. A. F., you can help the R.A.F. in 51 different ways.

Among them you can :—

Fly the balloons ;
Pack the parachutes;
Forecast the weather ;
Serve as a short-hand typist ;
Keep the accounts ;
Handle the stores ;
Arm the guns on the 'planes ;
Inspect and maintain engines and airframes ;
Train as a radio-operator ;

Join the administrative side and become responsible for welfare and discipline ; Cook and cater for R.A.F. and W. A. A. F. messes ; Act as batwoman to an R.A.F. officer.

Age limit 17½ to 43 (50 for ex-service women). Enrol at any R.A.F. or W.A.A.F. Recruiting Centre (Address from any Employment Exchange) or write to Air Ministry Information Bureau, Kingsway, London, W.C.2

"WOMEN IN UNIFORM"—No. 1
The W.A.A.F.

You Will See Her In Colour On Our Cover This Month

THE ROLE OF WOMEN'S MAGAZINES 1939-1945

JANE WALLER and MICHAEL VAUGHAN-REES

An OPTIMA book

© Jane Waller and Michael Vaughan-Rees 1987

First published in 1987 by
Macdonald Optima, a division of
Macdonald & Co. (Publishers) Ltd

A BPCC PLC company

British Library Cataloguing in Publication Data

Waller, Jane,
    Women in wartime.
    1. World War, 1939-1945 —— Women
    2. Women —— Great Britain —— Social
    conditions   3. World War, 1939-1945 ——
    Great Britain
    I. Title   II. Vaughan-Rees, Michael
    941.084′088042   D810.W7

    ISBN 0-356-12887-3

Macdonald & Co. (Publishers) Ltd
3rd Floor
Greater London House
Hampstead Road
London NW1 7QX

Typeset by Leaper & Gard Ltd, Bristol
Printed and bound in Great Britain

Contents

Introduction

The purpose of this book is to show how women's magazines during the Second World War reflected — and attempted to influence — the roles that women were playing in real life.

Some people may be surprised at any study of such magazines, dismissing them as mere easy-reading for bored housewives; others may consider the wartime magazines to have been no more than extensions of the Government's propaganda machine, encouraging women to give of their best while putting up with the worst. And it is true that much of their tone and contents were no doubt very pleasing to the Ministry of Information. Indeed their principal source of revenue came from the constant stream of adverts placed by the Ministries of Fuel and Power, Food, Health, Supply, and Agriculture, as well as the National Savings Committee and the various branches of the Services.

But, as we hope to demonstrate, the magazines were a forum for discussion of all the important issues of the time. Among the recipes, beauty tips and pleas to save any scrap of paper one can find articles on everything from the implications of the Beveridge Report to the role of women in the Soviet Union, from the spread of venereal disease to the 1944 Education Act. And while these publications concerned themselves primarily with the immediate needs and interests of women they looked increasingly, as the war progressed, at the place women should occupy in the new post-war Britain.

For the historical and social background we have consulted no original sources. Instead we have relied heavily on Angus Calder's admirable *The People's War* (Jonathan Cape, 1969; Granada paperback, 1971), essential reading for anyone interested in civilian life in Britain from 1939 to 1945. The following books also provided useful background information: *Speak for Yourself*, a Mass Observation Anthology, edited by Angus Calder and Dorothy Sheridan (Jonathan Cape, 1984; Oxford University Press paperback, 1985), *Mrs Milburn's Diaries*, edited by July Milburn and Peter Donnelly (George G Harrap, 1979), *One Family's War*, edited by Patrick Mayhew (Hutchinson, 1985), and the fascinating *Love, Sex and War: Changing values 1939-45* by John Costello (Guild, 1985). The recently published *A People's War* by Peter Lewis (Thames Methuen, 1986) can also be recommended, as can the television series with which it is linked.

As for the magazines, we have had no source other than the publications themselves, since — as far as we know — this is the first study of its kind. Nearly every section has been referred to, from editorial to agony column. The only major omission — for reasons of space — has been fiction. But we can briefly say that the roles of women in short stories failed lamentably to reflect the new roles women were taking on in real life. In 50 stories examined we found 69 male characters of working age, 51 of whom were in the forces — mostly as officers and NCOs — the rest being businessmen or scientists. Of the 66 female characters of working age, some 32 were without jobs (or at least not defined in terms of employment), four worked in factories and three were in the forces (not even reaching NCO status), while the rest worked in such traditional jobs as secretary or nurse or were actresses or singers.

For the sake of convenience we have tended to refer to 'the magazines', but this disguises a number of marked differences between individual publications. Some were published for particular audiences (such as *Farmer's Home* — supplement to *The Farmer and Stockbreeder*, or *Home and Country*, journal of the National Federation of Women's Institutes); others hoped for a much wider readership. Some would have considered an agony column rather vulgar; others considered it an essential service to their readers. Some, finally, are still flourishing, while others have long since disappeared.

Although we refer to or quote from some 20 different publications, not all are equally represented. This does not necessarily imply relative merit; it can be due to no more than ease of availability of one title rather than another. *Woman's Magazine* was an excellent magazine, but its presence is due to the fact that we have a couple of dozen copies in our private collection. If this were not so it would probably not be featured at all, since there are no copies either in the Lutterworth Press archives or the British Museum.

No study of women's magazines would be complete without mention of *Good Housekeeping*. Unfortunately we are not allowed to reproduce any articles from it, so we are confining ourselves to occasional references and paraphrases as well as selective quotations in quantities tolerated in a work of critical study.

Although we are not attempting to range the magazines in any order of merit, we would like to single out three titles for particular praise, *The Lady*, *Home and Country* and *Woman's Own*. When we started our research we assumed that the first two would confine themselves to what they considered to be the narrow interests of their particular readers, but we discovered to our delight that they were both ready to deal with matters of great import in a serious and even radical way. As for *Woman's Own*, we gradually developed great affection and respect for what we consider to be the magazine with the strongest editorial team, and we were delighted to see the wartime editor, Constance Holt, contributing to the recent television version of *A People's War*. We were impressed in particular by the writing of Leonora Eyles, probably the most warm-hearted and wise agony aunt of the period. Her work, and that of her fellow advice columnists from rival magazines, will be found throughout our book. And rightly so we think, because however interesting, however committed the editorials and features, it is from the letters that we can learn the most about what was confusing and worrying the readers during that six year period which did so much to change the way that women saw themselves.

London, January 1987

Chronology

1935	Baldwin government circular on Air Raid Precaution (ARP).
1937	Air raid warden service created.
1938	
Spring	Annexation of Austria.
August	Formation of WVS (Women's Voluntary Services). Building of Anderson shelters.
September	Czechoslovakia crisis. ARP services mobilised. Gas masks issued. Plans made for mass evacuations. First barrage balloons over London.
October 1st	Munich meeting 'Peace in our time'.
November	Schedule of reserved occupations.
1939	
June-September	Evacuation of 3½ million people from cities.
August 9th	Trial blackout in London.
August 23rd	Signing of Non-Agression Pact between Germany and the Soviet Union.
August 24th	Emergency Powers (Defence) Act passed, enabling the Government to introduce regulations without reference to Parliament. Censorship imposed on overseas mail.
September 1st	Germany invades Poland. Start of blackout and of official evacuation.
September 3rd	Declaration of War. Sirens first heard. Introduction of National Service Act.
September 29th	National Register introduced. Everyone issued with an identity card.
November	Introduction of possible 'deferment' of individual workers in key occupations.
December	By end of year, 43,000 women in women's services or nursing.
1940	
January	Start of rationing (butter, bacon and sugar).

March	Meat rationing.
Spring	Women as bus conductresses now a common sight.
May	Germany invades Belgium and Holland. Resignation of Chamberlain. Churchill asked to form coalition government.
May	Formation of Local Defence Volunteers (later called Home Guard). Evacuation of Dunkirk (May 26 to June 4). Limitation of Supplies Order (cutting production of non-essential consumer goods).
June 22nd	Fall of France.
July	Tea, margarine and other fats rationed. Free or cheap milk available to mothers. By July 1st over 50% of men between 20-25 in services — over 20% of all male population.
Summer	Battle of Britain.
September	Start of Blitz (and most intense period of London bombing). Nearly 1½ million Londoners (1 in 6) made homeless between September 1940 and May 1941.
November 14th	Bombing of Coventry.

1941

February	1,370,000 officially billeted evacuees. Arrival of Rommel in North Africa (no British land victories until October 1942).
Spring	Start of Battle of Atlantic — peak losses of shipping to submarine attacks.
March	Registration of Employment Act. People now directed towards essential war work. In March this applied to women of 20 and 21. By end of year extended to women up to 30. Formation of the Women's Consultative Committee to advise on wartime recruiting 'from the woman's point of view'. Members included two leading MPs, Dr Edith Summerskill (Labour) and Irene Ward (Conservative).
April	Women's services became part of the Armed Forces (hence subject to military discipline). By June there were 100,000 women in the services.
May 10th	Last and worst night of London blitz.

June	By June 19th, 2 million houses had been destroyed or damaged; 60% in London. Start of clothes rationing (cheese, eggs and preserves also put on ration at about this time).
June 22nd	Germany attacks Soviet Union.
Summer	Start of Lend Lease food supplies from USA. Expansion of provision of day nurseries.
November	'Points' rationing system extended to include many canned foods.
December 2nd	Full conscription of women. Unmarried women between 20 and 30 subject to call-up. Choice between services and important jobs in industry.
December 7th	Japanese air force attacks US fleet at Pearl Harbour. USA enters war.
December	Vitamin welfare scheme for children — cod liver oil, later, orange juice. By end of 1941 the following proportions of women were either at work or in uniform: 80% of single women aged 14 to 59 41% of wives and widows 13% of mothers with children under 14

1942

January 26th	First US troops arrive in UK.
February 15th	Fall of Singapore — surrender to Japanese. Increased austerity measures — no petrol for private use; clothes ration cut. During year rationing extended to include dried fruit, rice, pulses, canned fruit, condensed milk, breakfast cereals, syrup and treacle, biscuits, oakflakes, sweets and soap (note that bread was not rationed until *after* the war).
May	Introduction of UTILITY clothing.
Autumn	Extension of fuel rationing — 'baths should have no more than 5 inches of water'. Ministry of Health launch campaign to make people aware of facts about VD and possible treatment.
August	Germans reach Stalingrad.
October	Victory at El Alamein.
December	Publication of Beveridge Report on social security.

1943

By middle of year nearly 3 million married women and widows were employed (compared with a million and a quarter before the war). Of those between 18 and 40, nine single women out of ten and eight married women out of ten were in the forces or in industry (note that this included Princess Elizabeth, who joined the ATS Transport Corps in 1943).

National campaign for salvage, especially paper and rubber — 'make do and mend'.

Similar campaigns for National Savings.

January	Surrender of German army at Stalingrad.
May	End of North Africa campaign.
July	Allies land in Siciliy.
August	Russians push Germans back west.

1944

By middle of year 4½ million men in forces; 450,000 of the younger women.

February	White Paper on National Health Service.
May	Butler Education Act.
June 6th	D Day — Invasion of Normandy.
June	First V1 attacks, V2s followed in September.

1945

February	Yalta Conference. Attack on Dresden.
March	British and Americans cross the Rhine.
April	Russians reach Berlin. Death of Hitler.
May 7th	Germany surrenders.
July 26th	Labour victory in general election.
September 12th	Japan surrenders.

Outbreak of War

Role of magazines

On the first day of September 1939 Germany invaded Poland. Two days later we were at war. But the women's magazines for that month carried few references, if any, to the forthcoming conflict.

It was nearing the end of a fine, hot summer; the same kind of summer that older readers would have remembered from a quarter of a century earlier, before the start of the Great War. And if you look through the magazines you get the impression that they were deliberately avoiding any possibly unpleasant topic, just as we imagine people to have done in 1914.

Ovaltine advertised itself as '*The best summer drink yet — energising, refreshing, delicious. There is nothing like it for restoring the energy you spend so freely in the Summer*'. And the articles were on such topics as 'Weekends in the Royal country cottage', 'Corsetry for a living' and 'A better cup of coffee'. *Good Housekeeping*, it is true, had a story called 'Billeted', set in the autumn of 1938, but this turned out to be a love story about '*a boy and a girl who found each other*'. And the contents of *Woman's Magazine* showed something called 'Peacemaker', but this — far from being a study of the Prime Minister — was a story by Frances Ashby, with an illustration showing how '*the smiling little Chinese tailor stood unobtrusively against the wall until the Missies had finished shouting at each other*'.

Magazines, especially monthlies, have to plan their contents well ahead, of course. And there was no way that the September issue could mention the actual outbreak of the war. But war was in the air, and the civilian population was undoubtedly aware of its likelihood, and of their possible involvement.

The British people may well have gone about their business in the summer of 1914, not suspecting what was about to take place. No such ignorance was possible in the summer of 1939, however. The Czechoslovakia crisis the year before had lead to the mobilisation of ARP (Air Raid Precaution) services throughout Britain; gas masks had been issued; the first barrage balloons were seen over London; and plans were made for mass evacuations. Since June 1939, indeed, these very plans had been put into operation, with some three and a half million people leaving the cities. And in the minds of many there was the fear that a modern war would involve the bombing and gassing of major areas from the outset. Why, only three years before, the Alexander Korda film version of *Things to Come* had foreseen a war, starting in 1940, in which London would be destroyed and the population of Britain reduced to a disorganised remnant.

But we should not blame the magazines for failing to allude to these possibilities. After all, had not the Prime Minister promised 'Peace for our time' after his meeting with Herr Hitler the previous October? If Neville Chamberlain believed that there would be no war, why should readers be caused unnecessary alarm? This, we can infer, was probably the reason for the provision of such gentle, harmless material up to the last possible moment. But when the blitzkrieg hit Poland, and the deadline for the British ultimatum was reached and passed, then the editors put their magazines on a war footing:

'*Since September 3rd life has completely changed for every single one of us. The last was a soldier's war. This one is everybody's.*' (Elizabeth Lee, *Mother and Home*, November 1939)

And as this was everbody's war the women's magazines, saw it as their duty to advise women on the role that they could best play. The editor of *Weldon's Ladies Journal* intoned solemnly:

'*Now we have been at war for several weeks. Our lives have left the quiet, privileged backwaters of peace, and have now to stem the hazardous and unruly tide of war. We are only just at the beginning ... but I want to assure you that WLJ will set itself to help the women of this Country, whether their jobs are at home or afield, to keep a cheerful heart and to maintain a calm competence.*'

Mother and Home, its stable-mate, produced an almost identical editorial (see opposite), declaring itself, in even stronger terms:

'*... resolute in its determination to help the women of this country, wherever their jobs might be, to keep a cheerful heart and to maintain a calm competence.*'

Woman and Beauty, in that same month of November told its readers:

'*If you are lost and bewildered in this strange new existence, take your bearings from us, and we will chart your course.*'

While *Woman's Magazine*, going to the army rather than the navy for its metaphors, declaimed:

'*On our part we are marshalling our forces in an endeavour to give you of our best through this Magazine from month to month, against severe odds. We believe that the mental health of the population — as well as of the martial — is important, and that we can help you to uphold that mental health and poise by giving you mental and spiritual inspiration in these pages, and enlivening your leisure hours.*'

So their role, as they saw it, was twofold — they had to inspire, but also to enliven; to help women stay calm and competent, but also to keep up their spirits. And while they could be proud of the first of these tasks, they sometimes felt that they had to justify the second. '*Do NOT ever consider us frivolous when our articles are bright and progressive*', said the editor of *Woman's Magazine*, '*it is vital to keep cheerful and bright*'. And not only cheerful and bright, it was vital to keep up appearances, to look your best, not to let yourself go whatever the circumstances.

Some editors, in these first few weeks of war, were careful to explain the continuing appearance of articles on beauty care and fashion. *Woman and Beauty*, not surprisingly, put this high on their list of priorities, though not quite at the top:

'We are the women of England, the women behind the men who go and fight for her, and the best way we can help is by being brave — brave enough to keep normal however our nerves are frayed or our lives curtailed. WE can go on being beautiful, charming, graceful. Beauticians, couturiers, dieticians, shops are carrying on as normally as possible … It is our duty to go on being women whatever the uniform we wear — we can go on being feminine — we can go on being glamorous … We can, if we will, go down to posterity as the women of England's war who were beautiful as well as brave.'

In fact the need for women to be brave, bright and beautiful had already been stated in the weeklies, before the monthlies could come out that November. Rosita Forbes, of *Woman's Own*, brought up the theme of bravery as early as the last day of September:

'In these hard times, when the utmost is required of everyone, the most important virtues surely are

MOTHER AND HOME WILL CARRY ON . . .

Our lives have left the quiet, privileged backwaters of peace and have now to stem the hazardous and unruly tide of war.

And that is why I want to send you a personal message this month.

I want to assure you that "Mother and Home" is resolute in its determination to help the women of this country, wherever their jobs may be, to keep a cheerful heart and to maintain a calm competence.

Acknowledged now as being the ideal Family Magazine, "Mother and Home" will go all out to help family life in general by featuring enchanting Stories and helpful Articles. Practical Sew-and-save Home Dressmaking and Home Knitting will appear every month and, in addition, you can rely on the increasingly popular Mother Circle to keep you up-to-date and well-informed on every angle of Infant, Child and Adolescent Welfare.

In fact, "Mother and Home" will aim at being as much the good friend of the up-to-date home-loving woman in sad days as in sunny ones.

We have our part to play in wartime as in peace. Will you play yours now?

Will you Help us to Help the Government?

Until war broke out, magazines were sold to newsagents "on sale or return." This meant that unsold copies could be returned to the publishers and the newsagent was then credited accordingly.

But war restrictions have stopped all "sale or return" business, and all periodicals published on and after October 7, 1939 are being sold to all newsagents only on a "no-returns" basis.

In other words, all magazines are supplied only on a "firm order" basis. This means that all newsagents everywhere will order only their actual known needs.

Therefore, I appeal to you to place your regular order for "Mother and Home" with your Newsagent. Simply tell him that you want him to get your "Mother and Home" each month regularly and deliver it to your home with your other papers. You will be helping him. You will be helping us. You will be helping the Government, who have asked all publishing firms to save both paper and transport.

Will you do so at once, please? Thank you.

Your Editor

courage and kindliness. Women's courage is the valour of endurance, of standing up to endless small difficulties, of putting up with things and making things do. It is immensely brave to stand up to the endless bothers and boredoms of everyday life, to keep your head — and your heart — among the added difficulties of today. That is the very best thing you can do for your country and yourself. When you are tired and sick and frightened of the future as well, and you go on working without making a fuss, then you are quite as brave as the first person who flew across the Atlantic.'*

While Ursula Bloom added, a fortnight later:

'Put a bright face on it. A sad face won't win the war, It's the bright faces that win wars. It's your duty to your country to look your best at the least possible expenditure.' (Woman's Own, 14th October 1939*)*

The editor of *Woman's Magazine*, too, while starting with the need for a woman to be '*a bulwark of strength*' went on to state that she considered it:

'… of national importance — that women today should … make the most of their looks … You owe it to yourselves, you owe it to your country, to be beautiful, brave and of a grand cheerfulness at this time, as become British women.' (Woman's Magazine, November 1939*)*

Business as usual, then. Women were to be brave and competent, look their best and stand by — or possibly behind — their men. Family life must be held together, as Elizabeth Lee of *Woman's Magazine* said that same month:

'Nothing — not even National Service — is of more vital importance than home-making and home-keeping. On it, the whole of our future depends.'

And such a role was something to be proud of. Barbara Hedworth wrote in *Woman's Own*:

'No matter what happens we are going to have the consolation that is above all the jewels and riches of the world, that we are standing at our posts just as the men are standing at theirs; we are going to know, too, of their pride in us and our pride in them.' (Woman's Own, 14th October 1939*)*

But what were these posts to be? Many women thought that, at a time of national emergency, they should be doing more than keep the home fires burning. The previous war had brought women out of their homes and into jobs traditionally done by men. Surely now, a generation of voting women later, there would be even more for women to do.

During the course of this book we will be showing how, as the war progressed, the potential roles of women were redefined. But we will start by reproducing on pages 14 and 15 an article from *Woman's Journal* by the distinguished novelist Storm Jameson from the autumn of 1939. She, like many other writers of the period, could not foresee just how long the war would last, let alone the way that women would be asked to contribute to it over the following six years.

In Courage Keep Your Heart

There is a job that belongs peculiarly to WOMEN. In our determination to do it lies the hope of the FUTURE that will surely come

WHAT were your deepest feelings when war broke on us? Surely, after the first awful sense of unreality, the bewildered sense of being part of a nightmare—you felt uncertain and restless? I have never been in an earthquake, but I have been told that the worst terror is the sense that everything is crumbling. It is as though the ground turned suddenly to water, into which you fell.

The knowledge that we were at war was much like that. After a time another feeling took its place, the feeling that nothing was worth doing. And when that passed, many women still felt it almost their duty to be unhappy, unsettled, to find no pleasure in the ordinary things.

Looking with me at a sky of extraordinary clearness and beauty, a friend exclaimed: " But how can one enjoy this perfect day, with the war going on ? "

It is natural, and it is foolish. It is wrong.

Another woman came to me in the week war was declared and said agitatedly : " I must have some work to do ! " She has three children, one of them a boy of war age who will be called up very soon, and no servant. Her husband, a delicate and scholarly man, makes very little money, and the happiness and serenity of their home has been made by her. Now, because of the war, because of her eldest boy, she has taken the sudden decision to try to get paid war work and use her salary to pay a servant.

I told her what I honestly believe, that her most honourable war work consisted precisely in keeping her home what she had made it for her children and her husband, a small cell of warmth and peace in the noisy thoroughfare of this world, a place from which they will go out with strong nerves and sound minds, a place to which they will look back, and from which all their lives they will draw strength.

The supply of women to nurse, to drive ambulances, to wear a uniform, will not run short. Some of these, if they are honest, will admit to you that life has become more exciting. It is a feeling to be ashamed of, to be guarded against, that peculiar excitement to which some women succumb in war time. It can work in them like a very subtle form of madness, so that they are no longer capable of judging their own actions. And, like my poor friend, they want to hand over the work of a lifetime to the careless hands of a servant, and plunge into something new.

Some must drive ambulances, become air wardens, take on the exhausting and far from exciting work of a nurse. But there remains a task which belongs peculiarly to women. If we neglect it, not only will no one else do it, but our country will suffer an irreparable loss. It rests on all who are not actually fighting—but especially on women—to see to it that the life we shared with sons and lovers, the life we and they valued, is not spoiled by the war. We have to save both its forms and its spirit from destruction. Not for our own sake, not because it is a comfortable and familiar possession, but for those who have left it in our charge.

Think. What use, they might say to us, what use in risking our lives for the country we knew if, when we return, it has changed and grown dull or disorderly ?

In the last war many soldiers were bitterly disappointed when they came home. They went out believing in certain things, carrying with them precise images of what it was they wanted to defend—a house, a field, even only the corner of a room in which they had left one woman seated in a familiar attitude. They came back to find that we had changed. Our feelings, our ideas had altered. One soldier wrote : " When I got back to France I felt I was coming home. There is more of England out here, in our dug-out, than there was in London."

It will be a disgrace to us if this happens again. Even in small things we must try to keep the " home " intact. It is wrong, because they are not here, to be ashamed to enjoy a clear sky. Look at it and remember it. Say to yourself : " This was given me to encourage me." Last year in this month you gathered branches of berries. Gather them now. Fill the vases with them, make the rooms look as they looked when you were not alone. Take pleasure in their cheerful beauty in your home.

One October day in 1918, when sugar was very scarce, a woman who had always, in pre-war days, made cupboards full of jam, took the whole of a week's ration of sugar and began to make a very little bramble jam. She did it as a symbol, as a sign that the war had not destroyed every custom of a normal, pleasant life. She was stirring it in the kitchen when her soldier son walked in. He had been given leave unexpectedly, and had come unannounced because he knew better than to send a telegram in war time. As he came in, suddenly he ceased to be a soldier and

By Storm Jameson

Born in Whitby, Yorkshire, educated at Leeds University, where she was a research scholar, Margaret Storm Jameson married author Guy Chapman, has one son, lives at Reading. She's been advertising copywriter, sub-editor, publisher, has written a critical history of European drama, a historical essay on the Puritan Revolution, many novels including *The Lovely Ship, Delicate Monster, The Moon Is Making, No Time Like the Present, Here Comes a Candle*. Is President of the Pen Club, an association of writers in all parts of the world. Favourite hobbies are walking and travelling.

became the boy he had been. " Oh, mother," he said, " if I'd dreamed of coming home it would have been like this, with the smell of jam-making and you stirring it !'' She had her reward.

These small things, if you cherish them, will help you with the greater ones. A thing that deeply shocked soldiers in the last war was the spirit of hate and the lack of human feeling towards the enemy that met them when they came home. The face of a young lieutenant listening to the bellicose talk of an elderly civilian was a study in distaste and contempt.

At the moment there is very little hate or talk of hating the Germans. One reason for this is that we feel they have been tricked and misled by their leaders. There is a deeper reason. " Why should I hate Germans ? '' a soldier said in the last war ; " the poor devils are just as likely to be killed as I am.''

In this war, when we look at our loved ones and dread for them the agony of an air raid, the thought springs into our minds that a woman in Germany is suffering precisely the same sharp terror.

It will not be easy, once we have seen death in our streets, not to hate. We must find some way of preventing it in ourselves. Not so much out of any hard and fast morality, not because it is " wicked " to hate, but because hatred poisons the very life of the person who gives way to it, because it is impossible to hate another human being without hating ourselves, since we are not different from other people. A woman is not comforted for the death of her loved ones by punishing other women through theirs.

Will it seem unbearably ordinary and dull to go on as though life were normal ? It needs uncommon bravery to do it. But thousands of marriages, thousands of lives were ruined in the last war because this courage was lacking. Every tiny fragment of a quiet and peaceful country that can be kept unchanged is a victory. And not, in the end, a minor one. Do not give up country walks because last year you saw the bare-branched trees through two pairs of eyes. Do not put your book down because it seems wrong to enjoy a book in a quiet room. You and your quiet room, music, flowers, eating and walking, a children's party—these are the reality you are being trusted to protect. Protect it.

You have another task. Do not accept without reflecting on it anything you hear or read. Try to discover the deep reasons why this war started. Try—above all—try to imagine what sort of a world would make it unlikely that any nation would want to start another. You can see that things have been going wrong for a long time. Try with all your wits to see how they can be put right. Right enough to last.

On what you think, on what you feel today, depends the future of this land, the future of all the children in it. Let no one tell you what to think. Think for yourself. Think as a woman for all women. You will have time now.

Readers' problems

To many readers the problem and advice pages are the most fascinating, and often the most useful parts of women's magazines. And it is from these pages in particular that we can discover what was upsetting or confusing the women of Britain, especially in the first few months of the war.

Here is a selection of readers' letters from the period:

Wet warden

'I am an ARP warden and I quite frequently arrive home with my clothes soaking wet. Having no airing cupboard or hot room I very often have to put on a damp uniform again next day and I believe that is the way to get rheumatism. Have you any helpful ideas?'

'Fill your rubber hot water bottle with boiling water and hang it on a clothes hanger, placing the wet clothes over the bottle. This will make a sort of miniature hot room and dry the clothes perfectly in a few hours.' (*Woman's Own*, 14th October 1939)

Blackout query

'Is there any window covering I can use that won't spoil the look of my rooms in the dark?'

'Tack one half of a supply of very large press studs to the window frame with tiny nails, arranging them at intervals of a foot all round the window. Then cut squares of black sateen to stretch across each window, with the "twin" parts of the fasteners sewed to the edges. At nightfall, simply press-stud your squares to each window and the result is perfect. To recognize each one for the right window, make a french knot of a different colour for each room (relating to the furnishings of the room).' (*Woman's Own*, 28th October 1939)

Snug shelter

'Our "shelter" is a small room in the basement which will have to hold ten people. Chairs for ten will take up a lot of room, but we can't stand up for hours. We keep food and a tea making outfit down there, but there's nowhere to put it and, of course, a table is out of the question. I have a couple of old mattresses that have been replaced by modern ones. What can you suggest?'

'You seem to intend to make a picnic during the hours you spend in retirement, so why not carry it out by sitting on the floor, with a few chairs for folk with stiff joints? Give your mattresses covers of hessian; you could use both flat out, and each would seat four people. If that takes up too much space, put one on the floor and one at the back to lean against. If it's practical, have a dropleaf table on the wall to take the tea things. Hang also on the wall a rack full of magazines, a first-aid outfit, heater and a tin of cigarettes. These suggestions would have to be modified if the shelter is gas-proof, or you'd use up too much oxygen.' (*Mother and Home*, November 1939)

War bride

'I got married just as war began and my husband has already been called up. People were very kind about giving us presents, and I've got them carefully packed away for the duration. As it is, I'm still living in my "digs" and carrying on with my job. The money I had intended to spend on our home is lying idle, and with prices going up it'll be worth little by the time we furnish a house. Can you think of anything I ought to buy now and keep?'

'There are several good reasons for spending at least part of your savings. It is up to everyone to make life as bright as possible, so why not refurbish your "digs" with some new covers or accessories which in any case will have to be bought when you get that house? You might as well invest in a linen trousseau if it has not been given to you. If you and your husband are keen collectors — of prints, silver or antiques — you'll find prices favourable now.' (*Modern Home*, November 1939).

Rationing

'My husband seems to have got everything out of proportion since rationing started and refuses to eat butter or bacon in case the children should have to go without. I have tried persuasion; I have shown him the butter left at the end of the week, but it isn't any good.'

'Point out to him that his health is of paramount importance; he is the wage earner and if he falls ill then you might all have to go short. Make him eat bacon by saying it will be wasted if he doesn't. You can get round some things by giving him fish for breakfast instead of bacon, and the substitutes for butter that there are.' (*Woman's Own*, 17th February 1940)

Mother urges marriage

'I agreed to become engaged to a boy although I didn't want to, as I am not in the least in love with him, and it seemed the easiest way to avoid rows every day. Now that the war is on, Mother wants me to marry him at once so that I shall be sure of a separation allowance and pension, I simply hate the idea. What do you think?'

'I quite agree with you. It is loathsome and most unfair to both of you and to the country. Be honest with him, tell him your feelings, and then show your mother that you will not have anything to do with the affair. One of these days he will find someone who will love him surely and so will you. But I beg of you not to marry for such a sordid, horrible reason as your mother gave.' (*Woman's Own*, 7th October 1939)

Weekend together?

'I have been friendly with a man who has just been called up, and he wants to spend a weekend with me before he goes. I refused, but have been told that nine out of every ten couples do this and it is silly of me. I do love him, but don't want to do this.'

Nearest Our Hearts...

Watch this page every month. Never miss it. It is a free service—human, understanding and confidential—which Mother & Home is rendering to all its Readers, to meet the emergencies of war-saddened days, through the experienced and most sympathetic personality of ELIZABETH LEE. Read her messages. . . . Write for her advice—*The Editor.*

SINCE September 3 life has completely changed for every single one of us. The last was a soldiers' war. This one is Everybody's.

Our lives having been turned upside down, we must now get busy facing up to the facts of new difficulties. When we do that, we feel we can cope with them.

From your recent letters I realize that the personal problems about which you have written to me in the past still continue to bother you—as is only natural. But there will be others now in addition—problems that have not had to be tackled since the last war, and this time in an intensified form.

I want you to know that this page stands ready to help you in every sort of way. That is what I am here for. Should your problem happen to be one in which I cannot help you personally, you can be certain that I will put you in touch immediately with whatever organization can give you the advice you need.

It is a time of stress and strain for each one of us; war is such a wretched business. I feel sure, however, that we are all determined to make the best of a black job—and that goes for more things than satisfying the local warden in the matter of our window curtains !

Most of us are having odd experiences these days, and I do want to help you to bring your lives into a line of living to suit the altered circumstances : we have simply got to adapt ourselves to new conditions.

The husbands of some readers are away, and their children have been evacuated. Therefore they are suddenly faced with loneliness. We sympathize deeply with them. They are also experiencing the big new problem of unaccustomed spare time. I would like those who are having these difficulties to write to me, giving details of their circumstances, and I will suggest something that they can do.

Others of you, in the safety areas, are being "temporary mothers" to the children billeted on you. Judging from your letters, there are all kinds of problems here, too. Even when you do your best for your small guests, some of you say that you are finding it far from easy to run your homes smoothly now. Of course, time will iron out many of these creases. You have to remind yourselves that the little evacuees have been jerked into a new and (to them) strange routine. But children generally respond to love, and I can help you with suggestions which may enable you to make them feel quite at home.

The fact that numbers of readers are now at work under one of the Services doesn't mean that their own private worries have ceased. I want still to go on helping and advising in the same way as before. So please write to me whenever you feel like it, and remember that all letters will, as usual, be treated in the strictest confidence.

My address is c/o MOTHER AND HOME, 30 Southampton Street, Strand, London, W.C.2. *Please enclose a stamped addressed envelope when writing.*

I feel you will agree that it is specially up to the housewives now—the women who have the big responsibility of holding together family life. Nothing—not even National Service—is of more vital importance than home-making and home-keeping. On it, the whole of our future depends. There can be no possible doubt about that. These women—thousands of them all over the country—are not in uniform, but they play their parts splendidly. They just go on cheerfully, many with an ache in the heart. The human touch means a great deal at this moment when, in addition to our own personal troubles, we have been forced to stand up to a black-out of peace.

NEAREST OUR HEARTS page intends to help readers to search for the bright side of that black-out, and to suggest ways in which we can keep carrying on, until that happy day when we are able to step out into the sunshine of peace.

From My Post Bag

Anxious Mother

We have let our only girl be evacuated with her school, and she has had the luck to get into a very good home. But one thing is troubling us. We live very simply in a three-roomed flat, and where she is there are many servants. From her letters I can see she is thrilled about all this. She is thirteen, and we are afraid it will make her quite dissatisfied with our ways.

YES, I understand your anxiety, but could you not look at it in another way? Your child will get advantages—think what it will mean to her health in the coming winter. Even though temporarily she may have a "swelled head," this is certain to adjust itself. I am sure you are glad that your daughter is not in a crowded home. Don't be afraid, but welcome the fact that she is cared for.

Dissatisfied

Since war broke out I have been so dissatisfied with my work as a hairdresser and manicurist. Many of my friends have gone in for war work, while I just continue to wash and wave heads, and manicure hands. It seems so stupid in these times. I have a mother to support, so I am not entirely a free agent. What do you advise ?

A WAR is not won only by fighting, but by people carrying on in their own work, unexciting though it may be. As you have home responsibilities, it may be difficult to do war work, for you might be sent to some place away. Why not go on for the time being, and meanwhile send for the handbook prepared by the Women's Voluntary Service that outlines the various openings. You might find something to do in your spare time.

Moreover, I don't consider your present occupation at all stupid. Women must still make the best of themselves, so help to keep the beauty flag flying.

Marrying Young

My sister, aged eighteen, lives with us and when on holiday, she met a nice young man. He has joined up, and does not know where he will be sent, so he wants to marry her before he goes, as they are very much in love with each other. My husband and I are against this, she is so young. But I can see it will break her heart if she is not allowed to do so.

I THINK it depends on the kind of man—and you say you like him. Why not have a talk with his parents. Then, if you and they are satisfied, I think you should give your permission. Your sister will be able to live with you, and when he gets leave, it will mean that they have this happiness to look forward to.

A Helping Hand

I have been evacuated along with other expectant mothers, and when a friend came to see me the other day, she told me that my neighbour (whom I have never liked) is helping my husband with his meals, and taking advantage of my being away. I trust my husband, but I don't trust this woman. I feel so miserable. Please tell me what you would do about it.

OF course you are worried, and I sympathize with you. I think it probable that the other woman merely tried to be neighbourly, knowing that your husband had to prepare his own food. I expect you would do the same in her place. You have other friends at home, and I suggest you ask one or two of them to help you by asking him in for a meal as often as possible. That might be a happy solution to your problem. And you have one big comfort—the fact that you know you can trust your husband. *Elizabeth Lee*

'Then don't do it. Your informant is wrong, anyway; nine out of every ten couples do not do this. Even if they did, it is your life you are leading, not theirs, and you must choose for yourself. If a certain type of hat is fashionable you don't buy it unless it suits you, do you? So why should you behave in a certain way, even if it were fashionable, unless that way suited you? Besides this — fashion is no standard by which to judge right and wrong, is it?' (*Woman's Own*, 13th January 1940)

Anonymous letter

'It came three days ago, "I feel it is my duty to tell you … Everybody else knows about your husband's friendship with …" She is the wife of his works manager. I know that since the blackout he has stayed several times at their house which is close to the factory. I'm going through hell now, I suppose I should ignore an anonymous letter.'

'No! It is a challenge. Face up to it. Your husband felt the charm of a woman — you — and married her. His senses may still feel a woman's charm. He attracted you: he may attract other women. The thought of losing him makes you see him in a new light, doesn't it? Behave in a new way, as if he were an interesting stranger you had just met, whose presence stimulated you to be your best. A new hair style, new frock, a new perfume will help.

Soon your husband will say something appreciative — or just puzzled. Your response will be "But I *like* to look nice for you, darling! And I think I'm not the only one who does. It's a jealous creature who sends a wife a letter like this!" Then show him the letter. (Notice how tactfully you transfer the blame from the alleged "friend" to the writer of the letter).

If there is nothing in it, he will tell you, and I think you will know if he tells the truth. If there might be a *little* in it, the letter will be a warning and probably stop the affair. If there is a good deal in it, the letter will make him consider the cost of the attraction — losing you and his home. The bonds of long association are strong and comfortable. Only an unimaginative wife allows them to seem like fetters.' (*Modern Woman*, February 1940)

Evacuation

Some of these matters were trivial and easy to resolve; others were serious, even harrowing. But what was of pressing concern to hundreds of thousands of women were the problems associated with evacuation.

The wealthy looked after themselves. Many thousands decided to spend the war in the USA or the more pleasant parts of the Empire, while some two million people left for parts of Britain unlikely to be targets for bombs. Hotels and guest houses began to realise that the provision of '*separate liberal tables*' was no longer a sufficient draw; advertisements in newspapers, and in *The Lady* in particular, began to mention such attractions as '*large spacious air-raid*

THE CHILDREN SHOULD

Be sent to school at the proper times.
Be encouraged to "enjoy" their lessons.
Be helped to be punctual and tidy.
Be fed at regular hours.
Have the largest meal mid-day.
Get long hours of sleep.
Be given plenty to do in the way of occupation.
Be encouraged to give you their confidence.
Learn to respect other people's property.
Remember to close gates in the country.
Grow to love animals and birds and learn all about them.
Keep the hour before bed-time very quiet.
Not be allowed to become over-excited, or they'll get out of hand.
Understand that "no" is "no."
Realise that you will say "yes" whenever you can.
Know that you expect them to do the right thing.
Try always to help themselves.
Report sore throats, spots and colds at once to you.
Be seen by the local doctor and district nurse if ill.
Be made to feel they are really wanted and useful members of the community.

shelter', just as later — when the bombing had actually begun — readers would be tempted by reference to '*quiet nights*', '*safe area*' or '*no barrage*'.

But for most people affected by evacuation there was little choice. A mother living in an 'evacuation' area (where bombing raids were expected) could choose whether to send her children or not, or whether to go herself with the younger ones; but she had no choice of where they were to go. And people living in the safe 'reception' areas had little or no control over who might be billeted on them.

In chapter two of *The People's War*, Angus Calder describes what went wrong with the official scheme. When the children arrived at the railway stations on September 1st they were put into whatever trains happened to be waiting; parties of children from the same area, the same school, even from the same family, were split up and sent to different destinations. Arrangements for receiving them at the other end ranged from excellent, via disorganised to non-existent. At best, the volunteer billeting officers would have worked out in advance which families could take evacuees; at worst, local families came and helped themselves to the children as the trains and buses arrived (which meant that in rural areas the fittest-looking children were picked first).

Little or no attempt was made to match the social backgrounds of evacuees and host families. Children from city slums found themselves faced with bathrooms and indoor lavatories for the first time in their lives; occasionally, middle-class children ended up in Cold Comfort Farm conditions.

The very first letter in Elizabeth Lee's postbag (*Mother and Home*, November 1939 — see page 17) is from a mother worried that her daughter, billeted in '*a very good home*' where '*there are many servants*', will come back feeling that her own home isn't good enough for her. And magazine problem pages during 1939 and 1940 were full of letters from people affected by evacuation one way or another.

Country too quiet

'My two children and I have come up here for the duration of the war. It is a lovely spot and the kiddies look better already. But the youngest cannot get off to sleep at night. She has cried bitterly when put to bed ever since we arrived. Presumably it is the contrast between the noise of London and this absolute stillness?'

'Yes, undoubtedly that is what is wrong. After all, exciting as the change must be to the children, it is an upheaval and must take a bit of getting used to. Be patient with the child until she has become completely at ease in the fresh surroundings. Stay with her for a few minutes at night until she regains her confidence ... By the way, give girlie a cup of warm soup or malted food last thing.' (*Mother and Home*, November 1939)

Terrified of the dark

'I was sent into the country with my two small children and simply hate it, although I am willing to do my best and stand it for their sakes. But the children are terrified of the dark and scream for hours, can you help me?'

'You should get a night light for their room ... tell them dark is sent by God, so that everyone can have a nice sleep. If you appear to enjoy darkness, they will enjoy it too, while if you grumble, they will grumble.' (*Woman's Own*, 7th October 1939)

'Billetors' had their own problems, too. What happens if the children are badly brought up?

Bad manners

'We have three evacuated children with us; their accents and manners are very bad. I feel sorry for them, but don't want my children made rough and rude. Could I exchange these children for some others?'

'I don't think it would be possible, my dear. But why give way to the trouble — why not try to remedy it? Teach the children to speak and behave nicely; if you do it gently and tactfully, and are very patient they will soon learn to be much nicer. If you are firm, both with your own children and with these little strangers, I think you will soon find them falling in with your own ways. And, above all, do remember that things are probably very strange for them.' (*Woman's Own*, 14th October 1939)

GOVERNMENT GUESTS

And there can be problems when a strange young woman comes into your house:

Worried about her husband

'I am worried and do hope that you can help me. A woman with her child has been billeted on us and she is very nice and helpful. The trouble is, my husband is the sort of man who cannot leave a girl alone. I have to go out a lot to my work and he is often in the home when she's alone here. Ought I to warn her?'

'I feel you should be as loyal to him as you can, but you might tell her, casually, that he is rather inclined to say things to women he doesn't really mean. Say you know he loves you, and that you know you can trust him but she must take care he doesn't embarrass her by paying stupid compliments.' (*Woman's Own*, 21st October 1939)

Within a very short time evacuees started drifting back to their homes. Families wanted to be together again and many people, it is true, were unhappy about the place where they or their children had been sent to. But the main reason for the collapse of the first official evacuation scheme was that no bombs fell on the cities. Why put up with separation, discomfort, — even quiet nights (!) — when there was no danger in the cities? Not all hosts were relieved to see their evacuee guests leave, however, as the following letter shows:

A homing mother

'My evacuee mother wants to go home. I can't think how to stop her. And I know that with a little trying she and I could be friends and happy together. I love her baby!'

'I expect you would both be happy once she has made up her mind not to go home. Write to the National Baby Week Council ... and ask them to send you a copy of their leaflet, *Think First of the Baby* — it sets out, quite sensibly, good reasons why mothers and babies, moved from danger zones, should stay in their reception area.' (*Modern Woman*, January 1940)

The authorities, as one can see from the answer to the letter, were anxious to stop the mass trek back to the cities. They foresaw, correctly, that the major cities were still possible targets for bombing raids. And, indeed, there was a second official mass evacuation during the period May to July 1940, just before the Blitz actually started.

That there was still some resistance to the idea of evacuating children is shown by the following item written by Rosita Forbes as late as January 1941, by which time most cities had been ferociously bombed:

'Don't fight the recent evacuation plans. They are wholly for the benefit of your children. If your children have an opportunity of going off to the country, don't grudge it to them because you will be lonely. Apart from their health — and none of you can deny that space and fresh air and country food are best for growing boys and girls — they will benefit enormously from new experiences and new friendships. They will have a better chance in the future with every single new thing they learn. But if you can bear to let your children go for a while, you will give to them a better chance than you had yourself. It is you women who will have to build up the future. You can lay the first bricks with the health and education of your children. Use the best bricks you can. Stand up to Hitler's blitzkrieg yourselves.' (*Woman's Own*, 11th January 1941)

The women's magazines not only attempted to persuade mothers of the value of the evacuation scheme, they also did their best to ease tensions between evacuees and billetors. As part of their general approach, they stressed the need for 'smiling through', 'pulling together', 'keeping a brave face on it' and 'having a bit of give and take'. In particular they published articles and stories in which the topic of evacuation was dealt with in a positive, cheerful way. Evacuee children were not the little toughs, their mothers not the tarty slatterns of popular prejudice; nor were the people in reception areas all snobbish and condescending.

In the stories, evacuees and billetors grew to like each other, with both parties ending up the better for the experience. In the feature articles there was a similar emphasis on the positive aspects of the experience of evacuation.

Nurse Hale of *Woman's Own* suggested how people who had taken in evacuee children could handle problems of home-sickness. She also warned women not to talk about the horrors of war in the presence of the children. That this could be very alarming for young children was demonstrated by the following letter written some 18 months later:

Before a child

'My little niece, who is nearly five is on a visit to us in the country and when the sirens went the other morning, I discovered her in tears sobbing out that the Germans would get her. By tactful questioning I discovered that her mother had, all unwittingly, caused this state of affairs by saying unguarded things in front of the child ...'

'Five-year olds notice and understand far more than some suppose. I do wish mothers would remember this when indulging in "bomb-talk" with friends or neighbours and guard every word they say in front of the very young. Now for the antidote. Steer clear of repressing the expression of the children's fear by telling your niece that it is silly, even naughty to be jumpy when the siren goes. Luckily, children are as responsive to wise words as they are to foolish ones, so teach her a funny name for the warning, like "Whistling Willie", and tell her that if she hears gunfire she should be pleased, because it is our kind friendly guns taking care of us and telling the Germans to go away — and keep away.' (*Modern Home*, May 1941)

WELCOMING THE CHILDREN

During recent days many readers of "The Farmer's Home" will have been helping in the reception of children from the evacuation areas. Here is an account of the arrangements made in a rural district in the South of England

—By—

MARGARET FOX

Above: School children leaving a London station for the country. Left: Little Londoners set out to view their new surroundings.

WE hoped desperately that the children would not come, because of all that Evacuation implied; but we determined that if they did come (over a thousand of them) we would do all in our power to pack interest and happiness into their days while they remained with us as refugees.

The meal that was spread in the village hall to welcome them on their arrival in shifts was our first gesture. Since then the whole of our little community, organised into bands of willing helpers, has aimed to write HOSPITALITY in large letters everywhere for them.

Some of the homes where individual children or a couple or three children are being housed are humble. But our local Council has passed every one of them as suitably equipped with bedding, and where there has been any lack of sheets or blankets to meet the emergency supplies have been loaned by others in the village and surrounding district who have them to spare. Mattresses, too, have been loaned in these circumstances.

The big old houses near the Common that had stood empty for so long have been cleaned and curtained with generous curtains that not only entirely shut

in every gleam of light but bring some comfort to the rooms. Dozens of mattresses are neatly set in rows, giving the rooms a dormitory-like air. Up at The Court thirty young refugees are being treated as guests.

MEALS AND CLOTHING

Before the crisis, few of our womenfolk would have thought they had any time to spare. Now they are running communal kitchens with great efficiency, giving several hours every day of the week, including Sunday, to the job of preparing ample meals for the youngsters. Others have undertaken to wash the children's garments, others to mend and in some cases to make-over clothes given to the Council after an appeal was made for discarded garments of all sorts suitable for converting into children's wear.

Some of the little refugees, coming from very poor town homes, would have felt the need of a top coat and extra share the classrooms of their school, classes for them and the visiting children being held turn and turn about in morning and afternoon shifts.

Every fine day organised games are

underwear badly, except for the work of our needlewomen. Stockings are mended by the score—where they are mendable!

We are glad that our own school-children are able to do their bit. They played in the playing fields, and in the evening the older school-girls are giving their well-rehearsed school plays. Teachers, on duty on Saturdays and Sundays as well as all the week, are going to teach country dances, while between whiles willing helpers are leading the children in communal singing, assisting them in that way to dispense some of their energy and keep themselves happy.

Beautiful country stretches around our village, so little town children have every chance to enjoy themselves on blackberry picnics, nut gathering and nature walks in charge of elders and in search of those mysteries of hedgerow and meadow denied to them in the town.

Some of them are already finding the country a fascinating new world, some have yet to appreciate it. But all the children are breathing pure air, are feasting their eyes on new things and, above all, are learning to be able to sing, even with the war clouds above us, "Oh, peaceful England."

Later in the war, various accounts were written of the first period of evacuation by people involved in it. We haven't come across anything by evacuees, but there were many accounts by people on the receiving end. One, written for *The Lady* in early February 1941, gives an account of how a country village sheltered a group of London women and children for a night. Another account is part of a series called 'The Village and Us — in War Time' which Fay Inchfawn wrote for *Woman's Magazine* in 1942:

The Village and Us— in War Time

a series by Fay Inchfawn

The village entertains strangers. Never has it been so crowded, never have there been so many harassed housewives, nor so many cooks giving notice!

Dᴜʀɪɴɢ the next few days our house was the scene of great activity on the part of Self and Mate. They fitted pipes, fixed up the cooker and installed a separate meter.

Self thought we should have done better to have provided a gas ring for our evacuees.

"They won't need a cooker, Mam," said he. "All they wants is a tin-opener—they lives out of tins!"

Self had already made Mrs. Nonesuch's blood run cold with his tales of the doings of "them ladies from London!" He had been called in to every house of any size in the district.

Eyebrows rose to astonishing heights, hands exhausted themselves with frequent gestures

He hinted darkly that what he had seen and heard over the week-end at the Colonel's, at the Doctor's, and at *Mavoureen* would fill a book.

When Self and Mate had gone, some of these happenings, kindly edited by Mrs. Nonesuch, were related to me—and, truly, the circumstances seemed appalling. Mrs. Nonesuch stated with conviction that if she were required to harbour such folk in her house she would immediately go raving mad!

For three weeks Mrs. Nonesuch and I went on expecting the invasion of our homes. We lived as it were from hand to mouth—with our everyday things all crowded together in the kitchen, and nowhere to keep our table linen.

Certain articles began to creep back into the china pantry "just till the mothers arrive". The vessels we had appointed for their use had got pushed into cupboards, or were re-absorbed into household use again.

One evening at a meeting concerning the distribution of gas masks I met Mrs. Willis. She was up to her neck in village matters, and was almost worn to death with arranging and changing billets.

I said: "Oh, Mrs. Wills, our mothers have not arrived."

She replied: "There were not enough to go round. I hope you were not disappointed?"

I am ashamed to say it, but I went home harbouring feelings of relief —yet, if our turn came later, we were not unprepared. Thoughts of what we had done which need not have been done, and of what we had spent unnecessarily, were all swallowed up in feelings of release. We took our dustsheets from the dark place under the stairs and put them tidily in their own drawer, and Mrs. Nonesuch did her ironing in the sitting-room again.

Hitler seemed in no hurry to attack Britain, yet Britain, including our small corner of it, was at sixes and sevens.

A village, being a small community, is rather like a family. It is almost impossible for any member of it to do anything in secret. Every action is subjected to the most severe scrutiny, and as things of a surprising nature are always happening, we are never at a loss for conversation.

As a matter of fact we do not like too many interesting things to happen at once. We prefer to come to them one by one that we may extract the full flavour from each. Such events are turned inside out and upside down —viewed and re-viewed from every possible and impossible angle—and opinions are freely expressed.

Before the war we had enjoyed a running series of excitements which, after the manner of Bateman's celebrated sketches, might have been entitled:—

The Maid Who Addressed Her Mistress as Dear.

The Strange Lady Who Kissed the Policeman.

The Missing Daughter Who Was Followed to Gretna Green.

These had been very fruitful subjects for gossip, but now they took subordinate places. Only one topic was worthy of exploitation, and that topic was—the strangers within our gates.

Bᴇʜɪɴᴅ every darkened window pane at that delectable and elastic hour known as teatime, women's heads were bent together relating fresh enormities perpetrated by the aliens. Eyebrows rose to astonishing heights, hands exhausted themselves with frequent gestures, and lips were contorted into curious shapes, but all were expressive of dismay.

The Village which had stood on tiptoe with outstretched arms, anxious to succour those distressed sisters fleeing from fire and sudden death, was going through a stage of disillusionment. Excitement had given way to everyday-ness. Entertaining strangers, who could not by any stretch of imagination be described as angels, showed signs of becoming a wearisome performance.

Dejected-looking women with prams, and strange hair, were seen wandering up and down our steep lanes. They complained bitterly of the absence of cinemas and shops. There was not, they said, even an air raid shelter. One of them stated solemnly that she did not want to see another green tree as long as she lived.

These women were, most of them, small and sharp-featured, very quick at the uptake, noisy in laughter, and with—to us—a strange intonation in their speech. They had been suddenly transplanted from their usual environment; they had none of the amenities which had in the past kept them happy and interested from day to day—no cheap stores—no street stalls—no fried fish shops.

They found the country food "very dear" compared with that of the cities. It was true they could now obtain milk straight from the cow, and vegetables straight from the earth. But these quick little women liked such things better out of a tin. Why should they buy raw fish and have to fry it? Or raw vegetables and have to cook them? Why should they make milk puddings and have to wait while they baked? When a tin-opener could do nearly all their work for them, and made next to no washing-up?

It was not easy for the Village to feel any sympathy with such an outlook, and Mrs. Briggs, an elderly widow who had a boy and his sister billeted upon her, went to Mrs. Wills one evening with a sorrowful tale.

"They keeps asking me for biscuits which I haven't got, and for tinned milk which I don't hold with. I've brought up eight," said Mrs. Briggs tearfully, "and made 'em eat what was on their plates, but these have got me beat, Mam, and there it is."

Mrs. Wills sympathized with the difficulties, remarked on the greatly improved appearance of the children, and sent her away with a flush of gratification on her cheeks. Yes, she would try again, and, maybe, in time she would get them into the way of eating nice greens and proper gravy.

To Maxwell and his wife Mrs. Wills sent three little girls, who addressed them as Uncle and Auntie, and made themselves thoroughly at home. Mrs. Maxwell mothered them, and every week a letter of gratitude was received from the children's parents.

Of course, everything was not plain sailing. The little girls had their small accidents and ill-nesses; washing for them and cooking for them took considerable time. Mrs. Maxwell was kept busy ministering to ear-

Mrs. Maxwell mothered the three little girls who were sent to her

aches, toothaches and sore throats, and Maxwell often went down in the night to get the little evacuees a drink of warm milk, or a biscuit or two, to send them off to sleep again.

Mrs. Berringer, who lived at the big house opposite, and who employs Maxwell when Michael does not want him, was not quite so fortunate. She took in a stout, loud-voiced woman with two boys. Mrs. Berringer supplied vegetables and allowed numerous privileges, but the visitor intimated that she quite thought the Government would "find" everything for her.

When it was explained that the butcher and the grocer must be paid for the goods fetched, the stout woman, with a great flow of language, blamed Mrs. Berringer for the Government's deceptiveness! The two boys trampled over the begonias and poked the tame rabbits with sticks. They made queer faces at the cook, and spoke insolently to her, and then one Sunday morning when the family were at church, the stout woman's husband arrived with a car and took her and the two boys away.

MRS. NONESUCH was often in request to help to receive newcomers at the Village Hall. A great lover of children, she was an ideal welcomer of the shy and the homesick. She told me many stories of the pitiful little suitcases she unpacked, which contained badly washed and shrunken underwear, sadly in need of mending; of pretty and engaging mites who were quickly pounced upon by foster-mothers; of belligerent and none too clean little persons who were with difficulty provided with billets.

It was not an easy thing to be a billeting officer, and I view with veneration the people who undertake this difficult task. I think that out of all of them, Mr. Pedlar must be given the palm for showing tact, self-giving, and sheer goodness of heart when confronted with strange and harassing circumstances.

No one knows better than he the curious dilemmas which may quite suddenly arise when persons totally unknown to one another have to live under the same roof, and often in the same rooms. Mr. Pedlar has been fetched at all sorts of odd times to deal with queer customers, and to smooth down indignant house-mothers. He has been obliged to read the Riot Act as loudly, and as fiercely, as his kindly nature will let him.

This he was compelled to do in the case of Erbie's father.

Erbie's mother and Erbie an infant of fifteen months—were placed with Mrs. Tubbs. Erbie's mother went out one morning and did not return. She was seen boarding the London train.

Erbie's father, who appeared to have made a habit of stealing motor cars, was in prison for his last offence, and out of pity for "the little dear" Mrs. Tubbs agreed to look after Erbie. She had been doing this for some time, when late one night Erbie's father arrived in a car—also stolen—in search of his wife and child.

He was the worse for drink, and he was very abusive when he discovered his wife was not there. He insisted that Mrs. Tubbs must put him up. Mrs. Tubbs sent for Mr. Pedlar, who took Erbie's father in hand, and after administering the sobering influence of a strong cup of tea, miraculously found a room for him. The next morning he took Erbie's father to make his apologies to Mrs. Tubbs, and the situation which had seemed insoluble cleared up.

But many of Mr. Pedlar's experiences have been less sordid and much happier than this. One evening in the late autumn he took an elderly woman to her new home. She was to stay with Mrs. Thorn, and Mrs. Thorn's house stands in a lovely garden. Carrying her small case for her, Mr. Pedlar opened the gate and the elderly evacuee stepped inside. She looked around her with rapture—gazing at the Michaelmas daisies and at the brilliant dahlias, she exclaimed: "This here is just like my first place of service."

The old lady's contentment increased when she discovered that Mrs. Thorn had now only one general helper and that there were plenty of jobs to be done. This elderly stranger rubbed brasses, polished silver, did a good deal of washing up, and made herself responsible for preparing the vegetables. Each time she sees Mr. Pedlar, she says the same thing with the same expansive smile: "Ain't it lovely for me? This is just like being in service again."

THERE was, I remember, some perturbation among those who did the welcoming when out of one of the buses drawn up in the narrow lane stepped a woman whose face was the colour of parchment, and who carried two babies in her shawl. Twins! They were eleven weeks old, and two other children, Rosie and Ettie, were holding to their mother's skirts and sniffing.

Who was there who could and who would put up five? Mrs. Wills' comely face was puckered up with the problem of where to place them, when Miss Ventnor and Miss Watts offered to take them in.

The kindness of these two friends cannot be properly estimated until one remembers that they are two not-so-young gentlewomen who came to our village a year before the war, for the sake of quiet, after years of unrelenting work in the mission field.

Their house is one of those inconvenient places where steps and stairs abound, and which only by extreme tidiness can be kept in any sort of order. Miss Watts and Miss Ventnor gave the mother of the twins the lower floor of their house. They possessed only one spare bed, and for that first night they were put to great shifts to find sufficient bedding, and to manage sufficient food, for it was early closing day, when our grocer shuts up at one o'clock.

The tale of the twins spread far and wide, and the heart of the Village was moved with compassion. Almost every woman who had baby clothes put away found something for the service of the twins. The mother, wearing a blue coat and hat—given by Mrs. Wills—began to push a pram—given by Mrs. Brendon—up to the shop. Rosie and Ettie in red tam-o'-shanters and leggings—knitted by Mrs. Ellison—appeared at Sunday school.

Miss Ventnor and Miss Watts spoke eloquently of the mother's gratitude, and of the increasing prettiness and responsiveness of the twins. Of their own discomfort, want of peace and privacy they said nothing. These two ladies interpreted to the Village something which found a lodging place in its heart.

Indeed, it seemed impossible to set a limit to the goodness of spirit shown by Miss Ventnor and her friend. The mother of the twins pined for her two other children, and her hostesses suggested they should be sent for. Eventually the woman's husband put in an appearance, and he, too, took up his abode with them. He was a handy kind of man, and soon we heard he was doing the garden, mending door handles and putting washers on taps.

After a while he got regular work in Broadwater and moved there with his family—a very different family from the one which had first arrived in the village. The twins, so fat and so lively, able to chuckle and to make happy, bubbling noises; Ettie and Rosie chattering and singing; and the mother herself had regained a sprightliness of which she showed no sign that dour afternoon when she stepped out of the jolting bus.

THINKING of this family reminds me of the history of the seven. They began by being only two. Emma, red-haired, with shrewd, inquisitive eyes, and an air of never being gainsaid, was evacuated with her small boy of four to the little old town of Broadwater. Unknown to the authorities, she returned to London and fetched her sister Maud, and Maud's two little girls. Emma also collected her father and mother, a knowing old couple, seventyish or so.

These she brought back to the little old town, where the authorities groaned. Emma had been evacuated under the Government scheme, but these relations of hers had not, and accommodation could not be found for them. So the seven were put in the Town Hall for the night.

The next day the Evacuation Officer telephoned to our Mrs. Wills enquiring whether accommodation could be found in the village for seven. After scouting round Mrs. Wills decided that it could.

When Mrs. Nonesuch returned as usual to get our supper, we learned that Emma and Emma's little boy were billeted upon her. She would have to hurry home to get supper for them. Maud and her two children were settled in at Miss Moxam's, and Grandpa and Grandma were lodged up Corkscrew Hill, next door to the Maxwells.

That all sounded very well. We knew Mrs. Nonesuch would do her part, and good-natured Miss Moxam is the farmeress of the village. Her cows are the cleanest, silkiest-coated creatures, and we thought Maud exceedingly fortunate to be sent there.

Mrs. Nonesuch arrived the next morning, and Bunty and I leaned over the banisters and said: "Well?"

She looked up from rubbing the hall and began to laugh.

"I got their supper all ready and kept it hot until ten o'clock, and then Emma came to the door crying, to say she wasn't coming—all the seven of them were spending the night at the Village Hall."

Mrs. Nonesuch began polishing the front door knocker, knocking it with a kind of accompaniment while she talked.

"Emma didn't like her father and mother (knock-knock) being away up the hill, so she went and fetched them and their luggage down to Miss Moxam's (knock-knock), and she took her own luggage and her boy there as well.

"Miss Moxam wasn't there at the time, but Emma had everything figured out (knock-knock). They would all seven live in one room, and be no trouble to anyone; but Miss Moxam came home just as they were dragging the bedclothes on to the floor, and Miss Moxam went straight to Mrs. Wills, and she came down very upset indeed, and she took the seven to the Village Hall, and they had to sleep on the floor, as they said they wouldn't be separated, and there was nowhere else."

We felt very sorry for this united and distracted family. We also felt very sorry for Mrs. Wills, who had had so much trouble, and had not given satisfaction. Then the almost miraculous happened. Mrs. Fernley offered her furnished cottage for the use of the seven.

We—by which I mean the Village—gasped to think of their good fortune. For Mrs. Fernley's cottage was not just a cottage—it was *the* cottage.

In a village which has many beautiful homes, each in its own setting, Mrs. Fernley's home is something quite apart. Standing high upon the hillside, its foundations set quite literally upon rock, *The Chantry* has a beauty which is clear-cut and austere. Cars cannot approach very near to it —visitors must climb the rocky path, which gets steeper as it ascends.

The garden has to be entirely a rock garden, there is nothing softening nor accommodating, no pandering to easy ways. But when, more or less winded, the climber stands at the top and sees the view across the Frome Valley, he knows why the monks chose this place as a haven where they might turn their eyes away from the works of man, and look continually upon the handiwork of God.

Within a stone's throw of *The Chantry* stands the cottage. It had been a garden house for the young Fernleys, and a most delectable playhouse, but on the outbreak of war Mrs. Fernley, in collaboration with Mr. Flower, had the cottage made habitable, with special amenities for bombed-out mothers and their children.

Of this cottage the seven evacuees were very glad to take possession, and Mrs. Fernley, who is young, charming and beautiful as well, acted the part of Lady Bountiful.

Vegetables, cooked dinners, clothes for the children, and countless other benefits were showered upon the seven. Grandpa, who appears to have been rather a humorous old man, began to do a little weeding in the garden.

He and his Missis might have been the originals of one of George Belcher's sketches. Grandpa had wild hair and a moustache, baggy trousers and a wink. Grandma liked to sit by the cottage fire with her large arms folded over her capacious bodice.

Mr. Fernley paid Grandpa for working in the garden. The Village said he received a pound a week to do a little how and when he liked, and stared half enviously to think of such good fortune.

But in spite of everything that was done, the seven were not happy. One would have thought that they were, as the Village said, "on velvet", but the Fernleys found when they got up one morning that the seven had thrown up the sponge and were gone. The village was not their home and never would be

ALL these weeks the war against Poland had been proceeding—said the German High Command—according to plan; and that plan included the most barbaric and dastardly attack upon Warsaw. The Poles, in spite of valiant resistance, were crushed. We did not know then how ruthless, how devastating, how invincible mechanized forces could be against a people ill-prepared to meet them.

In the autumn the Queen of Holland and the King of the Belgians issued a joint peace plea to the belligerent powers. But the war went on, and the Village, like the rest of the country, was in for a difficult time. Evacuees kept coming and going. The little houses and the big houses were alike invaded. Those who were not harbouring Government evacuees were giving refuge to relations from danger zones.

The village had never been so crowded; never had there been so many harassed housewives; nor so many cooks giving notice. Circumstances were very hard all round in that first winter of the war.

I have been asking myself why it was that with so many good intentions, and with so much real sacrifice, things in the main turned out so awkwardly for so many people.

Part of the trouble was, I think, that nothing in the least sensational happened.

There was no sudden air attack upon London.

There were no breath-taking, fearsome odours of peardrops or geraniums to justify the troublesomeness of carrying gas masks.

There were no parachutists for the valiant L.D.V.'s to shoot at sight. Our leaders counselled us to look upon this interlude as the lull before the storm. They entreated us to remember that Hitler's attack upon the British Isles, airborne or sea-borne, or both together, might occur at any moment, but in spite of these warnings there was on the part of the evacuees a determined trek towards home.

When the village was almost deserted again, when the little houses and the big houses had only their own families to shelter, there was a distinct feeling of relief. But there was something else as well—the Village felt a disposition to recall the good points of the departed guests.

The Government had asked a hard thing—it is not easy to share one's own fireside indefinitely with anybody. But those who were least able—so it seemed—were the ones most willing to show the true Samaritan spirit.

In that season of testing our Village, so easily moved to compassion, and also to impatience, learned lessons which could not have been learned in any other way.

(*To be continued.*)

Carrying her small case for her, Mr. Pedlar opened the gate and the elderly evacuee stepped inside

Blackout time

While problems of evacuation concerned a minority of the British people, no-one could escape the blackout. The government was prepared for bombing raids from the outset of war, so the blackout was imposed on the evening of 1st September 1939, the day on which the ultimatum was delivered to the Hitler government. Street lights went out in towns and villages, and neon signs disappeared for the duration. No light could shine from any building after dark, and families had to spend several minutes a night making sure that the blackout was effective.

Blackout curtain material soon became difficult to find, and extremely expensive. Since any chink of light showing through a curtain was likely attract the attention of an air raid warden, the magazines soon started to advise their readers how to survive without breaking the law. Two such tips appeared in *Woman's Own* on 28 September 1939:

'Take a half pound cocoa tin and cut a hole in the lid the size of your electric light fitting; then fix the lid under your shade and hold it in place with a bulb. Cut a small hole in the base of the tin about an inch in diameter. You can easily fit the tin over the bulb into the lid every evening and you will get a beam of light sufficient to read by if you sit under the light, but the rest of the room will be in comparative darkness.'

'To stop bulbs from shining through curtains, take a block of Reckitts Blue and mix it to a cream with a drop of water. Paint your electric bulbs with this. Incidentally, the blue can be washed off instantly when the war is over.'

One wonders how many people followed these tips; and if so, did the blue last until 1945?

FATHER : No, dear, no! You're holding it all wrong!

Walking or driving in the blackout proved very dangerous, and the numbers of people killed on the roads doubled that September. Because of this the government allowed some relaxation of the original, severe restrictions including the use of dimmed torches and masked headlights. By October various products to help reduce blackout danger were being recommended in the magazines. *Woman's Magazine*, on a page of general tips, mentioned two such items:

'Lumic' arm band
'A new device for personal safety during blackout nights has just been put on the market. It is known as a "Lumic" Plastic Light Arm Band, and consists of an arm band half an inch wide which emits such a strong luminous glow that it illuminates adjacent objects two or three inches away from it. It is by far the strongest luminant that has been discovered. It is clearly visible at 25 feet, and is an essential safeguard that everyone will immediately appreciate the wisdom of wearing.'

For safety
'The necessary street lighting restrictions make it imperative that all approaches to one's house should be clearly marked. It is, therefore, a wise precaution to whiten front steps, kerbs, path edgings, garage runs, etc, with "WHITE CARDINAL" POLISH, which gives an intense whiteness to all stonework, and makes danger spots clearly visible on the darkest nights.'

Despite the use of such products many people, not surprisingly, were reluctant to brave the streets after dark. One woman wrote to *Woman's Sphere* in December 1940 complaining that her fiance wasn't prepared to drive out to see her after dark, and she received a well-deserved rebuke:

'We can't see each other during the week, and my fiance has now suggested that I should spend my weekends with his people. Apparently it's not worth the effort of coming to see me, what with the blackout and the distance between our houses. We have so little time together, as he usually has to work on Saturday and Sunday, that I think he might try to arrange something, especially as he has a car to make it easy.'

'Aren't you being rather selfish? After working long hours and a seven-day week the last thing you want to do is go driving around in the black-out. Apart from anything else, it's highly dangerous when you're tired. Do try to see his point of view.'

Not everyone chose to stay at home, however. Within a few months, in fact, cinemas, theatres and dance halls (which had at first been closed down) were even more popular than in pre-war days. Nevertheless there were very many who hesitated to step outdoors after dark.

It was for people such as these that the magazines printed suggestions for ways to enjoy yourself at home. 'Books to Brighten Black-out Evenings' was how *Woman's Magazine* renamed a regular feature (one recommended novel being *Mrs Miniver*, by Jan Struther, whose eponymous heroine was to stand as the most typical of British women in wartime).

In the same section was an advert for Harrap's *Black-out Book*, described as:

'... the perfect companion for Black-Out evenings. It contains amusement and interests for the whole family ... There are problems for Father, quiet corners for Mother, puzzles and things to make for the children ... and humorous odds and ends to suit the mood of everyone.'

You could, for instance:

'Look out the best and jolliest of your holiday snapshots, then buy a cheap papier maché tray and a pot of strong glue. Paste the snaps in the tray so that they overlap — not in rows or diagonally — but haphazardly here and there with the best bit of a snap showing, it is best to trim the snaps so that there is no quarter-inch border showing. Finally give the tray 2 coats of good colourless varnish.'

Woman's Magazine, from which this last tip came, tried to suggest how people could still keep up a social life without having to venture out after dark. In November they wrote:

'Take this question of entertaining. Many people are now inclined to say: "I never see any of my friends nowadays; no one wants to be out in the streets when everything is pitch dark." Well we must evolve a new technique of entertaining. First and foremost, why not get into the habit of asking folk to make a habit of "stopping the night" when they come over to see us in the evenings? This would save all question of groping about in dark streets, and of the risk of being held up by delayed road or rail transport.'

During this first winter of blackout much, and not just the entertaining, was new and makeshift. The blackout material was often unsuitable, having been bought in a hurry, while the heavily draped rooms were stuffy. In many houses, in fact, only the main rooms were blacked out, leaving people creeping along hallways and corridors. By the following autumn the magazines were full of practical suggestions for ways to live more comfortably with the blackout. There were detailed diagrams showing how to make pelmets so as to avoid light filtering through the top of the curtains; extractor fans were recommended, as well as miniature Miner's Lanterns for moving around the uncurtained parts of the house.

By the time the bombing started, careful families had their blackout precautions taken care of. Not only that, many homes had been equipped with some form of shelter.

The best known of these were the 'Anderson' shelters, named after Sir John Anderson, the Home Secretary (a reconstruction of one can be seen in the London Museum, equipped with contemporary furniture, books and so on). Even before war broke out over a million of these had been given free to families below a certain level of income; the number was to rise to over two and a quarter million by mid 1940.

The Anderson was cheap and relatively easy to install. The main drawback was that, although

originally planned for the inside of a house, it had — due to a design fault — to be put into a garden; and few working class families in the big cities possessed gardens.

Another problem was that these shelters, though quite effective as protection against blasts, failed to keep out the noise of bombs and anti-aircraft fire. And eventually, as steel became scarce, the government began to concentrate more on providing public shelters.

Many families, particularly the middle class, preferred to convert a cellar or strengthen an existing room. Soon, inevitably, the magazines began to fill up with suggestions for how to make the shelter that bit cosier. And in the run-up to Christmas 1940 suggested gifts included thermos sets, roll-up mattresses, sleeping bags and lighting and heating systems.

Anything that could make life more bearable during the Blitz was welcome, and 'shelter tips', such as the following from *Woman's Own*, began to appear regularly:

> *'Cold in your shelter? Miss your morning cup of tea? A woman told Miss Ellen Wilkinson she lights two candles inside an inverted flower pot and puts the kettle on top. It's boiling by morning and gives enough heat to warm the shelter.'*

But before the shelters were put to use, before the bombs actually began to fall, a great deal of waiting had to be done.

Phoney war

The waiting period eventually became known as the 'phoney war', a term invented by the Americans and later adopted in Britain.

Both government and people — as has been noted — had expected the war to affect mainland Britain early on. And the sight of our ally Poland being snapped up by the Germans '*blitzkrieg*' strategy (literally 'lightning war') did nothing to dispel this assumption (the Polish Air Force barely lasted two days). But by the early spring of 1940 the war seemed to have ground to a halt.

Poland had been divided up between Germany and the Soviet Union by the end of September, and the Soviet invasion of Finland was to end with the peace treaty of March 12th. Britain, meanwhile, seemed out of things.

The magazines had a hard job keeping up people's spirits and determination at this time. The initial flurry of activity had died down; most homes were well blacked-out, soldiers were kicking their heels in camp, people were drifting back from the safe areas, and the members of the AFS (Auxiliary Fire Service) spent most of their time pumping out water from flooded Anderson shelters. And it didn't help that the months of January and February 1940 provided Britain's coldest weather for 45 years.

An article by Trevor Allen, reproduced on page 27, from that frozen February advises the readers of *Woman's Own* on how to combat the frustration of waiting.

Within two months the allies had mined Norwegian waters, giving Hitler a pretext to march into Denmark and Norway. On April 12th, following an appeal from the Norwegians, British troops set sail. The phoney war was over.

The real war

Shortly before the war entered this new, active phase Trevor Allen was warning his readers not to worry too much about what lay ahead:

> *'Think of the people who worried themselves blue because they were sure London and the big cities would be heavily bombed immediately war started. They forgot the formidable anti-aircraft defences we had so resolutely built up, the barrage balloons, the coastal patrols, the bombing squadrons waiting to retaliate on German cities ... "Never trouble trouble till trouble troubles you" is a handy, ready-made philosophy for war even more than peace. If it comes we can do a lot of quick adaptation, just as we had to adapt ourselves to black-out nights and the coldest winter for half a century.'* (*Woman's Own*, 2nd March 1940)

What did lie ahead in the next few months needed all the quick adaptation the British people could muster. On 9th May a sick Chamberlain resigned, and Winston Churchill, his replacement, was far from having the confidence of the nation — to begin with at least. By the end of May the British Army had been driven back to Dunkirk. By the end of June, Italy had declared war on the allies and France — our only remaining ally — had surrendered.

What the new coalition government feared was an airborne invasion. In order to help combat such a threat, the formation of a new force was announced by radio on 14th May. It was open to all male British subjects, between the ages of 15 and 65, not already called up. This force was to be called the Local Defence Volunteers (later renamed 'The Home Guard') and by the evening of the following day over 250,000 men had reported to police stations to join up.

But there was to be no airborne invasion, or, indeed, an invasion of any kind. When the Germans struck it was through the bombers of the Luftwaffe. And though their principal targets, at first, were the airfields of southern England, in September they switched their attentions to the cities of Britain.

HURRICANE ON PATROL

The magnificent part played by the R.A.F. against Germany's numerically superior Luftwaffe will live always in the glorious traditions of the British Empire

Smiling through

Too much to do is hard—nothing to do is harder—but to be prepared is everyone's job and it's up to us to do it cheerfully

"WAITING," said the King in his Christmas broadcast to the Empire, "is a trial of nerve and discipline."

In the first few months of this war it seems to have been the job of half the nation and is there any that needs more "smiling through"?

Think of the A.R.P. squads, the First Aid Post workers, the A.F.S. men and girls, the Balloon Barrage units, the Police War Reserve. All trained and keyed up for vital emergency duties, and nothing to do but repetitive routine work devoid of excitement; little to do but wait for the "amber" and "red" warnings which would set a vast complicated machine in motion and make them feel that at last they were really "doing their bit."

I met a doctor friend recently. He had given up his practice to organise casualty-clearing services for the docks and convert pleasure steamers into hospital ships. He went into the job with terrific enthusiasm, worked day and night to get things ship-shape for any emergency. Nothing happened. After weeks of waiting he was told he would no longer be required.

"What am I doing now?" he said. "Nothing! I've lost most of my patients. I'm just hanging about, hoping for another Government job."

Another friend who flew his own Puss Moth before the war, left an important business to serve with the Fleet Air Arm. His luxury income dropped to zero; he had to shut his delightful Kensington flat and put his home into cold storage. A few weeks of training with Service machines, then monotonous waiting, waiting, waiting for something to happen.

A third friend, a commercial man, joined the Police War Reserve. I ran into him one day in his tin hat, haversack, gasmask, and civie suit when he was still waiting for his uniform. "If things had happened as we thought they would," he said, "I suppose we'd have been kept pretty busy. Now there's nothing to do except hang about and get bored. What a war!"

Neat, brisk A.F.S. girls attached to a sub-station near-by are quartered in my building. "Getting tired of all the waiting?" I asked one the other day. "Oh," she replied, "we play darts and knit!"

Make no mistake, we're all glad nothing has happened. Boredom is better than blood any day, and we can still get all the excitement we want at the pictures, thank you. But it is difficult to keep cheerful doing next to nothing if you're used to an active, working life.

I KNOW a young man who was crazy to join the R.A.F. and become a fighter pilot. After weeks of trying he was given a nice little "Reserve" badge and a schedule of abstruse mathematical books to study and told he *might* be wanted in a few more weeks—or months—hence. "I don't want to sit at home mugging up trigonometry," he said. "I want to be with the boys and get my hands on those controls!" Incidentally, I believe he also wanted to feel the inside of a nice blue uniform, the sooner the better. Well, he just had to wait.

BUT that, I suppose, is all part of the business of "smiling through." You just have to see the humour of sitting tight and doing nothing when you saw yourself in the Bomb Belt and danger areas doing the work of a National Hero. You just have to smile at the thought of donning a swagger war uniform to perform tame routine tasks which could be done equally well by a grubby gorblimey office-boy with a passion for peanuts and cigarette cards. There will be plenty of scope for heroism if the occasion arises; and no one knows when it may—perhaps before this talk has time to get into print.

Meantime, the sensible ones are putting the time on their hands to good advantage: reading books they have wanted to read for years, taking up some study-course, such as a foreign language, writing to old friends who in the past have been rather neglected, and, of course, in the women's services—knitting. I have heard of some who are studiously preparing for a new job when peace comes: learning shorthand and book-keeping, mastering the text-books of a technical trade.

They have to impose on themselves a hard discipline, for it is easy to kill time playing games, ragging, and wise-cracking with amusing colleagues when there is nothing else to do in a careless war atmosphere which tempts one to think: "Why worry? Why not have a good time?" But it can be done with determination, and bring added pride and self-respect and "power to the right hand."

There is an infinite amount of watching and waiting in the work of the Navy and Merchant Service, even in wartime, during long spells in which nothing dramatic is happening. I was once on manœuvres in a battle-cruiser in the North Sea, and noticed the amount of serious reading which helped to make sailors men of all-round knowledge and culture.

Behind the good-fellowship of ward-room, gun-room and mess there was often a mental discipline comparable to that of our Universities. In some of the cabins I saw shelves of books which reflected a very high individual taste and wide range of interest. Usually even the "hearty" type in the Navy is also a man who can converse intelligently on almost any subject. Self-culture is a part of their method of "smiling through" as well as riotous rags between rival messes and rollicking leg-pulling. That is why they are, as a body, as splendid men as you may meet in any walk of life, the Britisher at his best.

Let us forget the tedium of waiting, of drawing the black-out curtains every sundown, of longing for the return of children, and thank heaven if there is nothing graver and direr to be endured for the present, as there has been in stricken Poland and Finland.

TREVOR ALLEN.

The blitz

The magazines for September 1940 were very different from those of a year before. At that time, as the editor of *Woman's Magazine* put it:

'We had never seriously had to think of such a menace as invasion.'

And, as we have seen, they had not wanted to believe that war would come at all. But by the time the first anniversary editorials were being written, few people in Britain remained untouched by war.

Men had died trying to prevent the defeat of France; husbands and sons were prisoners of war in Germany. And during that summer of 1940 — the summer of the Battle of Britain — civilians in south-east England could watch Allied and German pilots fighting it out in the skies overhead, like some monstrous free spectator sport.

Everyday life was affected from dawn to dusk, marked by the rituals of letting in the day, then blacking it out again. Food rationing had been introduced, while goods of all types were in short supply.

Few people could take the traditional August holiday. Many were too busy; families were separated; most of the traditional south coast resorts were invasion targets, and barred to casual civilian visitors.

But not everything was gloomy, and the magazines took pains to point out what had been gained. The *Woman's Magazine* editorial printed below refers to some of them, including a greater relish for the ordinary things and an increase in self-reliance.

NEW VALUES

IT is just a year since that never-to-be-forgotten Sunday morning last September when the Prime Minister announced over the radio that this country had declared war on Germany. Although war clouds had hung over the horizon for months, forcing us nearer and nearer to the inescapable brink, and there had been preparations and plans and such visible warnings as gas mask issues and trenches dug in public parks and gardens, few of us had realized what the actuality of modern war would mean to each and all of us in our everyday lives. We had never seriously had to think of such a menace as invasion. It was even suggested by some of the most optimistic that the war would be a short one of a few months only.

Since then the grim realities have come very close to us, and in many homes bereavement has meant that family life can never be the same again in all its fullness. But now, at the end of this first year of the war, we have a moment to take stock of some of the far-reaching changes that the war has gradually made in the small matters of our daily round. We have already learned to live without a number of the little luxuries and comforts that we had regarded as essential or taken for granted—street lighting and unrestricted petrol and food. We are having to pay more, too, for very much less, and to work longer hours and then find energy for tasks of some special national urgency if our daily work is of more general character in the home or office.

As the weeks have gone by, however, we have developed new philosophies to meet them. We have grown slowly to value even small, commonplace things much more than we did. The very insecurities of life give new attraction to familiar sights . . . our garden that we once regarded as a matter of course, the sitting-room as we come into it and see a bit of fire in the evening hearth, or the outlook from the window, over to the hills, or the sea, or maybe even the city rooftops.

But as women particularly we are learning other new values; we are learning a wiser and more thrifty attitude as housewives, with a greater appreciation of the importance of planning menus for health and for avoiding waste, with an understanding of nutrition values of different foods. We are discovering, moreover, how to make our gardens productive of food as well as flowers, and to take a pride in the preparation of many home-grown dishes.

Perhaps even children may come in for their share in these discoveries of new values. We have in the past had readers couple " child care " and " beauty " articles as " superficial." Surely only superficial thought can make such comparisons of the greatest of our human trusteeships to civilization. One of the reasons given for France's tragedy was that too few children had been wanted; too few sons had resulted to defend her in her hour of need, and to uphold the great traditions of liberty for which she had so proudly stood until June 17th. " The spirit of pleasure has prevailed over the spirit of sacrifice. People have demanded more than they have given. They have wanted to spare themselves effort." We have made trite so many things by our own trite outlook. Even beauty culture and dress, if sensibly considered, have some contribution to offer to the social well-being. We certainly need urgently a new deal for families and for family life.

IN the freedom that science has given us as women from domestic drudgery, we have drifted into an escapism and an intellectual snobbery about the great fundamentals in our lives. The ideal has been too frequently the labour-saving flat from which dormitory we have chased outside pleasures that meant spending money, instead of doing anything of the least value to the community, forgetting that work is the greatest blessing that ever befell our race.

The war has brought us right back to " work " . . . work for the *common good*. It has been slowly showing us these new values to the community and bringing its own queer satisfaction, in spite of all the anxieties and difficulties. We are not being forced under an iron heel, but giving freely, according to our gifts, to the great democracy from which we have derived so rich a heritage.

We have still to go on struggling, and Mr. Churchill has promised us " blood and sweat and tears." But they are pangs of birth, of a new life, and a new era for our people. It is in the hands of women as much as men to make it so.

The Editor

The greatest gain, however, was in the way people's attitude to each other had changed, manifesting itself in a spirit of comradeship that had been noted even from the outbreak of the war. In that first autumn, two writers for *Woman's Own* used similar metaphors when referring to this phenomenon. Firstly David Garland in October:

Through the dark clouds shining
'People just don't need to be introduced nowadays. There's something about a darkened street that gives it a friendlier air than the most brilliantly lamp-lit one; and a collection of strangers in an air-raid shelter are a very different set of people from the same strangers in, say, a bus … War may be devastation and disaster, but at least it makes people understanding and helpful and human.'

Then Barbara Hedworth in November:

'Wherever I go in these darkened days, everyone I meet seems to be like a new friend. That, in my opinion, is the silver lining of the heavy clouds of war. All human beings in this country have become equal. We are no longer individuals, but part of a vast impregnable force with one aim and one common ambition — the resolve that liberty and freedom shall prevail.'

On 27th July 1940, with the invasion threat very real, the editor herself summed it up in the following words:

'It's a time to be specially kind and friendly and helpful to everybody possible — but if ever there was comfort in the thought that we are not alone it is now. We are all in it. Loneliness in anxiety doesn't exist for a single one of us today.'

But the editors couldn't foresee — even those writing for the September editions — just what was about to be unleashed and to what extent that spirit of comradeship was to be tested.

Bombs there had been already. The very first had fallen as far back as the 17th October 1939. But it had been on Hoy in the Orkneys. And it was in the Orkneys that the first civilian was killed by a bomb, on 16th March 1940, six months after the outbreak of the war.

The first bombs to land on the mainland of Britain fell near Canterbury on 9th May. Later that month, on the 24th, the first industrial town — Middlesborough — was attacked. And the first bombs in the London areas landed in fields outside Addington, Surrey, on 18th June.

During July and August there were civilian casualties as a result of bombing; but for the most part these were an incidental, almost casual, by-product of attacks on the primary targets — the airfields of southern England, or aircraft factories.

On 24th August a few German pilots, ordered to attack such factories, lost their way and bombed parts of central London by mistake. This was in direct contradiction to Hitler's express orders and — as the German leader had feared — led to a reprisal raid on Berlin the following night.

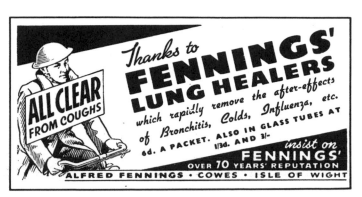
This series of raids on German soil infuriated Hitler, who decided to take counter-reprisals. It was also thought that a massive raid on London would bring out the British fighters so that the Luftwaffe could wipe them out and clear the way for the proposed invasion fleet. With winter approaching, it was time to step things up.

On the 7th September Goering, commander of the Luftwaffe, told the German people — *'This is the historic hour when our air force for the first time delivered its stroke right into the enemy's heart.'* That beautiful Saturday afternoon a force of some 375 bombers and fighters appeared over London; that evening a night raiding force including a further 250 bombers appeared. By the time this second wave had left, several thousand houses — mainly in the docklands — had been destroyed. Four hundred and thirty men, women and children had been killed and a further 1,600 seriously injured. The Germans soon abandoned daytime bombing — their losses from our fighters and anti-aircraft batteries were unacceptably high — but this still left the nights. And for 76 consecutive nights (except one, when the weather was too bad) London was raided, for the most part heavily. And London was not alone.

There is a hoary old cliche from westerns and war films which goes something like, *'It's the waiting I can't stand'*. And like all cliches it is based on reality. The following letter, written to Leonora Eyles of *Woman's Own* in July, showed what many people must have been feeling at the time:

Lost nerve
'I seem to have lost my nerve and am so depressed by the news. The thought of an air raid makes me feel quite ill; I have two children, a dog and an old father to care for. What can I do to make myself braver?'

'Try to look at it reasonably. You are one in millions and so far casualties have been very small. When you get frightened, make yourself read, or talk to a neighbour, and remind yourself that a lot depends on your courage. One thing I know: if real danger comes you won't turn a hair! You have imagination, which is a curse in some ways, but a blessing in a crisis. Get plenty of sleep and see that everyday rules of hygiene are strictly obeyed. That is most important. And if a time should come when you need courage, I am quite sure you will be equal to it and come out on top.'

And there were thousands of people fretting at enforced separation with no real danger to face. One such woman complained to Leonora Eyles in early August, but received a very stern reply:

Discontented wife
'I have been sent into the country with my two children as my husband got worried about us living in his town with air-raids. But I am bored to death — no shops, no cinema, nothing. What can I do? Should I put my foot down and insist on going back?'

'But if you do, you add terribly to his worries. Can't you find some work to do, helping a farmer's wife, or possibly doing something for evacuee children? Think of others, in Poland and Holland and Belgium, with no shelter or home, and for goodness sake call up all your sense and unselfishness and try to find a niche for yourself where you will be a use and not a nuisance.'
(*Woman's Own*, August 1940)

But when the Blitz hit Britain there was precious little grumbling. The voluntary services came into their own, with a sense of having a real job to do (air raid wardens stopped being referred to as blackout wardens very quickly). And the ordinary people felt what was often a pleasurable sense of exhilaration at the thought of danger. Most striking of all, the bombing stopped people complaining about the petty annoyances of wartime life. This was perhaps best exemplified by the much quoted case of a Clydebank woman, cleaning up broken glass and debris from her front path on the morning after a raid, who said to her neighbour — *'Well there's one thing about these raids, they do make you forget about the war.'*

In fact this exhilaration often manifested itself in a form of pride about how much *your* city, or *your* district, or *your* street had suffered compared with others. In February 1941 Trevor Allen in *Woman's Own* complained that:

'The trouble about all this competitive bomb talk is that it is tempting one to exaggerate, rather than to be outdone.'

That this tendency persisted is demonstrated by an indignant letter to Leonora Eyles some two years later:

Silly rumours
'How can I stop gossip? In a recent air raid on our town the casualty list was three; in queues and buses I hear women telling the most ghastly stories of hundreds of people killed and they seem annoyed when I burst in and tell them to go and look at the list in the Town Hall and only repeat the truth.'

'The fact is that most people unconsciously get a thrill out of repeating horrors to each other; they like to make a sensation. Few people enjoy air raids, but they enjoy talking about the dangers they have been through. It is a show-up of the dull lives they were living before the war. Keep on trying to squash silly rumours by pointing out the truth, my dear, but do it tactfully and pleasantly, or you'll do more harm than good.'
(*Woman's Own*, 16th July 1943)

During this period the magazines spent much of their time trying to help their readers cope with the demands of living with air-raids, which often meant sleepless or interrupted nights following hard days of work and shopping. Series of tips were common, like the one from *Modern Woman* in December 1940:

REMEMBER THIS ?

Noisy night? Then take odd naps by day if you can. Even a ten-minute doze in a chair helps. Train yourself to relax when you are not working; let your body go limp and keep your mind a blank.

* * *

Discipline your mind. Don't brood on the horrors of war—the best way of adding to them! Train yourself to switch your mind to the pleasant things of life. Read light, amusing books, thrillers—anything that grips your interest. And don't listen when the daily help brings in her night's bag of hair-raising "they-tell-me's."

* * *

Carry some barley sugar or other boiled sweets, or a packet of chocolate—good for the times when you have to skip a meal, or are delayed when travelling.

* * *

Never eat a large meal when you are tired out. Drink a glass of warm milk—sweetened with glucose or honey—or some other easily digested beverage. Rest for half an hour before the meal, or skip it altogether and go early to bed !

* * *

Keep your feet and ankles warm and comfortable. Wear warm stockings: shoes with thick, flexible, waterproof soles. Keep a spare pair at your office. For aching feet, lie down with a cushion or two under them: if you are sitting, put them up on a footstool— or another chair. Take your shoes off and wriggle your toes: move your ankle joints.

* * *

A pneumatic cushion, blown up as the sirens go, is a good comfort in a shelter.

And various products were advertised or recommended as being particularly suitable for Britain under the Blitz. Some were existing items — such as Bob Martin's Fit and Hysteria Powders 'to calm dogs and cats in air raids'; others were newly developed — such as INCENDEX, guaranteed to 'kill incendiary bombs in 20 seconds'.

Woman's Magazine's shopping reminders for December 1940 — nonchalantly sandwiched between Christmas cards and Letts diaries — included the following:

Protecting your home

'If your house has been hit by an incendiary bomb you will know something about the difficulties of dealing with these formidable weapons of war. You will have tested the ordinary methods of controlling them — have you found them successful? In many cases, no doubt you have, in others, no. For instance, using the stirrup-pump necessitates a certain amount of courage and steady nerves, at least three people on the job, and several gallons of water to extinguish a fire in a room of moderate size.

The best method so far produced is ... 'Chem-Control'. It is the only method which extinguishes the bomb entirely, and in half the time sand takes to smother it temporarily; its use allows close approach to the bomb for removal, and one person can deal with it easily ... 'Chem-Control' should be in every house in these dangerous times, for it will not only save the lives of you and your family, but will be the means also of preserving your possessions and your home.'

In fact, all the magazines for that December included similar timely suggestions among their ideas for Christmas gifts. *Modern Woman* was particularly rich in ideas. Those which were intended '*to please the man*' included a brandy flask and a bulletproof wallet; while those for the home ('*something useful, please!*') featured shelter bedding and a bomb snuffer.

These suggestions, it must not be forgotten, were directed at women, many of whom, before the war, would not have considered changing a fuse, let alone smothering an incendiary bomb. When we look at Chapter 3 on 'The Home Front' we will examine these changing roles further. Meanwhile let us note that the Blitz obliged many women — for the sake of survival — to pay much more attention to parts of the home which had traditionally been the domain of the man. With bombs around it was vital that everyone could, for example, cut off the gas and electricity in case of an attack. Even outside the home women were now expected to acquire such skills as a matter of course, in addition to all the traditional ones. *Woman's Own* in July 1941 claimed, for example, that:

'*... a capable secretary nowadays knows just how to deal with incendiary bombs, the exact position of water, gas and electricity mains, keeps a couple of candles in her desk against emergencies and carries a small first aid outfit in her handbag as well as her powder and make-up.*'

But the magazines saw that they had more to do than just provide tips for keeping the home and office

Smiling Through

We are doing all sorts of things we've never done before . . . and we might as well do them really well

Photo of Trevor Allen by Sasha

A TIME of ordeal is a great test of tolerance—I think most of us have discovered that during the past few weeks. Perhaps, under the strain, we have lost our temper at times, and said hasty things, and been irritated and annoyed. One of the kindest women I know, constantly thoughtful for others and inspired by a genuine religious faith, wrote me about her air-raid shelter in a large block of flats :—

"Last night, with the heightened despair which the hour brings, I felt I could not face one more session down below. Stifling air, strong smell of paint, innumerable people, including many aggressors—and most horrible of all, two equally selfish women quarrelling on the subject of whether they should or should not be allowed to talk. Utterly sordid—I nearly returned to my top flat and all its menacing possibilities."

The reply to that is : We are human beings, not angels, and cannot always fight down jangled nerves. Loving our privacy—at least at night—we hate pigging down with a crowd. Used to choosing our friends, we dislike having a horde of acquaintances thrust on us piecemeal, especially at a time when normally we should be sleeping or enjoying that good-night read.

Combine all this with physical discomfort, the din of gun-fire and bursting bombs, the sinister throb of cruising bombers that seem to be overhead, and we would indeed be saints if we could remain perfectly normal, and keep "smiling through" all the time. No one expects us to—or if they do they're just unlucky. Now and then perhaps we have to "let off steam." But it saves a heap of trouble if we can smile about it immediately afterwards—just to show there's no malice—and admit that we are usually a little comical when we lose our tempers !

THE whole thing, to me, is summed up in a story I heard of a fellow who was stung by a wasp in his garden air-raid shelter. He immediately forgot all about the falling bombs and whizzing fragments and chased it out into the open, swatting it with his handkerchief and muttering : "I'll get you, you little so-and-so !"

We are all like that. The bombs are bumping around us, but we must go and chase little wasps—the petty annoyances and irritations which really amount to nothing by comparison yet "get our goat." So long as we can see the incongruity of it all—in the end—we needn't greatly worry.

WE sat for an hour or two with guns banging away at night raiders, shells crumping overhead, that feeling of strain and apprehension you get when the din goes on indefinitely and promises to keep on all night. Said a young woman in the party, quietly : "When those people upstairs have finished shifting the furniture perhaps we can go to bed !"

I think it is the quiet ones who have proved such an asset during these difficult weeks—not the noisy and assertive. Suppose the two women in the air-raid shelter argu-

ment are of the noisy type. One will probably snap : "Stop talking—I want to get some sleep !" The other will retort : "If I want to talk to pass away the time, I shall !" At once there is enmity, hostility, and tempers are on edge.

Now suppose they are of the quiet type I have in mind. One will say : "I'd like to get some sleep, and it would be a great help if you'd talk very quietly. I know how difficult it is to please everybody in a place like this." Or the other will say : "Do you mind if we go on talking for a bit? We don't feel like sleeping. Naturally we'll be as quiet as we can."

EACH recognizes that the other has a "case," and must be considered—that a sensible balance must be struck between their respective wishes. After all, it is mainly a simple matter of good manners. Manners are not, as many people devoid of them seem to think, an artificial code of behaviour. They are just—thoughtfulness for the other person. They act as a brake when you feel like lunging out or going off the deep end. Infinite trouble, I believe, would be avoided if, whatever we wanted to do or say, we did it or said it *quietly*. If, at the same time, we can muster an understanding, friendly smile, we avoid the possibility of provocation and disarm our own tempers. It's almost impossible to be angry while you're smiling. It's equally difficult for the other person to be angry if your smile is a kind one.

During the worst raids, a dozen of us took refuge in a neighbour's cellar. We were a mixed lot—most of us would have been only on nodding terms in the ordinary course of events. We managed wonderfully because everyone tried to think of the others. If we wanted to smoke we said "Do you mind?" before lighting up. If we wanted to read we said "Will you mind the light?" and partly veiled it with a scarf. Late-comers crept in, resolved not to disturb those who had already parked down.

Above all, we saw the quaint and farcical side of our predicament, and smiled through it. No, we were not plaster saints; we simply realized the worth of—manners. They are a large part of the civilization for which we are fighting against a people who have repudiated them, with all the other finer virtues.

Next Week—Special Christmas Article by TREVOR ALLEN

Be a Success

Our popular writer has given her views on the important question " to shelter or not to shelter " question.

Rosita Forbes

YOU can't be a success unless you have enough sleep. So you have just *got* to sleep in spite of air raids.

When the guns begin in earnest, or the enemy is dropping high explosives quite close to us—then and *then only* it is time to stop work. Do you know how small the risk is ? During the first fortnight of Hitler's intensive bombing, casualties among the civilian population were one to every hundred thousand people.

I am living in a district which is constantly bombed. High explosives and incendiaries have fallen within 200 yards. Yet I have only once been in a shelter since the war began. Every night I put soft wax in my ears and I sleep through the noise of sirens and gunfire. Only the nearest bombs wake me and then I go to sleep again. So I am able to go on with my work in the daytime. Remember, this is not in the least brave, for I am only taking a hundred thousand to one chance. It's just common sense.

In the daytime it is quite easy to go on with the work—on which our chance of salvation depends—if you realize that bombs do not necessarily fall when a siren shrieks. This warning is given as 'planes cross the coast.

DO you remember I told you how one of the Foreign Ministers told me, "It's the ordinary men and women in Britain who will win the war." But we can only win it with the tools of our various trades in our hands, staying put behind desks and counters, carrying on as usual in spite of Hitler's raids. It is not the slightest use patting ourselves on the back because we "go calmly" to the nearest shelters. We can't contribute anything to victory, sitting—however "calmly"—underground. Workers are just as important as soldiers to-day. When Hitler puts a whole city's workers out of action underground, he has won as big a victory as if he had defeated a British army.

This talk is not meant for the old or the justifiably idle, nor for mothers at home with children to look after, and, of course, it is most certainly not intended for people living in danger zones, beside the sea or military aerodromes or any other objectives likely to be bombed at any second. It is meant for the women who work in offices, factories, munition plants and mills, as clerks in Government departments, and secretaries or forewomen in businesses. At this moment while I write in a small top room with windows looking over the roofs of London, there is an air raid on. I can hear the guns in a neighbouring park. For a minute I saw two German planes like enormous silver fish dip into and out of a cloud not so very far above the balloons. Previously, there had been one loud thump when a bomb dropped and two farther away explosions. So you see I *am* doing myself what I advise you all to do.

I know it is not your fault when you are hustled into cellars by the heads of your businesses. But remember this war may go on for three or four years. There may be one or two or half a dozen air-raid warnings a day during all that time. Hitler, after his success of the last weeks, will certainly do his best to go on slowing down our work—because he cannot otherwise defeat us. So every one of you should make up your mind that you won't stop working—just to please Hitler ! And in time the Government will be influenced by your own sense and courage. We are terribly slow in England. That is why we have lost so much to our enemies in the last year. But if every English worker is determined to carry on through raids—as our brothers, sons and husbands in the fighting services and all the women enlisted as auxiliaries are carrying on—then the Government and the heads of factories and businesses will have to face the real situation. Germany is *not* wasting one moment of time. We are wasting millions of hours. Our worst enemies at the moment are not German bombs, but our own sirens. If you have nothing serious to do, by all means take shelter. But if you are on a job of work, you are a soldier. Carry on !

going; their job was to keep up the morale of women fighting on the Home Front at this time. And on page 32 we print two examples of articles designed for just this purpose, both from the period October-December 1940.

Courage

There was much talk at this time about the nature of heroism. In 'traditional' wars groups of men go off and attempt to hack each other to bits, blow each other up or whatever. In those circumstances 'heroic' as against 'non-heroic' (or even 'cowardly') behaviour is fairly easy to define. The mechanism appears to be more or less constant; the only variable is the form that the means of slaughter takes. But when war comes to the civilian population, and on a daily basis what's more, then we are forced to redefine what is meant by heroism.

'*Never was there such a call for the heroic spirit as in these critical times*', declared *Woman's Own* on the 7th October 1939. And to help their readers decide if they were made of heroic stuff they even gave them a little check-list. If you answered 'yes' to the majority of the questions you were '*already mentally and spiritually armed for any eventuality*'.

By July 1940 the magazine was making a clear parallel between the war proper, the traditional war, and what had to be endured at home:

'You may be thinking it's a bit difficult these days. If so, it is all the more worthwhile. There are two wars to be won. The first is in the hands of our soldiers and sailors and flying-men who who seem to be able to take on any odds and come out on top. The second war is at home. It is very hard because — in many cases — it is one of discomfort rather than danger. We cannot hinder the men who are fighting by giving way to nerves, or grumbling ... Every one of us has got a job. It is to keep as fit as possible, spiritually and physically. If you must criticize, criticize yourself. We've got to be calm and assured and full of sense. The things that are happening now will not last forever.'

And Trevor Allen, that same month, drew attention to the calm courage of the men being evacuated from Dunkirk a few weeks earlier and said that:

'The least we at home can do is emulate the cheery courage, the defiant optimism of the fighter on whom falls the brunt of the worst that's happening or may happen. If he can smile through hell itself we should be able to smile through a bit of bad news, which is probably no more than a temporary setback.' (Woman's Own, July 1940)

So it was women's job to be as courageous as their menfolk, even if there was little actual danger. But within a matter of months the danger was very real, and Rosita Forbes felt that she had to tell her readers that:

'Being afraid does not mean you are a coward. Just realise there is another self way down in each of us in which you can do everything that is asked of it — quite extraordinary things that you would not have believed. When Hitler's doing his worst overhead we can carry on. We have an ally, another self, strong and cool, which is our real self — somewhere inside us.' (Woman's Own, 9th November 1940)

In January 1941 (by which time the bombers had attacked not only London, but Coventry, Bristol, Birmingham, Southampton, Liverpool and a dozen more cities) Ursula Bloom in *Woman's Own* could write that:

'For the first time in the history of the world ... the women of a nation are fighting in the front-line trenches.'

And magazines were happy to print examples of individual heroism, such as the following from the *Woman's Magazine* editorial in November 1941:

'I must tell you something about a reader that, I know you will agree, does testify to the magnificent fighting spirit of the women of Britain. She lives in an area which has been bombed, so much so that practically all the families have moved out of the road. She is alone most nights, her son fighting and her husband on ARP duty. One night when there was a big blitz and the guns were unusually heavy, her flat received such a shaking that every plate on her dresser was thrown to the ground — and not one was broken! Instead of stacking them up in a pile as so many of us might have done, she put them back in their original places. This happened again and again, and each time her anger against Hitler increased and she became more and more determined that she would not give in, but she would put these plates back in their right places! That took some courage and determination, don't you think? And it is that sort of courage that is going to help us win through.'

So common were the words 'courage' and 'heroism' to denote matters of ordinary endurance that they were in danger of becoming devalued. It may well have actually reached that point in a *Britannia and Eve* feature in December 1940 on furnishing 'Homes for Heroines', where they claimed that:

'In such times as these, it is a very special sort of heroism that incites a woman to continue placidly, even stubbornly, making plans for a home and a future that are so heavily obscured by the clouds of war.'

It was up to Rosita Forbes, with her usual commonsense, to write that same month an article for *Modern Woman*, in which she pleaded for '*less cheap talk of heroes and heroines ... All we want is to be allowed to get on with our work as hard and as fast as we can.*'

And so they did, in spite of all the bombs. But bombs were not the only thing that the women of wartime Britain had to face. There was rationing, of food, petrol and fuel; there were long queues, often after a hard week's work. And there were constant pleas to scrimp, save and salvage; all matters which we will be looking at in the next chapter.

Home life

'Never more in our lives, perhaps, have our homes meant more to us.' (Woman's Own, 20th April 1940)

The Second World War came into everyone's home, and by the time it was over, one in every three dwellings had been damaged or destroyed. Families separated, or shrank — through conscription, evacuation or death. Families moved or were expanded by having others billeted on them. No family was left unscathed, even if it was only the oppressive blackout that closed the household in.

The women's magazines helped to lift spirits and offer assistance to the housewife who was often left to fight alone on the Home Front. The best way to cope was to make yourself and your home as cheerful as possible, especially in the long blackout evenings of winter. The most touching homily came from *Mother and Home*, in January 1940:

'Make your home as bright as possible. In these days, above all others, home is your biggest asset. And you do want it to be a cheery spot for the dear ones to come home to, don't you? You may be missing the children, but you can comfort yourself by remembering that they are safer anyway — so hang onto your courage, and, if possible, to a laugh. Remember, you used to teach your child to turn up the corner of her mouth to make a pretty smile? Well, do the same yourself today — and every day of 1940.'

Home life should appear normal even if you had to hide your sorrow. The same magazine gave a tip to mother:

'Wash away traces of tears with warm weak tea — a secret which saw great grandmamma through many a crisis.'

The practical housewife's first duty was to equip the home with a well-stocked medicine chest (the number of accidents sustained in the home and in the roadway due to the blackout, was appalling). But she also needed a good set of tools — and the knowledge to use them. For with the man of the house away, and most electricians, plumbers and so on transferred to Government work, you had — as *Everywoman* said in October 1941 — to learn to *'be your own handy man'*. The magazines explained how to carry out minor repairs like changing a fuse or an electric plug and made it clear that such tasks were not beyond a woman's competence:

'Many women have a nervous dislike of anything to do with electricity, but there is no need for this; as long as you take the proper precautions when doing repairs or handling apparatus you will be quite safe. Think how useful it is to be able to do any little job yourself without having to send for an electrician — and how much cheaper.' (Woman's Own, October 1942)

If larger repairs were too daunting, smaller improvements could be made:

'If a door jams, a drawer sticks or the leaves of your table squeak, a little candlegrease spread on the parts exposed to friction will stop the trouble.' (Everywoman, October 1941)

When a household needed to expand to accommodate extra members, the magazines proposed ways of turning the loft into an extra room or constructing a shelter with a bed under the stairs. They also explained what had to be done when a household shrank in numbers (through the departure of evacuated children or of domestic servants). Unused rooms had to be shut up and unnecessary items such as brass, silver or pewter stored away under a thin layer of vaseline to protect them for better times. Such self-denial was considered patriotic, and the Royal Family itself was proposed as a worthy model:

DECORATING AN ATTIC BEDROOM
A Carefully Chosen Scheme Makes It An Attractive Little Room

I have been advised to paper my attic-bedroom with striped paper to make it appear taller. How will this look? Also, how would you arrange the dressing-table which is now in front of the window and hides the bed?

Above you see how the room looks with striped wallpaper. On the right you see how much more attractive it looks with walls and ceiling done in a plain colour. The dressing-table no longer hides the bed as it has been cut to fit into the window recess.

ARE YOU BRAVE?

Can you come out victorious from the extra difficulties and problems of to-day? These questions will help pull you up to scratch !

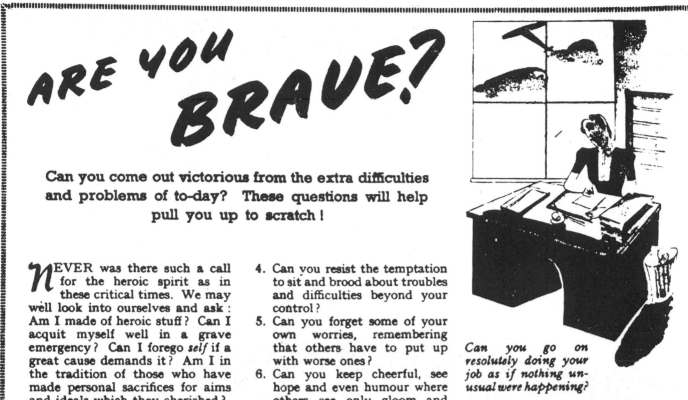

Can you go on resolutely doing your job as if nothing unusual were happening?

*N*EVER was there such a call for the heroic spirit as in these critical times. We may well look into ourselves and ask : Am I made of heroic stuff? Can I acquit myself well in a grave emergency? Can I forego *self* if a great cause demands it? Am I in the tradition of those who have made personal sacrifices for aims and ideals which they cherished?

Answer these questions truthfully, be prepared to act on them in emergency, and you will know roughly of what you are capable. If the majority of your replies are "Yes" you will not fail yourself or others in the hour of trial. You are already mentally and spiritually armed for any eventuality.

1. In times of crisis and emergency can you keep cool and calm and refuse to be panicked?
2. Can you go on resolutely doing your job as if nothing unusual were happening?
3. Do you eagerly undertake emergency service, believing that the best antidote to worry is to have definite, valuable work to do?

Can you resist the temptation to sit and brood

4. Can you resist the temptation to sit and brood about troubles and difficulties beyond your control?
5. Can you forget some of your own worries, remembering that others have to put up with worse ones?
6. Can you keep cheerful, see hope and even humour where others see only gloom and despair?
7. Are you busy consoling others instead of bewailing your own fate?
8. Have you a religion or philosophy which compensates you for loss and helps you to see even disaster in proper perspective?
9. Have you a deep-seated faith that right triumphs over might, justice over wrong, in the long run, whatever the immediate set-backs?
10. In temporary defeats, can you say, "Well, that's that, it can't be helped," and fight on with your back to the wall?
11. Can you keep control, remain level-headed, in face of extreme provocation designed to make you lose your temper.
12. Can you so behave in a severe ordeal that you emerge from it finer in every way—morally and spiritually braced instead of weakened?
13. At times of great national stress do you impose more self-denial and discipline on yourself, instead of expecting more indulgence and licence because conditions are abnormal?
14. Can you make supreme sacrifices ungrudgingly, if they seem necessary, without questioning the whys and wherefores unduly?
15. Can you serve a cause wholeheartedly without expecting it to be 100 per cent. worthy and perfect in a very imperfect world?
16. Do you count certain ideals of liberty, freedom, fairness more precious than life itself without them?—worth defending even at the risk of life?
17. Would you suffer yourself to save children suffering? Part from them indefinitely to strangers rather than submit them to grave risks by keeping them with you?
18. Would you prefer that husband or lover left you to serve an urgent cause, if his conscience demanded, rather than remain behind solely because he loved you?
19. If he lost his life in that cause, would you accept the loss courageously and consider his love for you greater on account of the sacrifice?
20. Can you forego *self* at a time of dire need for the sake of community, nation, a brotherhood of nations defending their common liberties, the bulk of humanity ?

POINTS : Yes......... No.........

IF there is one thing harder than squeezing a quart into a pint pot it is attempting to get as much as you need from a flat or an old house into a one-room home.

At first it seems impossible. And yet just now hundreds of women are forced to cram themselves and their belongings into tiny one-roomed homes with varying degrees of success.

In America we are more efficient—and more proficient—crowders. We have had more practice. Here one-rooming is almost a new art. An art that has to be learned.

Amateurs go to extremes. Ten to one the young girl who is setting up house will go "gadget crazy." Her bed will turn into a mock sideboard. Her dressing-table disguise itself as a table. Every single bit of furniture she possesses will be doomed to a double use.

All very well if you can command two essentials :—

(1) Money to buy well-made, easily adjusted furniture. This is emphatically a case where cheap built-for-effect pieces are not worth while.

(2) Leisure and a tidy nature so that automatically you transform your small abode from night to day. It is not as easy as you might think to find paid help to do the job efficiently if you have not the time or the temperament to indulge in daily scene-shifting.

The older woman tends to one of two extremes. Either she discards and discards until she is living in a monastic cell, devoid of comfort and furnished only with the barest necessities, or she develops a possession complex and can hardly bear to part

with as much as an empty cigarette box in case it may one day come in handy for buttons.

IN America the first essential that a one-roomer who wants to settle down looks for is a *big room*—preferably with one or more plain, straight walls.

A favourite dodge in the States is to steal a long, narrow strip right along one wall—or, even two. Then a perfectly plain "dummy" wall is built-in right up to the ceiling. This wall hides all the skeletons in the cupboard—a sink, a stove, a refrigerator, and plenty of cupboard space—domestic conveniences that make all the difference to a one-room home.

The illustration shows you what I mean. The different parts of the room are cleverly grouped together so that within four walls you have bedroom, sitting-room and kitchen.

In this room you have two walls partitioned off. If your room already has a large built-in cupboard you can probably manage with one wall, or, if you cannot afford to have these partitions specially built, make the most of alcoves and curtains and adapt your own furniture to fit some of these labour-saving ideas.

DECORATION and furniture are both important. Remember if you live continuously in one room you *must* keep to light, plain colours ; parchment, deep cream, or a light shade of blue, green or apricot. Avoid patterns and all strong colours.

If you want an individual touch and the room is high—as so many old rooms are—try parchment paint and walls and a coloured ceiling.

For the scheme we show here we have chosen off-green walls and cupboard fittings. In the dining-room view on the right the divan and banquettes are in palest oatmeal, the curtains in rich pink fabric lined for a complete black-out.

The lower left hand elevation features the same walls with an alternative fabric—russet printed with small white motifs. The cushions are in rich wallflower tones as contrast to the lightness of the walls.

This plan will give you some idea of the clever arrangement of space possible with built-in furniture. The fireplace—gas, coal, or electric—serves as the centre of interest, dividing the sitting-room from the dining part of the room.

LOOK at the dining-corner first. The banquette seats three people. One at the top of the narrow table, the other two along the side.

This also forms two sides of a bridge table. The two chairs, which usually stand one at the foot of the table and the other at the desk between the windows, are easily pushed up to complete the bridge four.

I have never seen anything more beautifully fitted-up than the wall cupboards. As the proud owner assured me when she allowed me to take a sketch of it before I came over here (I thought I might copy it for myself) : "My brother fixed it all up for me for about fifty dollars"—that's £12 or so to you ! A little jobbing carpenter helped him.

Of course, that price did not include refrigerator, stove or sink fittings. But take a look round the walls. Starting right up by the divan, you have a dressing-chest

Planned for ONE-ROOMERS

SADIE SCOTT. Ideas Scout, passes you some bright notes on living cosily inside four walls

Full details of furniture and fabrics shown are in "We'll Tell You."

SCALE ⅛" = 1'-0"

KEY TO PLAN OF ONE-ROOMED HOME

A. "Hall" Cupboard—for visitors' coats, golf clubs, etc. (Door in entrance passage B.)
B. Door—level with the inner, dummy wall.
C. "Service cupboard." At bottom, space for rubbish bin. Tradesman's delivery hatch and post box on top. Entrance both from passage and from inside room.
D. Refrigerator.
E. Sink.
F. Working Bench. (Cupboards under and over.)
G. Cooker.
   (*Note.*—Working equipment D to G screened by curtains or by doors that fold back screen wise. Use asbestos near stove.)
H. Built-in Banquettes (round dining table).
I. Bookcase.
J. Fireplace.
K. Desk.
L. Dressing Chest. (Can be built-in if preferred.)
M. Store Cupboard.
N. Wardrobe in use.
O. Chest of Drawers. (Shoe rail under . . . hat nests over.)
P. Divan.
Q. Bedside table with space for books underneath and lamp on top.
R. Chair for desk.
S. Chair for foot or dining-table.
T. Dining Table.
U. Easy Chair.

containing all toilet articles and dress accessories.

Behind the well-sprung divan you have storage space and hanging space which can be added to the wardrobe in use as required.

The built-in chest of drawers has a shoe rail below and hat nests above, and the store cupboard at the extreme end—at right angles to the door—is used for visitors' coats, golf clubs, umbrellas and suchlike. It is opened from the entrance hall.

ON the other side of the front door there is a cute contraption. At the bottom there is an airtight space for the rubbish container. Over it is a tradesman's delivery hatch and on top of all the post box. All these "service niches" can be unlocked and locked again by the porter from outside so that parcels can be delivered and rubbish emptied during the tenant's absence.

Now you have reached the kitchen side of the room. Refrigerator, sink, working bench and cooker are all in a row. The cupboards above are amply big enough for china and glass ; below the working-bench you have space for pots and pans and the dozen odd cookery gadgets that even the tiniest home demands.

And—believe me—if you are living in a room like this, it *is* a home, not just a lodging. There is even somewhere to put the linen. It is safely stored away in the long drawer under the divan bed . . . built right down to the ground so that there is never any dust.

This may all sound like a dream room at the moment, but with a little ingenuity you will easily be able to copy some of these bright ideas in your present room.

'Among the Queen's wartime economy changes at Buckingham Palace, the two Princesses' suites and many other rooms have been closed, state liveries, gold braid abolished; no flowers in rooms except from Royal gardens; private cinema suspended. More than one third of the staff away on war service.' (Woman's Own, 24th February 1940)

Frequently a family was on the move. During the war there were 60 million changes of address. Many migrant families had to fit into someone else's house. Here the magazines offered consolation and ways to adapt. Trevor Allen in an article on moving home in *Woman's Own*, July 1940:

'I wonder, is there a worse trial for a woman than having to leave a loved home, with all its personal links and intimate associations, … yet home is not only what you make it but where you make it. You can take its spirit with you, I believe, even in the pack on your back … yes, the soldier takes his home with him on his back — and in his memories, knows what miracles can be worked with cheerful adaptation … Most women have that same adaptability. Instead of bewailing too much the loss of old surroundings … they can add those little personal touches that make it different.'

Even if the new home was only one room … the 'bed-sit' could be made as comfortable as possible. Sadie Scott in *Modern Woman*, January 1940 inspired the new one-roomers to plan their room in ways already much-practised in the States — one piece of furniture could perform several functions; items not needed could be cleverly stored away so that a feeling of space was achieved. 'Hilary', in *Woman's Own*, said that constantly changing around the furniture in her own room was a tonic, Esther Murray, in *Woman's Journal*, showed that unwanted pieces of furniture from elsewhere in the house could be put into use with a little ingenuity. She recommended readers to:

'Shorten the legs of that ugly old iron bedstead in what was the maid's bedroom long ago. Hack off the top and bottom rails. Shorten the legs and send the scrap to your salvage centre. The result will be a low, modern divan when you have covered it.'

The greatest problem was faced by newly-weds wanting to set up home. By 1941, over two million houses had been destroyed, 60 per cent of them in London, and in the following year, when the birthrate was the highest since 1931, more space was needed for the new baby. Even if a house or part of a house was acquired, it was difficult to furnish and equip it. Everything was in short supply and wholesale prices had soared.

The 'Utility' scheme, started in December 1941, helped to ease the situation. The principle of Utility production was that only a few lines of each item were to be manufactured, and these chosen by teams led by the top designers in the country. Each product had to be simple, serviceable and of a sound quality. The first category of goods to be produced to utility specifications was hollow-ware such as kettles and saucepans. Later the scheme covered curtains, sheets, blankets, linoleum, mattresses and furniture. The manufacture of certain luxury goods was prohibited in

the summer of 1942, and the magazines helped by suggesting ingenious alternatives. For example, if you had no egg poacher, a Mrs Twigg of Glasgow told readers of *Woman's Own* in November 1943 to:

'Use your tea strainer. It saves the precious egg from spreading and the water drains off as the strainer is lifted.'

Furniture was a great problem for everybody, not just newly-weds. If you had been bombed out, local authorities lent a certain amount for a period of three months, after which it could either be bought or returned. From July 1940, the supply of imported timber had been cut drastically, and much shoddy, cheap furniture was produced using inferior woods. *My Home* in April 1940 thought of ways round the problem, saying:

'By careful planning with whitewood furniture, astonishingly pretty results can be obtained when painted with blue enamel paint.'

But Roger Smithell in *Woman's Magazine*, May 1941 suggested:

'If you have to start a new home, why not refurnish with antiques? Sale-rooms all over the country are crowded with good, honest, period furniture for sale at prices which were moderate in peacetime and remain unaffected by wartime conditions.'

Utility furniture arrived in 1942, and the manufacture of all but 22 articles of two qualities and three designs, was prohibited. Newly-weds and those setting up home to have children were 'priority' customers and given permits to purchase up to a number of units of furniture at a fixed price. Even so, utility furniture was expensive because of the high price of materials. People were asked to make unused furniture available to those in need. The editor of *The Lady* went so far as to say:

'Hoarding furniture in your attics will be unpatriotic. Hard up new householders can no longer perform amusing ingenuities from packing cases and banana crates as they could before the war.'

Many brides decided to delay setting up a home until the war was over. *My Home* thought that a bride was wise if she packed her wedding presents and other treasures away carefully until happier days came along.

But such days seemed a long way off. At the peak of the V1 attacks in 1944, more than 200,000 houses a day were being damaged or destroyed. Thousands of families lived in houses that were deemed unfit, millions occupied houses which had received only first aid repairs. Heating them was difficult — if not impossible with the fuel shortage; cleaning them a tricky operation since soap had been rationed to 16 ounces for every four weeks in 1942. Taking their tips from the magazines, people were now using crushed eggshell as a scouring compound for dish-clothes made out of old silk stockings cut into inch-wide strips and crocheted into squares, or they were saving old tea to clean up the woodwork.

Some relief came in the September of 1944, when the blackout came to an end at last. Esther Murray reported in *Woman's Journal*:

'The sun seems to shine just that little bit more these days — but, oh, how it shows up the dingy pieces of furniture, how it spotlights the threadbare patches! The passwords are camouflage and initiative. With a little bit of both there's no need to yearn for that bargain in wood that you saw in Oxford Street, and you can yawn next time you pass those lampshades.'

Now it was time to brighten the house for the family's return. Touches of paint and pretty gingham curtains could freshen the kitchen, and some garden furniture, pressed into indoor service, would do for the nursery, after the walls had been decorated with a frieze of animal transfers. Even blackout curtains could be put to use. *Woman's Journal* in January 1945 suggested that '*they make very good loose covers or bedspreads if you sew wide bands of coloured braid round the edges*', while *Woman's Own* in the same month thought that you could:

'Bleach your discarded curtains in strong household bleach until quite white and then make pillow cases, tablemats, tray clothes or even cot sheets from them.'

The true ending to war on the Home Front came at Christmas 1945. In November, *Home and Country* wrote:

'This is the Christmas for which we have been waiting six years. Once again there will be lights in every window; parents and children, husbands and wives, friends and sweethearts will be reunited in their own home.'

But in many cases it was still far from being the dream home. Although by January 1945 nearly 800,000 houses had been repaired and many bombed-out families had moved into prefabricated dwellings, the housing problem was being solved far too slowly. In March 1945, Rosita Forbes wrote in Woman's Own:

'Optimists prophesy "milk and honey flowing" and an easier time for everybody. Realists, with perhaps a touch of liver, look forward gloomily to a lot of disorganisation while houses, ports, railways, lives and countries are re-built.'

Christmas on a Shoestring

Percy Pea-Nut is threaded through with string. He has a cotton suit and cardboard hands and hat. Connie the Coco-Nut has a paper cap. Her features are made of paper pasted on her nice hairy old face!

Brightly coloured fruit, scarlet ribbons and candles, a big jug of cider-cup, all help to make a festive table!

No sugar icing must be compensated for by brightly coloured paper frills and plenty of sweets as decoration

A big bow of scarlet or silver ribbon, makes a very little mistletoe look important!

Candles Everywhere!

Just ordinary twigs, dipped in white-wash or silver paint, and decorated with Xmas baubles, make a Fairy Tree!

Dreams of homes for the future had started early in the war. In 1940, Goering's bombers had started up the first great slum clearance programme. And once it became clear that much of Britain's housing stock would need replacing, the magazines began to print articles with titles such as 'Building for the Future — Now!', 'Design of Dwellings', 'Homes for Young Parents', and 'Your Home in Tomorrow's Britain'. There was general condemnation of a system where men plan the houses while women work in them, and women were encouraged to write in and say what they expected of the home of tomorrow. What they wanted most of all, it seems, were houses which were cheap to heat, free of clutter, with room to move around and as many labour saving devices as possible.

Such equipment was, of course, impossible to find during the war, since the factories were geared to war production. But the manufacturers of many unavailable goods made sure that their names remained familiar by means of adverts geared to peacetime expectations.

'*Tanks can't run on toasters*' women were told in early 1944, '*so GEC toasters are temporarily unavailable, the same as most other of the company's Household Electrical Appliances, to reappear after the war in new and better designs ...*' A competitor countered with a campaign whose message was, '*thank goodness Hotpoint are going to make life easier after the war*', while a third, in early 1945, urged women to '*post early to get on the Kelvinator Priority List ... to make certain of getting even better Kelvinator Refrigeration at the earliest possible moment*'.

As for the housing itself, women wanted it to be close to green spaces where children could play in safety, ideally with nurseries close at hand. The new 'Council Houses' were much admired, with their individual gardens and feeling of neighbourliness. But most of the new dwellings which did get built after the war lacked spirit and pride. The insides might have been utility inspired, but they were dull. The outside appearance was not considered at all. Reginald Lester, in his article for *Woman's Magazine* in 1944, looked gloomily at the prospect ahead, summing up rather aptly what was going wrong. He wrote:

'Many of us are occupied with the problem of finding a new house, and during the next year or two, thousands of women leaving the services will be faced with a like task. The defects of modern planning arise from faulty design and lack of imagination and interest in detail, excessive pressure for speed and economy, and failure to study the site, its limitations and possibilities ... it is by means of variety of lay-out and clever positioning of the houses — taking advantage of varying levels and any accidental features of the site — that individuality can be obtained.'

Children

'What a highly satisfactory state of affairs it is that, after close on four years of the war ... not only are there more babies but bonnier and healthier ones — due to their mother's co-operation in taking advantage of the many opportunities offered them, such as free clinical advice, free immunisation, the splendid Government vitamin scheme, and many others — not forgetting our baby circle!' (Woman's Own, 13 August 1943)

The above quotation shows the positive side of having a baby in wartime, and many of the schemes began in and because of the war were to continue afterwards, radically altering the health and welfare of children for the better.

During the Blitz, the Government was anxious that epidemics of diptheria would break out, and as a direct result of this vaccinated nearly seven million children between 1940 and 1945. Campaigns were launched in the magazines encouraging mothers to take advantage of the vaccine which was free of charge. As a result, deaths from this disease showed a marked decline.

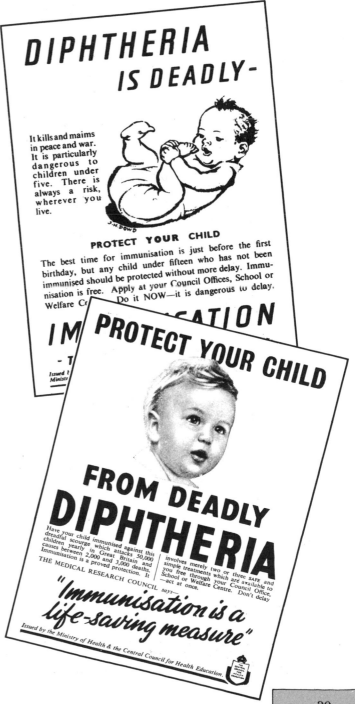

Children benefited also from the provision of cod liver oil, orange or blackcurrant juice and cheap or free milk, so that *Mother and Home* was able to say that the vast majority of wartime children '*pass through the various stages of childhood the picture of health*'.

But this apart, wartime was not an encouraging time to have a child. There was a shortage of prams, push-chairs, baby baths, chamber pots and rubber teats. There was a shortage of midwives, hospital beds, nurseries and nannies, and a shortage, too, of fathers, teachers, and settled homes.

COMMANDO *in training?*

He is on a tough job, at any rate. All babies are. So are their slightly older brothers and sisters. They are busy growing, laying the foundation of the men and women they are to be; and one of their greatest needs is vitamins.

If children are to grow up sturdy and happy, with healthy bodies, good strong bones, fine teeth and sound constitutions, they must have plenty of vitamins *now*. That is why the Government provides orange juice and cod liver oil — products particularly rich in the vitamins children need — for babies and for all children holding R.B.2 Ration Book. And not only for these children, but for expectant mothers also; for baby's life begins before he is born.

You want to give your little ones the best chance in life you can. The Government's vitamins scheme is a long step towards it; so for your babies' sakes, please join the scheme *at once*.

How you get your Orange Juice & Cod Liver Oil

EXPECTANT MOTHERS

If you are already getting milk under the National Scheme, you are reminded that your 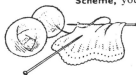 present National Milk Scheme authority expired on February 6th. To obtain benefit after that date you must take or send your ration book to your local Food Office. See that your authority for *priority* milk (Form R.G.48) is attached to the ration book. You will receive coupon sheets for your orange juice and cod liver oil from the Food Office.

If you have not yet entered the National Milk Scheme and have not already given the Food Office a medical certificate in respect to priority eggs and milk, first get a medical certificate from your doctor, certified midwife or health visitor. Hand or send this with your ration book to the Food Office. You will then receive coupons sheets for your vitamin products and authorities to obtain seven pints of milk a week at 2d. a pint and priority supplies of eggs as well.

Please try to take the cod liver oil. It will give baby such a splendid start. And in any event please do accept the offer of orange juice. Diluted with at least 4 parts of water you will find it a most refreshing addition to you diet.

CHILDREN HOLDING THE R.B.2 RATION BOOKS

Your children's authorities and coupon sheets also expired on February 6th. In future they will receive seven pints of milk a week under the National Milk Scheme automatically, at 2d. a pint. For their milk no application of any sort is necessary. But you must apply at the Food Office for coupon sheets for orange juice and cod liver oil. Take the children's ration books with you. You can send the ration books if you cannot call.

WHERE YOU GET YOUR ORANGE JUICE AND COD LIVER OIL. Your Food Office will tell you your nearest distributing centre. At least one is sure to be reasonably near to you. You needn't go to the same centre each time.

WHAT YOU PAY. Expectant mothers and children who, by reason of family income, etc., are entitled to *free* milk under the National Milk Scheme (the Food Office will give you particulars) will get their *vitamin products free also*. Otherwise the price is 10d. a bottle for the cod liver oil and 5d. a bottle for the orange juice. You "buy" these products with postage stamps — not cash — and they should be 5d. or 2½d. stamps, so get them from the Post Office beforehand. The stamps should be stuck on to the appropriate coupons in your ration books.

Ration books must be presented every time you apply for your vitamin supplies. Loose coupons cannot be accepted.

The first decision was whether to have a baby at all with a war going on. Many young wives wrote to Leonora Eyles apprehensively, with problems like:

'My husband and I are both on war work, but I am longing to have a baby. Do you think it would be wrong to stop war work for that, and is it right to have a baby in this troubled world?'

'If you don't, what are we fighting for? Having a baby is definitely war work, my dear, and by doing so you will be helping to build the new world afterwards. And you could go back to your work afterwards, you know, leaving baby in a day nursery.' (*Woman's Own*, 5th June 1942)

The 'Baby Circles' and 'Baby Clubs' formed by the magazines encouraged new mothers to take advantage of post-natal care and of the Government welfare schemes, details of which were issued as bulletins from the Ministries of Food and Health. They also gave advice on the correct way for a mother to breast feed during wartime:

'Never feed baby while you are anxious. Sit down for 15 minutes on a low chair before each feed and compose yourself. The mother who sits perched on the edge of a high chair with her eyes anxiously on the clock, wondering how she will get through all her work if baby does not hurry up, will never make a good nurse. Not only will her baby be cross and disconcerted, but she will probably lose her milk. If you find yourself doing this, take yourself in hand and remember that feeding your baby is your warwork.' (Woman's Own, 18th January 1941)

There were problems, too, with older children, many of whom suffered from psychological strain or boredom during the war. The magazines helped mothers to cope, especially when an air raid was on. In an article called 'Happy Christmas In Spite Of Hitler', Len Chaloner wrote:

'Try to stop in yourself the inclination to nag in the shelter because your own nerves are frayed, and think of the odd little things to do or play with the children, and if the children are tiny, you should avoid talking in front of them about air raid tragedies and damage. Above all, if they are "borrowed children" particularly, go out of your way to make them feel really loved and wanted.' (Woman's Magazine, December 1940)

Leonora Eyles suggested a little weekly book that might keep the children amused:

'It is called Enid Blyton's Sunny Stories. Enid Blyton has the knack of knowing what children love to read, and at the same time she manages to teach them the value of such things as courage, kindness and common sense.' (Woman's Own, 13th January 1940)

Some mothers were unable to cope. A distraught woman wrote to 'Nurse Hale' in 1941:

'My little girl, two years old, is terrified of her gas mask and screams when she sees us in ours. I just cannot make her put it on. Can you suggest any way of making her wear it?'

'I know what difficulty this is sometimes and I think your best plan will be to have a talk with your air raid warden, who must have some considerable experience. I'm sure he (or she) will be able to help you. Try to make it a game if you can.' (*Woman's Own*, 10th May 1941)

Despite the mother's care, many children experienced such bad shocks during the bombing that they developed nervous disabilities for long after. Some mothers were worried about what would happen to their evacuated children while they were away. Not every child was as fortunate as the Royal Princesses who had only been evacuated to another Royal Residence away from London ... and they had been allowed to take familiar things with them. One harassed mother wrote to Rosita Forbes after the children had crossed the Atlantic:

'I am afraid of my children coming back to me as strangers.'

To which the reply came ...

'It's splendid for your children to start travelling and meeting new people while their minds are forming. They'll come back much more adaptable and capable of thinking for themselves.' (Woman's Own, 17th August 1940)

Later in the war when most women were employed,

To help overcome such problems, Ernest Bevin organized Nursery Schools and Nursery Centres throughout the land as well as Emergency Day Nurseries attached to the big munitions factories for the children of women workers. In these, children were encouraged to mix and play under trained guidance and were expected to participate in such things as laying the tables at meal times or clearing away. However the numbers of Centres were at first inadequate and the rate at which they were opened, far too slow. Moreover, there were many children who had no Nursery School close at hand, with the result that they had little to occupy their energetic minds. And it did not help matters that, as part of the austerity measures of 1942, many toys were banned — especially those made from rubber, kapok, hemp, cork, synthetic resins and cellulose. All kites were prohibited, and there were often no paper hats, crackers, balloons or iced cakes for a party. *Woman's Own* assured mothers that this would not present any problems because for the older child ... '*a piece of pastry or a hammer and nails give more thrills, and children are no happier for having elaborate or costly toys*'.

And for the younger child, you could cut out the shape of a duck in a scrap of towelling and stuff it with pieces of your large bath-sponge after this had disintegrated, or even '*try half a coconut shell as a soap dish for baby's bath. It floats on the surface, amuses baby and is always at hand.*'

Clothing, too, was a problem. Rationing was introduced in May 1942 and coupons never seemed to go far enough. The magazines helped out with ingenious suggestions whereby discarded mackintoshes could be made into an apron for baby or father's old plus fours into a suit for the boy. The children's own garments were liable to undergo all kinds of strange transformations. *Woman's Pictorial* in December 1943 revealed that:

'*... a useful suit can often be made from a dress that your little girl has outgrown. The bodice can be used to make over the shoulder straps and the patch pockets a waist-band.*'

Children's shoes were a particular problem. In 1940, *Womans Own* suggested that you should:

'*Varnish the soles of the children's shoes to make them last longer ... and use pieces cut from an old inner tyre to stick to the soles of your children's plimsolls. You've no idea how it increases their life.*'

Utility material, available from 1942, did much to improve the quality of clothing, at no greater cost. The following year *The Lady* commented that '*little girls never looked prettier in utility Drayella and gingham*', while, in February 1944, they printed a delightful letter from a mother who said:

'*Yes, mine is definitely a utility baby; utility cot, utility pram, utility clothes — everything about her except, bless her, the little self. It has taken a lot of planning, queueing and counting of coupons to produce this tiny scrap that blinks so*

some mothers hardly ever saw their children who had been farmed out to aunts or grandmothers while they went to work. The reaction of *Woman's Own* was:

'*Have you ever noticed that children grow up more enlightened, less inhibited, where the mother has interests outside as well as inside the home?*' (*Woman's Own*, 9th July 1943)

But the absence of the mother could be positively dangerous, as *The Lady* reported in 1943:

'*Children are being injured on the roads at the rate of nearly 100 per day. The fact of so many women needed in war work away from home may partly account for this.*'

There were also unhealthy stories of working couples who tried to keep their children with them despite their long hours of work. *The Lady* in February 1943 revealed that:

'*There are women on night duty who have to keep their under school-age children in bed with them all day, their husbands taking over bed and children at night.*'

These wartime problems — together with the growing attention to what life should be like after the war — created great interest in the future of the educational system. Articles on various aspects of education appeared regularly in all the magazines, increasing quickly in number once Butler's proposals for reform were made public in January 1944.

Butler's new Education Act was to change the whole structure of the schooling system. It was to ensure that State aided places in schools could be awarded on merit rather than parental income. The school leaving age was to be raised to 15, and eventually to 16. There were to be Young People's Colleges, Youth Services and other technical and adult classes. And school meals were to be free, together with medical treatment.

The magazines which devoted most space to the proposed reforms were *The Lady* and the Women's Institute *Home and Country* magazine. In the latter, Kenneth Lindsey M.P. was to write:

'We shall need first rate women as well as men on all education committees, and lively, active pressure groups in every county. These pressure groups must muster the main clauses of the Bill, they must know the new powers and duties of their local education authorities. After the Bill is passed, the real work starts.'

Many new teachers would be required for the working of the new act, and *The Lady* said of the future:

'If we ever do build Jerusalem, it will be partly through the schools, and the new Education Bill promises to help with the foundations. It will depend on a sufficiency of good teachers rather than on buildings and equipment — a school can be built more quickly than a teacher can be trained.'

The climate of reform in which the Education Act was passed had been largely established by the publication of the Beveridge Report in December 1942. The report described itself as 'a plan for social security to abolish physical want by ensuring for all citizens at all times a subsistence income and the means of meeting exceptional expenditure at birth, marriage and death.'

The Report was greeted with almost universal enthusiasm, though Churchill ordered that any resulting legislation should be shelved until after the war. In the magazines one of the issues debated most fiercely was the question of Family Allowances. Some aspects of the subsequent government proposals were successfully resisted — notably, that the allowance should be paid to the father rather than the mother. The reaction of women was summed up by Eleanor Rathbone MP in a letter to *Home and Country*, August 1944, in which she said:

'... payment to the mother has a symbolic value as a sign that the nation thinks of her not just as a "dependent", which literally means a hanger-on, but as standing on her feet and as the child's natural guardian.'

unconcernedly at her surroundings. Nor does she realize that the vehicle which transferred me to the hospital for her arrival was not the peacetime taxi but a most official looking ARP car driven by a slip of a girl.'

Children of school age were, perhaps, the most severely affected. During the war, approximately one in every five schools was destroyed. Teachers moved from one place to another, as did their pupils. Evacuated children changed billets sometimes as much as four times. Naturally education was erratic and suffered enormously. Some children were even taken from school for a few hours daily (paid at Government rates) to help bring in the potato crops. It was not surprising that many could not read by the age of seven, or that the juvenile crime rate soared during the war years.

Una is a welcome guest,

(Reproduced by courtesy of the Lancet)

Secondus scarcely crowds the nest,

Tertia makes a tighter fit,

Quartus pinches things a bit,

Quintus, Quintus, luckless Quintus,
Woe the day you came to stint us.

FAMILY ALLOWANCES
by Eva Hubbock

THE case for Family Allowances, strong as it was before the war, has been still further strengthened by war-time conditions.

Even in normal times the wife of the low-wage worker has been expected to perform daily miracles in making ends meet. The recent rise in the cost of living has made her struggle harder than ever, but it has also complicated life for a great many other women—mothers of young families—living on a limited income.

It has been estimated that the number of workers living in this country whose total earnings are lower than the Rowntree standard of minimum needs reaches a total—including the dependents—of at least ten million people. It is an appalling figure if considered in terms of human lives deprived of the opportunities of healthy life and proper development. And it is important to remember that the Rowntree standard is an extremely low one, which is concerned only with the barest essentials, such as food and rent, and ignores all the ordinary day-to-day expenses such as postage stamps, fares, clubs and tobacco.

Families as a Cause of Poverty

As Sir William Beveridge has pointed out, it is the possession of several small children which must rank as the greatest single cause of poverty. Social surveys, taken in different parts of the country before the war, showed that even then something like 25 per cent. of the rising generation came from families where the income was too low to provide nutrition adequate for normal health. With the war-time increase in prices, the percentage has undoubtedly risen—even though, admittedly, many fathers of families are receiving higher wages than in pre-war days. Unfortunately it is a fact that the greatest number of children come from families where the father works in low-paid, casual or unskilled employment: and in these industries wages, generally speaking, have not advanced, due to the lack of effective organization usually to be found in them.

Here, then, is the first argument in favour of Family Allowances. Higher wages which chase after higher prices do not provide a satisfactory solution: they put spending power equally in the hands of those who require it for necessaries and of those who, having no family obligations, use it for the undesired purchase of luxuries.

A Second Argument

A second war-time argument arises out of the confusion of all sorts of different children's allowances now being paid by the Government. There seems to be no guiding principle on which these are based, and they vary so greatly—from 3s. in some instances to as much as 12s. 6d. and even more in others—that it is not unnatural that a sense of injustice should have resulted. There would be no occasion for these discrepancies if the Government abolished the lot and replaced them with a single, scientifically determined scale, to cover all the present recipients and include many others no less in need.

A Third Reason

A third point centres around the population question. It has been calculated that, for various causes—death, separation, anxiety for the future, and economic hardship—half a million fewer births took place during the War of 1914–1918 than would otherwise have been the case. This war is likely to have a similar result, in proportion, of course, to its length and extent: and although Family Allowances have never been advocated solely as a means of increasing the birth-rate in times like these, they certainly would help to relieve the financial stress, which is the main cause of hindering parents from deciding, in spite of everything else, to start, or add to, a family.

Women in Employment

Argument number four is an important one to women at work. Family Allowances are, perhaps, the only just solution to the vexed question of equal pay for men and women who are doing work of equal value. The reason for men's wages being normally higher is said to be on account of their family responsibilities. It is an excellent reason when men actually *have* such responsibilities, but a very large proportion have not ; whereas, of course, a small percentage of women are actually the sole supporters of a family; and anyway, the inequality of wage-rates is the means of turning women into involuntary blacklegs and of turning men out of employment. How much more sensible and just to pay not according to the sex of the worker, but according to the value of the work done—leaving the children of the worker to be provided for *far more adequately* by a system of Family Allowances.

These are some of the main arguments which have brought this subject so much to the fore in recent months. It is because they would provide a commonsense solution to so many present problems that Family Allowances are now being recognized and advocated by Members of Parliament, social workers, and leading economists.

There is nothing new or revolutionary about them. They were introduced some years ago in New Zealand and Australia: France, Belgium and many other European countries have adopted the principle, in one form or another.

In France and Belgium, for instance, employers were compelled to participate in an industrial pool scheme; elsewhere schemes based on contributory insurance are the means of family provision. In this country, the greatest measure of support would undoubtedly be for a really comprehensive State scheme, with allowances of not less than 5s. weekly for every child, starting, perhaps, with the second child in the family.

The child of the income-tax payer would be included on the same terms as the docker labourer's child; and the present system of income-tax rebates would, of course be abolished. Such a State scheme would probably cost the Exchequer about £50 million a year: a large sum, perhaps, but a cheap price for the purchase of a better national health bill and a more constructive social policy !

Great Britain could solve many of her problems by the introduction of such a system, whereby her children would be given the chance of growing up into strong, healthy men and women, and her young married couples would have less fear of bringing babies into a world that had made no adequate provision for their coming.

And women, increasingly, did choose to make their voices felt, whether individually or through women's groups. Some, it is true, felt that they should only speak about matters of direct relevance to them as wives and mothers; but — as we shall see in the final section — the magazines encouraged them to think that women should have a voice in everything concerning the new world after the war.

Food

At the outbreak of war the most pressing need on the Home Front was to start preparations to produce and store enough food for the coming year. 'Digging for Victory' had begun. Appeals were launched in every magazine with instructions on how to proceed. People were encouraged to obtain an allotment, but if you only had a garden that would do. *Womans Journal* included a plan showing how to make the best use of your land ... after sacrificing the lawn. Although it was September, there was still time to plant certain crops:

'Have you ever grown the vegetable called prickly spinach which is hardy enough to stand the severest winter and is regarded with great favour by doctors? ... This may not be a suitable time to grow lettuce but it is just right for corn salad, a closely allied crop which, if anything, possesses a superior flavour.' (Mother and Home, November 1939)

By growing enough food for itself, Britain could save valuable shipping space that would be needed for essential imports. This was to prove vital over the following years. Even those with small gardens or yards could help save shipping by usefully employing themselves in animal husbandry:

'Chicks? Ever kept any? Even if you keep a few in town or suburban gardens, you'll know they can be fed almost entirely on household waste. Breeding rabbits is another hugely valuable way of using that bit of garden or yard, too. They aren't expensive to feed, you know. And — don't laugh — you COULD keep a goat, and help your country by lessening demands on milk supplies ... A normal goat will give six pints of rich milk every day for nearly a year. And the cheese and butter you get from it is excellent.' (Woman's Own, November 1939)

As it was still autumn when war was announced, there was a plentiful supply of free food to be found in the hedgerows ready to be eaten or preserved. Everything that was edible, such as rosehips and elderberries, should be experimented with. The magazines urged their readers to go into the countryside with their baskets and gather, in their seasons:

'... hawthorn and elderflowers and make them into wine. Tender dandelion leaves lend a tang to salads, while sorrel, with its spear-shaped sour-tasting leaves, can be used as a salad vegetable or made into soup. Have you tried young nettles boiled as a vegetable? They are done spinach-fashion and make a very good substitute for that vegetable.' (Woman's Own, September 1939)

It was to the Women's Institutes that the Government turned to organise a communal preservation of home-grown produce throughout the land. This was backed up by articles in the magazines showing the housewife how to bottle plums, salt down beans, preserve vegetables in sand and dry apple rings over the stove.

Meanwhile, food prices climbed with appalling speed. In November the Government decided to subsidise the cost of staple foods in order to avoid an inevitable round of pay claims. But supplies of sugar, bacon and butter were dwindling and the unscrupulous rich could motor into poorer districts and buy up supplies. Rationing was the only solution.

Ration books had been issued to everyone at the end of September and people had to register with a retailer of their choice before 23rd November. Retailers could then obtain supplies in accordance with the number of customers registered with them. On presentation of the ration book, they would cancel the coupons for each portion of food received. Rationing was due to begin on January 8, but before then, the women on the Home Front were asked to try to make the first war-time Christmas as normal as possible:

'However divided our families may be, we should try as hard as we can to celebrate Christmas as usual. We owe this to the young folks, whether they belong to us, or are in our care for the time being. We also owe this to "someone in France" who will feel all the happier if he knows we're holding the home fortress in the time honoured way. In spite of that empty chair, we should carry on.' (Woman's Journal, December 1939)

Elizabeth Craig, cookery editor for *Woman's Journal* gives a recipe for Christmas pudding without an egg and another for 'a goose with one leg' which turns out to be a small plump boned leg of mutton stuffed with a mixture of stale breadcrumbs, minced onion and ham, a sheep's kidney, celery and seasoning.

On 8th January 1940 — the coldest January for 45 years — rationing began. Each person was entitled to 12 ounces of sugar, four ounces of butter and four ounces of bacon or ham per week. By 29th January, the bacon ration was raised to eight ounces, which was greater than the pre-war consumption per head! Perhaps the amount of bacon available was due to the Pig Clubs that had sprung up throughout the land. A few people would club together to buy a pig which they would feed, fatten, then slaughter. But for those not so lucky, every scrap of the ration should be saved. The bacon rinds were crisped in the oven and mixed with brown breadcrumbs to sprinkle on savoury dishes. For those who could not afford real bacon, there was a substitute called 'macon' which was really made out of mutton.

On 11th March, meat was rationed, though offal — heart, kidney, sweetbreads and liver etc — was left unrationed. The magazines celebrated its nutritious qualities and good value — '*Ox tongue*', promised *Mother and Home*, '*is a lordly dish — being almost all meat, it will go a very long way!*'

During May, bacon rations came down to four ounces per week, sugar to eight ounces; and in June, tea was rationed at two ounces. By July, cooking fats and margarine joined butter on the ration. The only good news during this month was an announcement by the Government that free or cheap milk was to be given to mothers and small children.

Britain was becoming increasingly dependent on its own produce. By the end of June 1940 — with Germany occupying most of Northern Europe — many sources of food supplies were no longer available. Most of our green vegetables, for example, had come from the Channel Islands or the Low Countries. Bacon, butter and milk were similarly affected. And the entry of Italy into the war as an ally of Germany (10th June) meant that the Mediterranean was closed. Supplies of fruit and tomatoes were now severely restricted. *Modern Home* suggested that with orange juice so desperately expensive, children should be given swede or tomato juice to obtain their vitamin C.

In the Autumn, the Government fixed the prices of onions, turkeys and rabbits, and later in December put price orders on many other foods including poultry and nuts. But fixing prices without imposing rationing meant that many goods either sold out quickly or disappeared under the counter.

Households which kept chickens had been able to preserve their extra eggs in a mixture of borax and water or in waterglass, and the Women's Institutes had managed to open 2650 Preserving Centres with a resulting 1000 tons of fruit saved ... In the December issue of their magazine *Home and Country* they announced that '*even salvage dumps and cemeteries were scoured for extra jam-jars!*'

1941 was the poorest year both for food and food shortages. By May, U-boats had sunk 142 merchant ships, with air attacks accounting for 179 more. Imports were now running at only two-thirds of their pre-war level, while wholesale prices had risen almost 50 per cent between 1940 and 1941. British farmers would have to grow more crops than ever — and this at the expense of livestock, which was too costly to produce for its return.

There was precious little choice in the shops. Many people took to relying more and more on canned food. In 1940 *Mother and Home* had stated that '*the war has made us realize the value of canned foods — in fact we wonder how we should manage without them these days.*' The favourite of all wartime canned foods was tinned salmon. In February 1941 Elizabeth Craig wrote in *Woman's Journal*:

'Now that our menus are so dependent on not only rations but on other supplies, cooking for the family sometimes needs a little juggling, and, when I go out shopping, I just take whatever I can get without a murmur and then give my imagination full rein. If you find the butcher's slab bare, hie to the fishmonger. If he is wrapping up the last haddock, don't blame him, give thanks for the salmon in your store.'

But by Spring 1941, the Government decided to step in to persuade the housewife to eat more home-produced, fresh food — especially vegetables. The person in charge of this operaton was Lord Woolton, the Minister of Food. As early as Autumn 1940 he had issued 'food bulletins' in the magazines, aimed specifically at teaching the housewife the rudiments of nutrition.

In early 1941 there was a potato glut, and in the April Lord Woolton launched a campaign to make people eat more of them.

Potatoes, it appeared, could be used for anything — but they should not be peeled prior to cooking, as the most nutritious parts lay immediately under the skin. They could be grated raw and used to lighten batters and puddings; usefully employed as a basis for every meal — and the potato-water incorporated into soups and stews or used to mix the gravy powder. Before long, people complained of becoming fat:

'You would think war conditions might make all of us thinner, but that isn't the way it works. Maybe it's the greater proportion of starch in our diet; at any rate, lots of quite young women are having to let out their buttons.' (Modern Home, April 1941)

In March, jams, margarine, syrup and treacle were rationed on the basis of a minimum of eight ounces per person per month, according to availability. This

Simple But FESTIVE

By

Elizabeth CRAIG, *M.C.A., M.I.H.*

HOWEVER divided our families may be just now, we should try as hard as we can to celebrate Christmas as usual this season. We owe this to the young folks, whether they belong to us, or are in our care for the time being. We also owe this to "Someone in France" who will feel all the happier if he knows we're holding the home fortress in the time-honoured way. You see, these men of ours who are in France or on sea protecting our shores and our food supplies will be keeping Christmas with us in spirit. So let's all try to make as many people as happy as possible on Christmas Day in spite of that empty chair. It's quite easy to prepare festive fare, even though you may have to employ substitutes for certain of the ingredients you would normally use.

Eggless Puddings

You needn't stint your family of nourishing puddings even when eggs are scarce, because you can make them without eggs.

Spiced Raisin Puddings

½ lb. flour	**¼ teaspoon mixed spice**
¾ teaspoon baking soda	**¼ cup golden syrup**
¼ cup treacle	**2 tablespoons melted butter or margarine**
½ cup weak coffee	**Little fat for greasing moulds**
½ cup chopped raisins	
½ teaspoon salt	

Grease 6 fair-sized pudding moulds. Sift the flour with the salt, soda and spice. Heat the fat slowly with the syrup and treacle until the latter are tepid, then add the coffee. If you've any sour milk you can substitute it for the coffee. Stir into dry ingredients. Add raisins. Three-quarter fill the moulds. Cover with greased greaseproof paper. Steam for ¾ hour. Serve with custard or sweet white sauce, flavoured with vanilla essence to taste.

If liked, you can steam the mixture in a large greased mould instead, when it will require about 1½ hours.

If you haven't any raisins, add ½ cup Robertson's mincemeat or use ¼ cup chopped candied orange peel and the same of sultanas, or chopped stoned dates

Hawaiian Grapefruit

3 large grapefruit	**6 teaspoons crushed pineapple**

Chill, then cut the grapefruit in halves, crosswise. Remove, the pips and cores, then carefully run a curved grapefruit knife between the peel and the fruit to separate one from the other. Now with a sharp, pointed knife, carefully separate the fruit from the membrane encircling each section by cutting from the centre to the peel. Place a teaspoon of crushed pineapple in the centre of each. Serve with sugar. Enough for six persons.

Lentil and Tomato Soup

1 pint lentils	**1 oz. grated cheese**
1 pint of tinned tomatoes	**Salt and pepper to taste**
2 large onions	**Water as required**
1 oz. butter or margarine	**1 scraped carrot**
	1 sprig of parsley
Fried croûtons	

Rinse the lentils in a colander under the cold water tap. Drain well and place in a basin. Cover with cold water and soak overnight. Peel and slice the onions. Slice the carrot. Melt the butter or margarine in a saucepan. Add the onion and carrot. Cover and cook slowly for 10 minutes, shaking frequently. Uncover and add the lentils, tomatoes, parsley, salt and pepper to taste and 1 quart of water. Bring to simmering point and simmer for 1½ to 2 hours, or till tender. Rub through a fine sieve. Reheat. Add more salt and pepper to taste if necessary. Stir in the cheese and serve at once with the croûtons. Enough for eight persons.

If you have any left over gravy, or liquor in which salt beef or ham has been boiled, use the gravy for the same quantity of the water, or substitute 1 pint of the salt beef or ham liquor for 1 pint of the water.

To Make this Soup Go Further.—Stir in 1 pint of milk, mixed with 1 tablespoon cornflour, dissolved in ¼ gill of the milk, brought to the boil and boiled gently for 5 minutes.

Santa Claus Salad

3 cups shredded cabbage heart	**Mayonnaise as required**
1½ cups sliced celery	**Roasted peanuts**
1 teaspoon minced onion	**Salt and cayenne pepper to taste**
1 pimento	**1 small sprig berried holly**
1 cream cheese	

Chill the cabbage in ice-cold water. Meanwhile, take a pimento from a tin, and drain it well. Cut into tiny short "matches." Divide the cheese into small portions the size of a walnut. Roll each into a ball. Crush enough of the peanuts to cover the cheese balls, then dip each ball in the nuts. Drain and dry the cabbage. Mix with the celery, then with mayonnaise to moisten. Stir in the onion and salt and cayenne pepper to taste. Pile the cabbage and celery salad in the centre of a salad bowl. Make a hollow in the centre, and lay the cheese balls in this hollow. Decorate the fringe of the salad with crosses of pimento. Wrap the holly sprig stalk in waxed paper, and plant in the centre. Enough for six persons.

This salad goes best with cold pork, pork or veal and ham pie, brawn, or cold boiled or baked ham or turkey.

A Goose with One Leg

1 small plump leg of mutton	**Salt and pepper to taste**
2 cups stale breadcrumbs	**2 tablespoons shredded celery**
2 tablespoons minced onion	**Pinch of crushed herbs**
2 ozs. minced ham	**Milk or water as required**
½ cup shredded suet	
1 sheep's kidney	

Before taking this "goose" home, see that the butcher bones it. Now skin, core and mince the kidney. Place the suet in a frying pan. Add the celery, ham and kidney. Cook slowly for 5 minutes, stirring frequently. Turn into a basin. Add the crumbs, herbs, onion, salt and pepper to taste and milk or water to moisten. Fill the hollow in the leg with the stuffing. Skewer and sew up. Weigh, cover with caul, and roast in a hot oven, skin side next rack, allowing 20 minutes to the pound and 25 minutes over. Lower temperature at the end of 25 minutes after sealing in the juices. Serve with gravy, roast potatoes, Brussels sprouts, and caper or red currant jelly.

Make sure of your Woman's Journal by ordering in advance.

soon proved difficult to administer in practice and, in July, this system was replaced by a 'straight' ration, which later rose to a pound. In May, cheese was rationed for the first time at a meagre one ounce per week. Good Housekeeping suggested grating one's cheese ration and putting it in a screw-top jar so as to use it more sparingly.

At the end of May, the first 'Lend-Lease' food from America got through; by the end of the year such shipments were to account for one fifteenth of all food arriving in Britain.

That first cargo contained the first supplies of dried egg to be seen in British shops. Each person was rationed to one packet every eight weeks, the equivalent of 12 eggs in the shell, while children under six had two packets.

People soon got into 'the dried egg habit'. You first had to reconstitute the egg by dissolving one tablespoonful of the powder in two tablespoonsfuls of lukewarm water or milk. Then you could make a wide variety of dishes, including a quite passable omelette.

And the ships brought other novelties, notably canned foods with names like 'Prem', 'Tang', and 'Spam', made from who knew which parts of various animals. But the housewife was rapidly losing her prejudices about what was suitable for the family table. Recipes appeared in the magazines for 'sheep's head broth', 'pig's head pudding' and 'calf's head pie'. Even horse-meat began to be featured on restaurant menus.

People were also encouraged to go further afield and gather seaweed and shellfish from the shores. In Scotland, cormorant's eggs were eaten; and the cormorants themselves, could be soaked in the sea, boiled then roasted. *Good Housekeeping* even revived ancient gypsy tradition by suggesting that whilst on your summer holiday, '*if you are lucky enough to acquire a hedgehog or a squirrel you will find them both good to eat.*'

In *Woman's Magazine*, however, Mrs Stanley Wrench suggested alternative sources of protein. There was, after all, no need for meat at all:

> '*This season we do not expect to have large meat supplies, so we must try to grow these crops that are meat substitutes — peas and beans, and dry them.*'

That Autumn Lord Woolton urged the housewife to preserve fruits from the hedgerow and garden; everyone should gather rosehips for marmalade, damsons for jam, chestnuts to roast and blackberries for jelly.

In November, he announced a points rationing scheme for a group of canned foods that included meat, fish and vegetables. Each person had a given number of points, and could decide how these should be allocated. If you had eight points left at the end of the week you could obtain, for example, two pounds of baked beans or half a pound of sardines. This was a popular measure as it did much to curtail the unfair distribution of unrationed foods.

In December, Woolton introduced perhaps the

finest welfare scheme of the war. Children under two were to be allocated a free issue of blackcurrant juice and cod-liver oil. (Later, the blackcurrant was replaced by lend-lease orange-juice, for which there was a small charge). Sadly, however, many mothers failed to take advantage of this scheme.

1942 was the year of conscription for unmarried women between 19 and 30. Since most women were working now, which made shopping very difficult, many found it more convenient to eat in works canteens or the 'British Restaurants', which had sprung up everywhere to cater for such needs. Many of the better class restaurants, however, were adept at cornering the supplies of unrationed food, so in the spring, the Government restricted them to serving one main course which was not to cost over five shillings.

Walt Disney

Clara Carrot

Clara Carrot is the picture of health, though the neighbours say she leads a double life. Sometimes she's a sweet, sometimes she's a savoury: it all depends on how you treat her. She adds piquancy to meat, fish and vegetable dishes ; and in puddings, pies and cakes, she's sweet and spicy. She's the making of

Portman Pudding

6 ozs. flour, 4 ozs. each grated raw carrot and potato. Teaspoon mixed spice, 2 tablespoons sugar. Level tcaspoon bicarbonate of soda, pinch of salt. ½ cupful of sultanas and raisins, 2 ozs. fat. Cream fat and sugar, add carrot, potato, flour, spice and soda. Mix well together. Add fruit. Add water if necessary to make a stiff dropping consistency. Steam for 2 hours at least. Serves 3 or 4. **A sweet that needs little sugar !**

EYES IN THE BLACKOUT

Some odd, unexpected little talents Doctor Carrot possesses. Not only does he entertain you at mealtimes, giving savour to your sweets and sweetness to your savouries, but he can actually—did you know?—help you to see better in the blackout. Meet Doctor Carrot: you'll like him.

Here's a recipe that will be new to most British housewives :

Boston Bake

Soak 2 breakfastcupfuls small white beans in cold water for 24 hours. Put into a stew-jar with 3 ozs. of diced fat bacon, and 1 lb. sliced carrots. Mix thoroughly 1 level teaspoonful dry mustard and 1 tablespoonful golden syrup with enough hot water to make ¼ pint. Pour over beans, and add enough water to cover. Put on lid, and bake in moderate oven for 2 to 2½ hours. For the last half-hour remove the lid, and bring some of the bits of bacon to the top to brown off. Delicious !

Six million acres were now under cultivation. Farmers produced oat, barley, wheat, sugarbeet, flax and clover for the home market. Over half a million tons of green vegetables were produced; but the largest crops by far were potatoes and carrots. There was such a glut of carrots that Lord Woolton launched another food campaign, encouraging everyone to eat more of this healthy vegetable. From January to May, 'Clara Carrot' and 'Doctor Carrot' stalked through the magazines expounding their own worth; they even hinted that eating carrots could help you to see in the black-out.

Food itself was now considered a munition of war. 'DIG, COOK, AND STORE' were to be the watchwords. Vegetables such as onions, broccoli, cabbage and brussel sprouts should be grown in the home gardens, thereby releasing field space for farmers to grow essential staple crops. The last remaining scraps of land were dug up and planted. There was a demonstration allotment in Hyde Park and many of London's Georgian squares were taken over for food production.

Rationing intensified throughout the year, with dried fruit, rice, sago, tapioca and the pulses affected in January, and canned fruit, tomatoes and peas following in February. In March the Government halted the production of white bread, in order to save the cargo space taken up by white North American flour. They had already tried, unsuccessfully, to promote the 'National Wholemeal Loaf'. Now, despite its unpopularity, the National Loaf was made compulsory. *Womans Own* gave a tip on how to tackle it:

'The new wholemeal loaf is difficult to cut thinly; try dipping your knife in boiling water between each slice, it makes thin slices easy to cut.'
(*Woman's Own,* 3rd July 1942)

By April, breakfast cereals and condensed milk were rationed. With most of Britain under the plough, dairy produce and milk was in short supply. Expectant mothers and nursing mothers, children and invalids were guaranteed a pint of milk a day, while the general public had what remained — usually two pints a week in winter supplemented by dried milk, and possibly three or four in the summer.

In July, syrup, treacle, chocolate and sweets joined the points rationing scheme. Now the good cook sweetened her cakes and biscuits with grated carrot or swede. Those who made their own preserves, however, were entitled to part of their preserves ration in extra sugar.

By the end of the year, rationing had reached its peak, with biscuits going on points in August and oatmeal and rolled oats in December. When Christmas 1942 arrived, it must have seemed as if enjoyment itself was rationed. December 25th with dried egg Christmas cake and pudding was, for most people, a dull affair.

On the whole, rationing had worked well. People accepted that it was the fairest way of distributing scarce resources. There were some people, though, who complained that it was not right that everyone over the age of six should get the same rations. The scheme took no regard of whether one had a heavy physical job or a sedentary one (only certain categories of heavy workers had been given an extra ration, in the form of cheese.) Also, why did children under six receive extra food in the form of orange juice and cod liver oil when growing teenagers were denied these supplements?

But in April 1943, *The Lady* summed up most people's feelings by saying:

'An overwhelming majority of women of all classes are thankful for the food controls and praise their efficient running. Many wives and mothers are able to give their families better and more regular meals under war conditions than ever before. The medical reports on the health of children of the Nation are the best arguments for wartime control.'

To encourage the consumption of more home-produced foods, new patriotic items called 'Victory Dishes' found their way into restaurants, works canteens and pubs. These were starred with a V sign and contained mainly potatoes and other home-grown vegetables ... though 'ship savers' such as dried egg, milk or cheese could be added.

Lord Woolton's final food campaign was almost certainly prompted by the fuel crisis of 1943 (see page 52). The British housewife's habit of cooking her food for long periods meant not only that excessive amounts of fuel were being used but also that much of the nutritional value was being wasted. Back in 1942, Dr Thompson, of the Food Education Society had stated in *Good Housekeeping* that:

'It is perfectly true to say that we grow in Britain the finest vegetables in the world, ... yet probably cook them the worst.'

Now Lord Woolton's bulletins insisted that vegetables should not be overcooked. Indeed, it was good to eat them raw at least once a day.
Conditions in 1944 remained very similar to 1943.

Potatoes (now referred to by Lord Woolton as 'the insurance crop') were still the mainstay. These together with carrots had doubled their acreage by 1944, achieving record tonnage. The farmers had ploughed up and planted another seven hundred thousand acres and were calling for extra Land Army Workers to get the harvest in.

With everyone working hard, there was little time to cook. Now the stock-pot came into its own to furnish a good casserole which could be left cooking slowly all day on the range or in a hay-box. Meat was now used more as a flavouring than as an integral part of the meal. *Woman's Magazine* suggested:

'If you can obtain a beef or mutton bone for flavouring, so much the better, but a bunch of scalded bacon rinds, tied together, will also serve the purpose, or you could add a bouquet of herbs.'

By the end of the war, the British public had virtually become vegetarians. *My Home* reported that:

'Although we are still among the world's greatest meat eaters, we have realized that too much meat is a bad thing ... the vegetable was regarded as a necessary evil; now we appreciate it as the essence of a good meal and a valuable aid to beauty ... we have become more sensible and thoughtful about food ... but I suppose all our good resolutions will be thrown overboard when we sit down to Victory dinners.'

When peace came people were obliged to keep their wartime habits for some time to come, however. In 1945, with a world shortage of food, there was no chance of stopping rationing at once. There was even less meat available than in 1944. In 1946 bread was rationed, and rationing was not finally abolished until the fifties.

But, as they gradually became available, people pounced with glee on all the pre-war luxuries. The scientific ways of cooking were mostly forgotten. Low-fibre white bread, sugar, meat and alcohol were devoured in quantity, vegetables were cooked from convenient tins or packets, fresh vegetables were overcooked and the water thrown away. Only recently has the wartime diet been acknowledged to be a good, healthy way of eating.

Fuel

'Let's get together — you and me and the people next door, and the Smiths down the road and cook for ten instead of two.' (*Woman's Own*, 14th September 1940)

The magazines were full of tips on saving fuel, showing that it was individual carelessness which caused waste of national resources. Many of the reminders to conserve energy started with the word 'if'. If you kept your electric lamp bulbs spotlessly clean by washing them weekly in soapy water, they would give out more light. Or, if every household saved two pounds of coal a day for a year, the fuel conserved would supply about 8000 tanks ...

Further economies could be made by lighting no unnecessary fires. A clever idea was to shut the dining room altogether or have breakfast and lunch at least in the kitchen. But the best idea of all was to close up your home (after turning off the gas and water in case of an air raid) and go to eat with a friend. *My Home* said in April 1941:

> *'The Government wants you to save by forming "cookery pools" with other wives and other families. You're saving the nation the fuel it needs for making tanks, planes, and guns and you're saving yourself time, money and trouble. Arrange yourselves to take turns cooking dinner, in asking each other to dinner in your respective homes.'*

There was a shortage of both domestic and imported coal during the war. Many of the young miners had joined the forces, abandoning without regret the appalling conditions of the pits where they were underpaid and lacked decent equipment. The older men were left to work the pits alone. Hilary Brett in a *Woman's Own* of October 1942 gave some ingenious ideas for spinning out the supply:

- *'Collect slack and dust in empty sugar cartons or strong brown bags, dampen it and use as brickettes.'*
- *'Mix ten parts of coal dust to one of clay to a paste with water. Shape into lumps and put onto fire while still damp. They burn for ages.'*
- *'Fill fruit cans with a mixture of damp tea-leaves and coal dust. Placed on a red fire, they give a lovely glow and plenty of heat.'*
- *'Heat a quantity of chalk in the grate and place in equal proportions to coal at the back of the fire. It throws out a tremendous heat and will continue burning forever almost!'*
- *'Throw potato peelings on a good, clear fire. They burn nicely and act as a sort of disinfectant.'*

'Remember, every careful day saves lives of sons, husbands, sweethearts', said *Woman's Own*.

Many housewives took to their bicycles, fitting them with shopping baskets. After petrol was banned for personal use in 1942, most people put their cars away for the duration unless their vehicles were needed for war work. The Ministry of Transport had already announced in March 1941, *'please finish travelling by 4 o'clock . . . and leave the bus, trams, and trains free for war workers'*. Holidays, too, were cancelled (the beaches were covered in barbed wire anyway), and *Woman and Home* in July 1942 said:

> *'Better to stay at home. The trains are still packed with troops and goods, more vital than our sun-suits and buckets.'*

So now the main saving of fuel was carried on in the home. The most sensible way to begin was to wear warmer underwear and woolies yourself, then you should lag your hot water tank with a blanket of kapok and calico, and finally, cover every interior and exterior waterpipe with old pieces of carpet, overcoats and even dressing gowns, sacking or felting.

In 1942, the Government urged 100,000 young miners to return to the pits but only a quarter responded. Then, after a wave of strikes in the coal mines that summer, people were asked to restrict the depth of their baths to five inches to save fuel. *Ideal Home* suggested that it was more patriotic to use a big sponge and a small amount of water, and in *The Lady* it was divulged that:

> *'The President of the Board of Trade has cut in two the large bath towels he used to enjoy to cut down laundry bills and hopes his plan will be followed all over the country.'*

A mild winter followed and the public responded so well that they saved half a million tons of coal more than they had been required to. But in 1943 and 1944, one in ten of the youngsters just joining up was forced to go down the mines, though many of these 'Bevin Boys', as they were called, managed to get out of it. There was still a severe shortage, and at the end of 1943, households were asked to save five pounds of coal per day. This they might manage by sieving the cinders, thus saving one pound per day per fire, or they could place a fire brick at the back of the grate which would glow red hot and radiate heat. If they went out or left a fire burning overnight, the coals needed to be banked up:

'... with slack, ashes, tea leaves, hedge or grass clippings or a mixture of all of them, you will keep the fire going for hours with no attention, and the amount of fuel it burns is less than you would need to re-kindle it if you let it go out. (Ideal Home, September, 1943)

By now, many people had dispensed with coal fires altogether. This was the age when those 'ugly' fireplaces were boarded up and replaced with an 'attractive' gas or electric fire set into the front with a hardboard surround. The Family was urged to snuggle closely round this, turn the gas down low (or switch off one bar), and draw the standard lamp nearer before continuing to knit, read and sew.

Perhaps the greatest saving of fuel could be managed through changing ways of cooking: in particular, cooking food for less time. Countless tips appeared in the magazines showing how energy could be conserved. For example:

- *'Never put more water in the kettle than you need at one time.'*
- *'A three- or four-tier steamer is a great saver — a whole meal of fish, vegetables, potatoes and steamed pudding can be done in one.'*
- *'Use a biscuit tin or sponge tin lid instead of a saucepan lid, when you are cooking for a long time; a kettle or a saucepan of potatoes will boil if placed on top.'*
- *'Put as many dishes as possible in the oven at the same time and have the food ready to be cooked near the oven so that little heat is wasted before putting it in.'*
- *'After you've lit the gas oven, open the door for a few seconds after it has been going for two minutes. This lets out the steam and heats the oven quicker.'*

It was also found that a washing-up bowl of water if used instead of a saucepan lid, or left in the oven after turning off, would warm up ready for use. Also, if a guest was staying, an ordinary building brick heated in the oven would retain its heat for a long time, and make for the visitor an efficient bed warmer when wrapped in several layers of flannel. The guest room could be aired well enough if a candle was lit and placed inside a flower-pot, and this saved a fire.

In hot weather, the cook was persuaded to give up cooking altogether and prepare a raw salad to save fuel. As well as adopting salad days, 'hay days' were a good idea as they saved fuel and precious time. Pauline Fry from *Woman's Own* said:

'That useful contraption, the hay box, once more comes into its own. Food placed in the hay box will continue to cook quietly for hours by itself with no risks of burning or over cooking meanwhile.'

But fuel and time — as the magazines never stopped saying — were not the only things that needed saving.

5 lbs. OF COAL SAVED IN ONE DAY BY 40,000 HOMES WILL PROVIDE ENOUGH FUEL TO BUILD A CHURCHILL TANK

NOTE : 5 lbs. of coal are used in 2 hours by a gas fire or electric oven.

Is YOUR home saving fuel to make Churchill tanks?

Save FUEL for BATTLE

ISSUED BY THE MINISTRY OF FUEL AND POWER

Salvage

'So few purchases are wrapped up now that one may see almost anything from a corset to a stick of celery being carried naked along Knightsbridge by distinguished shoppers.' (The Lady, December 1943)

Britain devoted more of her resources towards the War Effort than any other nation, Germany included. Re-cycling of waste was vital, especially with imports of raw materials so badly restricted. It was the housewife's job to salvage things from her home such as paper, bones, metal, gramophone records, old film, jam jars, metal, rubber and rags. Because each category had to be put into a different container, salvage stewards were appointed to carry out these duties. Salvage shops were opened throughout the country where people could deposit their scrap materials. Collections of food waste were made from special bins placed at the end of each street. Even children were roped in to help with good effect, for this job, it was felt, would give them interest and responsibility. Junior salvage collectors, known as 'Cogs', were enthusiastic about doing their bit.

Iron and metal were easy to collect. From 1940 onwards, a compulsory campaign had deprived parks, gardens and squares of their ornamental railings. Fifteen tons of scrap metal would make one medium sized tank. Aluminium saucepans, including those from the royal households, had been collected in July 1940. But, sadly, the aluminium was not of the right grade and many households suffered by having to cook with inferior pans for the rest of the war.

After Japan had joined the war, the supplies of rubber from the Far East dwindled fast. Housewives were asked to collect and hand in their old rubber corsets, boots, children's toys, punctured tennis balls, hot water-bottles, old bicycle tyres and rubber rings. To help stimulate the flow of scrap rubber from households, *Woman's Own* made up a 'Rubber Rhyme' in August 1943 (see opposite).

Paper was collected in every form without much difficulty. It was needed badly. One hundred tons alone, for example, were used to plan and build a battleship — high quality paper for the charts, preliminary drawings and log-books; waste paper for the engine gaskets, wall-boards and gun fuses. The invasion of Norway had cut major supplies of paper pulp, and the only way of balancing this deficit was to avoid buying new paper or recycle the old. Paper itself grew thinner as the war progressed, and the magazines helped by slimming down their issues, *Woman's Magazine*, for example, reduced its pages, then adopted a smaller format twice. In July 1942, the editor apologised for this:

'Once again we are having to save paper by having smaller pages. I have no doubts as to how my readers will react — you will accept the situation with a smile as you have the previous reductions we have made and be glad to know that in doing so you are dealing Hitler another blow and helping towards victory.'

Theatre programmes, bill heads, cheque books and

RUBBER RHYME

R stands for Rubber — peculiar stuff! It stretches, it bends and it bounces. And to give a gun-sight to a Churchill tank you merely need six or eight ounces.

R stands for Rafts to save the brave men who fight on the broad ocean highways ... and R's for the dinghies to save the R.A.F. boys when they have to crash down from the skyways.

R stands for R.A.F., as you've already seen, for Mae Wests when a fighter-plane's reeling, for life-saving jackets, reconnaissance boats and petrol tanks safely self-sealing.

R is for Rhyme — yes, of this I'm aware — and for bath-mats that may have gone rotten. And R's for the bottle that leaked in your bed and rubber toys you have almost forgotten.

Bring out your racquet grips, bring out your tyres — the ones that can never be mended. Salvage your doorstops, your old bathing-caps — the seaside, alas, is suspended.

R stands for Road-immune tyres for the tanks plus bullet-proof suits for snipers. R's for balloons and for oxygen masks — and a Lancaster's anti-freeze wipers.

R stands for Rags, household Refuse and Rope. And R stands for wise reclamation. But remember that rubber's more vital than most — and please help the whole British nation.

R's for the Riches in garage and cupboards, R's for the Rubbish discarded. And R's for those golf balls you think you might need and — ah! — the war effort retarded.

R's for the Runs — and I modestly blush! — R's for the Runs in your girdle. May I suggest, if the wreck is worn-out, 'twill help us to jump the last hurdle?

R is for victory swift if you heap you scrap rubber neat for the dustman. R stands for the Rewards that we all hope to reap when an R stands for joyous Re-union.

Bring out your rubber
Rub out That Man
Rub out the Japs and the Eyties
The sooner you do it
The sooner you can
Buy coupon-free nighties.

---

bus tickets became diminutive. People were asked to buy a slate or wipe-off pad to write their shopping-lists on. Envelopes were reused by sticking a label over them. A clever housewife would buy her household supplies in larger sizes thus saving cardboard. Private receipts and old cheques were taken straight back to the bank to be disposed of in secret, but ordinary waste paper such as used bills, old photographs and postcards would probably be collected. Drawers were to be turned out and anything of paper not needed was sent for scrap. The Ford Motor Company, in one of its advertisements in June 1942, helped towards paper salvage by saying:

'Solicitor's letters are as sweet as love letters to your local waste paper collector; the happiest ending a book can have is to go in the making of munitions.'

Knowing that six old books provided enough material to make one mortar shell carrier, the Government promoted special book drives up and down the country during 1943. Although people were needing and reading in wartime more books than they had ever done before, *Good Housekeeping* happily ran the slogan *'Few books bear second reading!'*, while *Woman's Own* asked their readers to make sure whether they really wanted every book in their bookcase. Interesting novels should go to the Post Office for the army, 'Dry-as-dust' books and old music to the paper salvage. By October, 56 million books had been collected, from which only six million were spared, so heaven knows what was destroyed.

Collecting waste for the many 'Pig Clubs' which had been formed was easier still. Practically everything could be made into swill except for poisonous things like tea-leaves, coffee-grounds, rhubarb leaves, fish-bones and, of course, no glass should get in. People now had to stop throwing their potato peelings onto the fire, the pigs needed them more. Once collected, the contents of the bins were sterilised, processed and fed to the voracious creatures.

Rags proved more difficult to collect. '*We're wearing them*' the housewives remarked. But generally speaking, when they were told that their rags would go to make battledresses, gun wadding, tyres, haversacks, padding for tank seats, maps for airmen, surgical dressings, camouflage netting, ground sheets, balloons, webbing, caps and wipers, as well as paper, they responded well. Even father's worn out soft collars would do to make maps for tank commanders.

Bones proved the most difficult to collect of all, especially if there were dogs or flies around. But housewives were told to hand them in AFTER the dog had been at them. They were to dry them in the oven once the gas had been turned off and then put them in a tin. '*Everything except for the backbone of a kipper*' could be used, said the Ministry of Supply — fish bones were not needed. The bones went into making explosives like nitro-glycerine, and as the Editor of *The Lady* pointed out:

> '*... it is interesting to know that household salvage bones made the glue used in distemper with which the thousands of aeroplanes used on D-Day were given their distinctive zebra markings.*'

Savings

JACK'S IN THE NAVY
saving our ships at sea

JILL'S IN THE POST OFFICE
saving her money to help him

Jill's the girl!

She'll never let it be said that the boys who are risking their lives for us were let down because people at home could not make sacrifices.

She thinks before she spends now.

Something saved here by giving up a luxury, something else saved there by doing without a treat. Every penny of it is invested in National Savings. In next to no time she's got a useful investment that grows greater as time goes on. Wise Jill! Some day these Savings may help to start a home — meanwhile they're helping to win the War!

HOW TO LEND TO HELP WIN THE WAR

NATIONAL SAVINGS CERTIFICATES
Free of Income Tax
Price 15s. Value after 5 years 17s. 6d. After 10 years 20s. 6d. which equals interest at £3 3s. 5d. per cent. Maximum holding 500 Certificates including earlier Issues.

3% DEFENCE BONDS
£5 and multiples of £5. Income Tax NOT deducted at source. Maximum holding £1,000.

POST OFFICE SAVINGS BANK & TRUSTEE SAVINGS BANKS
Any sum from 1/- upwards with annual limit of £500. Interest 2½% per annum.

Lend to Defend the Right to be Free

ISSUED BY THE NATIONAL SAVINGS COMMITTEE

'Money is needed as much as munition' ran the slogan for those left on the Home Front, for in no other war had the women to play such a prominent part in saving money for the nation. The National Savings Campaign was set up in November 1939. A Defence Bond was issued at the same time which allowed people to hold up to £1000. Ever since the outbreak of war, people had had to modify their spending, whether to meet the increase in income tax or the rise in the cost of living. But they were expected to do more, and the magazines supported the country by asking the housewife to give up a luxury or do without a treat and save the money instead. *Woman and Home* in December 1940 said:

> *'Now your family has to help buy guns, tanks and planes to defend a bigger family — the family of Britain.'*

By August 1940, £200,000,000 had been saved, and the National Savings Committee had issued countless pamphlets in the magazines exhorting people to do their 'bit'. People were asked to give National Savings Stamps for Christmas rather than bulky presents which would, incidentally, add to transport costs as well as use up precious wrapping paper. In many

"I'm the 5/- National Savings Stamp."

I make your War Savings still simpler and I tempt you to save still faster. Simply stick me in your book with your 2/6 and 6d. stamps and 'swop' every now and then for Savings Certificates, Defence Bonds, Savings Bonds or National War Bonds of the Savings Bank Issues, or use me to make deposits in the Post Office or Trustee Savings Bank. Ask for me next time you do your War Savings.

Obtainable from any Post Office or Trustee Savings Bank, War Savings Selling Centres, Honorary Official Agents, and Savings Groups

Issued by the NATIONAL SAVINGS COMMITTEE

towns and villages throughout the country, housewives were acting as honorary secretaries and collectors for street savings groups. There were also special savings weeks.

By 1943 saving was almost a national obsession. Private individuals were putting aside something like a quarter of their disposible incomes. But with more women working than ever before, it was tempting to be a little thoughtless with that extra money coming in. A nasty little individual — the 'Squander Bug' — was created to help the propaganda, and he made his way into the Saving's pamphlets, covered with swastikas (so that you knew which side he was on). He incited the housewife to spend her savings:

'He's artful, he's insidious, always at your ear, whispering suggestions for spending.' (September 1943)

Or …

'The Squander Bug is always lurking in the background, ready to pounce on your housekeeping money. Be on your guard against him — keep your cash out of his clutches by putting more and more into War Savings every week.' (November 1943)

Conspicuous spending, however, was virtually impossible. A purchase tax had been put on most luxury goods and many people preferred to wait until better things appeared in the shops anyway. Even at the end of the war, when conditions hadn't improved, people went on saving for a better life for their children in the future.

THE BEACHES ARE CLEARED! These have been hard years for children. They have missed so much that *we* once enjoyed. Let us now build for them a land and a life worth having. When the Jap is beaten there will be much to do and our savings will be vital. For the children's sake — *give thanks by saving.*

GIVE THANKS BY SAVING

Issued by the National Savings Committee

DON'T LISTEN TO HER; SHE RUNS A SAVINGS GROUP

THE SQUANDER BUG
WORKS FOR HITLER!

When your Savings Group Secretary calls there's always a third party present. That little saboteur, the Squander Bug, is with you, doing his stuff. He can't bear to see you putting by a little fund for a rainy day! He hates to see money going to help the boys who are fighting. Of course, *you're* not going to listen to him!

Savings Certificates costing 15/- are worth 20/6 in 10 years — increase free of income tax. They can be bought outright, or by instalments with 6d., 2/6 or 5/- Savings Stamps through your Savings Group or Centre or at any Post Office or Trustee Savings Bank. Buy now!

ISSUED BY THE NATIONAL SAVINGS COMMITTEE

Women at Work

In May 1944, 11 days before the invasion of Normandy, Rosita Forbes wondered if people realised that:

'... in Britain just about seven women out of every available eight are doing wholetime war jobs.'
(*Woman's Own*, 26th May 1944)

She was writing from America *'where women's lives and home life generally seem — to the outsider — to go on very much as usual'*. In Britain, on the other hand, there seemed to be few women who failed to contribute actively to the war effort, whether in the forces, the factories or as unpaid volunteers.

When war started it found many women in full-time employment, it is true. But for something like a third of them this meant domestic service. Even a fairly modest lower middle class income could ensure the services of a young girl from the country. For many others employment meant repetitive tasks in the still flourishing textile industry. And for the majority of women — whatever their background — work was something you had to give up on marriage (or when the children arrived).

In the early days of the war the magazines tended to support the idea that women — particularly those with children — should stay at home. Even later, when women workers were desperately needed, *Woman's Own* felt obliged to state, on 19th April 1941, that:

'Whether or not we agree with Mr Bevin's plans for sending women to needed jobs (and to be honest we must admit that our sex isn't without members who might learn a lot by having to do a job of work) we all agree that it is home that matters.'

But while many women *did* agree, there were others who had had the foresight to realise, well before September 1939, that women would need to serve in many other capacities in the event of another major war.

Women had, in fact, come out of the home in their hundreds of thousands during the previous World War. By February 1940, according to *Woman's Own*, though it was true that *'of over 100,000 women in engineering industry, a large proportion are in arms factories, filling shells, making cartridges cases and small arms ammunition'*, their numbers had not reached the level of 1914-18, when *'women munition workers exceeded 800,000'*.

And there were the women's forces, all branches of which had been formed during the First World War. By 1918 the WRNS (Women's Royal Navy Service) and the WRAF (Women's Royal Air Force) each had some 5,000 recruits. Strongest of all was the WAAC (Women's Army Auxiliary Corps), whose members —

at first confined to nursing or the kitchen — soon took on duties in administration and communications.

All these were disbanded when the peace came. Since a future war was unthinkable, there was no need for a peace-time women's army. But some of these veterans continued to meet at women's branches of the British Legion. And it was they who, in 1934, began to organise a Voluntary Emergency Service (VES) which, gradually, began to receive support from official sources, including the War Office and the Air Ministry. This included the provision of instructors for summer training camps, for example.

In September 1938, following the Czech crisis, the VES was turned into the Auxiliary Territorial Service (ATS). This, as the successor to the WAAC, was to be the principal branch of the women's services, having under it such organisations as the First Aid Nursing Yeomanry (inevitably referred to as the FANY's).

During the following year, with war increasingly probable, the other two branches came into existence. In March the WRNS were reformed, and in July the WRAF re-emerged under the new name of the Women's Auxiliary Air Force, the WAAF.

By the end of 1939 there were some 43,000 women in the various auxiliary forces, the 'Ats', 'Wrens' and 'Waafs' as they came to be called, together with members of the nursing services. All at this time were volunteers, and, most of them came from the wealthier sections of society.

Within four and a half years their numbers would swell to over two and a half million, and they would come from all sections of society, providing a social mix which did much to increase women's awareness of each other's interests and concerns.

As in the previous war, women were at first needed to perform traditionally female tasks. And, indeed, this remained a major role. Since women were not to be sent into combat, every woman cook, for example, meant a man available for front line service.

But, as the war stepped up, women were allowed to volunteer for jobs which had hitherto been considered very unfeminine. Many, for example, served in mixed 'Ack-Ack' (anti-aircraft) batteries, alongside men soldiers. At first, however, they were treated in a pettily separate way. Though doing the same tasks and taking the same risks as the men, these women gunners were not supposed to consider themselves part of the battery. Nor were they allowed to wear the badges to which their male comrades were entitled. It took a visit to such a battery by Churchill himself to change this. The Prime Minister — not particularly noted for his feminist leanings — shot off a memo to

WOMEN OF BRITAIN

This fine tribute to the work our women
are doing for the war effort has been
specially written for 'Woman's Magazine'

by FAY INCHFAWN

Hark! It is the summons of
  The bugle of the Lord.

He who called the men of Britain
  To become His living sword
Sounds once more His royal challenge;
  Calls with no uncertain claim
To the women of Great Britain
  To become His living flame.

They have heard it! They have heard
  That compelling mighty word.
They have answered in their thousands—
  Body willing—spirit stirred!

Up with haste the British women
  Rise responsive to the call—
Women stout—and women slender—
  Women queenly—women small.

Proud—ah! proud—the British women;
  Quick—how quick!—their hasting feet
March from parlour and from palace,
  Castled gate and battered street;

Women young—and women old—
Women shy—and women bold—
  Bringing for an offering
Hands to lend
And backs to bend;
Women with their lives to spend
  In the service of their king.

They are willing! They are willing!
  British women, here and now,
Drive with skill Britannia's lorries,
  Run to guide Britannia's plough;
They will mind Britannia's children,
  Scrub, and shop, and wash, and mend,
Crochet, knit, and sew for Britain
  Till her hour of need shall end.

Swift to do Britannia's bidding—
  Never asking why, nor when;
Toiling in Britannia's kitchens,
  They will feed her fighting men;
In machine shops, in munitions,
  Toiling hard for Britain's sake;
Nothing—*nothing*—British women
  Cannot—will not—undertake.

They are giving! They are giving
Time and treasure, strength and skill;
Smooth hands—rough hands—
Soft hands—tough hands—
Resolute and toiling still.

Gently on Britannia's wounded,
  Free from hurry as from fear,
They are laying hands of healing,
  Hands of sympathy and cheer.

Yes, and loyal British women,
  With the faith which understands,
From their beds of pain and anguish
  Lift up faithful praying hands.

Can they fail? The splendid answer
  Thunders over land and sea:
*Shout with gladness, British women!
  For the coming victory!*

They have hearkened to the summons of
  The bugle of the Lord—
He who called the men of Britain
  To become His living sword!
They have taken up the challenge
  And acknowledging His claim:

British women! British women!
  You shall be His living flame!

the Secretary of State for War (marked '*Action this Day: 18/10/41*') pointing out that this state of affairs was particularly wounding to the servicewomen. He ordered that they were not only to be allowed to wear the various insignia but could also call themselves 'Gunners' and 'Members of the Royal Regiment of Artillery', since that was a wish universally expressed.

The changing roles that women were expected to play in the services can be worked out from an examination of the recruiting advertisements placed by the government. These were found in a wide variety of magazines in great profusion from 1941 onwards (though they were halted in 1943).

The messages in such advertisements ranged from the emotive — '*No woman will ever have peace in her heart unless she helps this man!*' — to the patronising — '*Joan's doing a real job*' — or the soberly informative — '*Why married women are asked to volunteer for the Services*'. It is tempting, perhaps, to dismiss them as simple propaganda, but there was a vital need to attract women to the Services, and, even after conscription was introduced in late 1941, it still relied to a great extent on volunteers.

By early 1942 women were being trained for a wide variety of jobs, and over an age range from 17½ to 43. By the middle of the year there were advertisements for cooks up to the age of 50. But for a whole year, from mid 1943, the advertisements for servicewomen disappeared, since the demand for womanpower had shifted towards Industry. When more women were needed for the Services in late 1944 recruiting was restricted to those between the ages of 17½ and 19.

Until Churchill became Prime Minister little thought had been given, at an official level, to the role of women in the war effort. From then on, however, the move away from what were now considered inessential industries was accelerated. The textile industry, in particular, was slimmed down, and many factories with a predominantly female workforce went over to war production. Women found themselves doing new and demanding jobs, while often being asked to do 10 to 12 hour shifts.

Following the fall of France there was an obvious need to increase the size of the British armed forces. Sir William Beveridge was asked to work out the figures. In late 1940 he reported that, by the end of 1941, the Services and Civil Defence would need an extra 1,750,000 men and 84,000 women. This, he calculated, would mean taking half a million men out of the munitions factories and putting them in uniform. But a larger army would use more munitions, so the factories needed more workers, not fewer. The only answer was to train more women in skilled work, thereby freeing greater numbers of men.

In March 1941 Parliament passed the Registration of Employment Act, by which people could be directed towards essential war work. At first the only women to whom this applied were between the ages of 20 and 21, but by the end of the year the upper limit had been extended to 30 years. (Eventually it was to affect all women between the ages of 18 and 50). Early that same year centres were set up throughout Britain where women could go for engineering training. A massive advertising campaign was launched to

FOUR GIRLS AND *their job*

Their factory once made boots. Now they are making electrical parts for the Allies all over the world

No, she is not a Russian. Although there is the same directness, courage and determination in her face as in the photographs we have seen of Russian women. She is British all right—she was nine when this war broke out! She is only fourteen now. Her name is Beryl Haycock. For six months she was in the office, but Beryl was not satisfied until she was given a machine to operate. Here you see her assembling a cartridge fuse carrier. Let us hope that victory is near so that Beryl can spend her youth in the world we want a fourteen-year old girl to have.

Some of the girls in this Midland factory are making electrical parts the size of a small hairpin (a bent wire contrivance for pinning up curls, if you've forgotten) but Mrs. Winifred Brandrick has something bigger to occupy her time. She is taping the coil ends of a giant armature for a directcurrent generator which will soon find itself in use as part of a rolling mill equipment in a South African steel works.

Twenty-year-old Barbara Wren is not standing in this attractive frame just to have her photograph taken. She is showing you her job, which is punching core plates for electrical machines. Once upon a time in this town, small cosy factories made boots and shoes. Leather meant a job for local girls. Beryl Wren was one of them. She was a shoe operator but is now quite content to give leather a miss until coupons are things of the past.

Dorothy Deakin is twentyone and met her husband in the works where she is doing her war job. You see her soldering elements in an Admiralty pattern cartridge fuse which is used in fuse gear for the protection of electrical apparatus against excess current. Dorothy is doing another step in the same job as fourteen-year-old Beryl Haycock. Other girls are producing giant rotors for one of Russia's armament plants.

persuade as many women as possible to opt for the Services or Industry.

This turned out to be a failure for two reasons. First, not enough women volunteered; secondly, there was not the machinery for processing those who did come forward. Of 2 million who registered by August 1941 only 500,000 were interviewed, and of those only 87,000 had gone into the women's auxiliary services or Industry.

The answer was to extend conscription. All unmarried women aged between 20 and 30 were subject to call-up, with the choice limited to the Services or 'vital war work'. (Under the latter heading came munitions, aircraft, transport, tank or radio industries, Civil Defence, the Woman's Land Army, nursing and the Royal Observer Corps.)

There were various reasons why there were not enough volunteers. Many women (or their parents) were put off the idea of the Services by the widespread rumours of immorality that swept through Britain in 1941. The auxiliary forces, it seems, were a hotbed of vice, with women dropping out from pregnancy or riddled with venereal disease. Questions were asked in the House and an investigating committee set up. After six months it reported that the rates of pregnancy and veneral disease in the women's forces were everywhere lower — often considerably lower — than in the civilian population. The report blamed the rumours on the blatant sexism of male soldiers.

The reasons why the factories were unpopular were more varied. The main ones were that many of the factories were located in the Midlands or the north-west (which often meant that women would have to move away from home), and many industrial jobs were still repetitive and boring; there was often resentment on the part of men workers, who felt that their skills were belittled if women could acquire them; and a predominantly male trade union leadership showed little sympathy for the problems of women. Also there was, at the beginning, little or no provision of nursery schools for the young children of women working in factories; women factory workers, like all full-time working women, had to do the shopping outside work hours; and, finally, husbands were often reluctant to allow their wives to take up industrial work.

Recruitment

These, then, were some of the reasons why many women were reluctant to join the Services or engage in vital war work. What, however, were the magazines doing to persuade them to volunteer?

Their efforts in this direction seem to fall into five categories. First — and most noticeably — they emphasised the positive side of whatever they were describing, while attempting to correct any false impressions that their readers might have. Secondly, they set out to give women a feeling of pride in their achievements and those of their sisters. Thirdly, they lobbied for any reforms that they thought needed to

"*Joan's doing a real job*"

"*That's what I like about her. She's not playing at war work. Once she heard my story of what women could do for our chaps she was off like a flash to join the W.A.A.F. Gets her stripe soon . . . and deserves it.*"

The R.A.F. wants more women like Joan . . . and that means more women like *You*. You'll wear a proud uniform. You'll get a close-up of the war. *And you'll share responsibility with airmen who are making history.*

The age limits for all trades are 17½ to 43 with few exceptions. Go to the R.A.F. Section of the nearest Combined Recruiting Centre (address from any Employment Exchange) or fill in the coupon for leaflet giving full particulars.

be introduced. Fourthly, they advised their readers how to adapt to the demands of their new jobs. And finally they attempted to influence those people — particularly parents or menfolk — who might be holding women back from doing their duty.

The first two categories were often combined in articles with titles such as 'Battling ATS', 'Women can make it', or 'Down on the farm with the land girls'. Some of these concentrated on individual forms of service or war work; others looked at the wide range of work that women were taking up.

Often, however, individual items could be seen as having one clear function. There were, for example, many attempts to soften the somewhat forbidding image of the women's services in a bid to make them more attractive to young women. On 9th September 1939, six days after war started *Woman's Own* wrote that:

'The Women's Army is a very human institution. The use of powder is allowed and even a touch of natural lipstick. Heavy make-up and brightly varnished nails are frowned upon, and so is hair that hangs down below the tunic collar. Smoking is allowed in "off-duty" hours but not in uniform. Not an easy life, perhaps, but a healthy, friendly one.'

And they were clearly reflecting women's pride in the acquisition of new skills when they asked:

'Can you strip, clean, reassemble an Army gun in record time? Rose Waltho, 24, of Stafford, in Midlands ATS can do this with Hotchkiss, Browning, Bren, anti-tank rifles, Tommy and Lewis guns: she says "All my time is taken up studying guns. It's a responsible job. One slip might mean a jam and the death of the gunner".' (Woman's Own, 26th September 1941*)*

Once it became clear that women were needed to take up industrial work there was less emphasis on the ATS and WAAF, while the WRENS (which seemed to have more volunteers than places) were rarely mentioned. Positive accounts of factory life and women's achievements in the work-place abounded, however. *Woman's Own*, in particular, was rich in these. The magazine's attitude was neatly summed up in December 1941 when the editor reported indignantly that:

'Many women and girls still hesitate to volunteer for factory work because it's not "quite nice". Don't they know that some of the finest women in Britain are in industry now? In any case, factory hands have always been among the most human, likeable friendly folk anywhere.

Do the particular people think the Nazis are quite nice? Would they feel more refined working for them?'

And on 1st January 1943 she was able to point to a whole string of advantages that could be gained from industrial work:

GO TO IT!

You can see from these pictures how splendidly women are tackling every kind of war work. One of their latest efforts is on gun sites. On the left is an A.T.S. volunteer in a special uniform relaying spotting orders by field telephones

The trousered postwoman of to-day

Women do valuable work in overhauling aeroplanes. These two are stringing a tailplane

W.A.A.F. at company drill

A.T.S. girls being taught to handle motor-cycles

JEEPERS

Those of you who have been chased up trees and frightened to death by these comical looking little vehicles will be pleased to see one of your own sex getting even with the aid of a spanner.

The A.T.S. have come to the rescue of re-conditioning the Jeep in many parts of the country, and this expert mechanic will soon have this one back in service with the army.

'Listen to a supervisor in a Birmingham factory. "Factory work benefits women, helps them forget small worries," she says.

Medical and welfare officers in factory towns attribute better health of women workers to simpler foods, medical supervision, no time to develop petty illnesses, less overcrowding in cities, shorter hair, less coddling, and losing superfluous weight doing active work.'

The magazine was rich in items showing the growing contribution of women to the industrial war effort, particularly in areas hitherto the domain of men. Most of these were put in the regular column called 'What Women are Doing and Saying', with sub-heads such as 'Hats off to these feminine achievements'.

We're proud of you

'I'm employed as a bus-driver driving a double decker bus, and drive through blackouts, working the same shift as the men. I'm told I am the only woman in the country doing the job and holding a Public Service Vehicle Utility Certificate. Can you tell me if this is true?

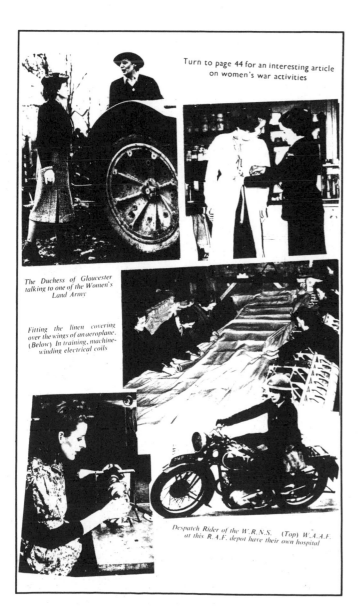

Turn to page 44 for an interesting article on women's war activities

The Duchess of Gloucester talking to one of the Women's Land Army

Fitting the linen covering over the wings of an aeroplane. (Below) In training, machine-winding electrical coils

Despatch Rider of the W.R.N.S. (Top) W.A.A.F. at this R.A.F. depot have their own hospital

'I've just made enquiries but cannot find out. Perhaps some other reader can tell us. I have never heard of any girl driving a bus ... We are very proud to have such a clever and enterprising girl as one of our readers.' (*Woman's Own*, 8th March 1941)

Dundee woman railway porter

'When I registered at the Employment Exchange and obtained a job as a railway porter my friends all said I could never manage the heavy work. Not only do I handle trunks and all other packages, but I deliver them within a radius of a mile on a wheelbarrow. My hubby is a POW and doesn't know I hold this job. I also have a girl of 3. It can be done.' (*Woman's Own*, 20th March 1942)

Post girls

'Postgirls are the unheralded heroines of Britain's least sung women's civilian army. Whether working in London or big provincial cities which the blitz has visited, with puzzles of changed addresses to work out, letters to deliver to a heap of rubble; or on long country roads, where isolated cottages must have their mail as regularly as home in the village high street.' (*Woman's Own*, 4th September 1942)

Jobs no woman could do

'Job experts said no woman could do: boring, screwing a breech ring for the barrel of a 6-pounder tank gun on a giant lathe. But Miss Megan Lewis, 22, from Wales, ex-clerk at a London hospital, has been doing it at the Home Counties Ordinance factory where 80% of machine operatives are women. "I learned by watching the setter at work on the machine." Officials were astounded.' (*Woman's Own*, 27th August 1943)

By the end of the war the range of jobs taken over by women was staggering. On 21st April 1945 *Woman* under the title 'Seeing's believing' produced a series of photographs of women steeplejacks, bricklayers, pipe-layers and brewery workers.

The magazines took very seriously what they obviously saw as their duty to press for any reforms which would improve woman's lot, particularly when this could also help the war effort. A good example comes from *Good Housekeeping*, which, though diligent in plugging the Government line, was nevertheless prepared on many occasions to point out shortcomings in the system.

In October 1941 they commissioned Cicely Fraser to find out what life in the factories was really like. She came back so impressed with what she had seen that she worried whether the resulting article, 'Be fair to the factories', was '*too propagandist*'. Much of it was, indeed, close to the standard morale-boosting account of sturdy, happy women wielding spanners while singing along to 'Music while you work'. She made no mention of 12-hour night shifts or of the health hazards, it is true. But she did refer to the high rate of absenteeism, caused by women taking time off to shop for those scarce, unrationed foods which were unlikely to be available late in the evening or on Saturday afternoon. And she sympathised with mothers of young children who had to choose between sending them away to safe areas or keeping them close by, in danger. Both these problems, she concluded, were for the Ministry of Labour to do something about.

And an anonymous male contributor to *Woman's Own* in July 1941 referred to the Minister of Labour by name with the words:

> 'I'm inclined to warn Mr Bevin that his conscription scheme for young married women is causing uneasiness which could be avoided.'

The article went on to recommend that the Government should set up schemes to enable young married women, whose husbands were in industry, to work with them, rather than be sent to other parts of the country. Family life as well as the war effort would be the winners.

Much of the advice, however, was addressed to women themselves; notably on how best to adapt to the changing circumstances in which they found themselves. Some of this was of the type, '*My complexion is sallow and I look dreadful in khaki, what kind of powder should I choose?*' But it was often measured and serious, for example advising new factory workers on matters of health and safety.

More serious still were the articles aimed at those people who were holding women back from volunteering. In mid 1941, *Good Housekeeping* printed an 'Open letter to parents and husbands' which stated forcefully that the entire woman-power of Britain had to be fully mobilised. The writer appealed to husbands and parents not to stand in the way of their wives or grown-up daughters. Separation was difficult to bear, but it was nothing compared to what had happened to people in occupied Europe, and what would happen in Britain if Hitler took over.

By December 1942 there were even fewer woman available for work. Victoria Stevenson, writing in *Woman's Own*, urged servicemen to allow their wives to leave the home — '*Why do you wish to keep a young, healthy girl back from doing her duty just because she is your wife? Is it that you dread competition? Or do you feel that, working side by side with other men and women, she will become coarsened, changed into a woman who prefers the company of a public bar to that of her own home?*' Tough words perhaps, but women were changing and men were not always happy about it.

Forgotten jobs

With all the talk of women in the Services and the factories, it might be easy to forget some of the other jobs women were doing in the NAAFI, domestic work, the Women's Land Army and voluntary work.

NAAFI stood for the 'Navy, Army and Air Force Institutes', but the average service man and woman would have been hard-pushed to tell you what it meant. To them the NAAFI was just the place where you could relax, have a cup of tea and a bite to eat after a tough day. And as the item on page 65 from

Conscripted Wives

SEPARATION—that is one of the biggest hardships of any war. In this war it is a trial that has to be borne by men and women all over the country — whether they are in uniform or not. The children were the first victims of this heartache in Evacuation Week, 1939.

As the war effort develops, fresh problems arise and many of them have to do with the burning question of home life and how to keep it going in spite of the absolute necessity that many men and women should be sent here and there, irrespective of where their human roots lie. We have to accept personal hardships to avoid a world-wide tragedy, which would affect not only ourselves but our children in grievous and terrible ways.

But there is no doubt about the fact that forethought can prevent and cure at least some of the hardships caused by present conditions. Probably you and your friends get together sometimes to enjoy a good old indignation meeting—as we all do—and re-organize wartime life in your own way. Probably you have some good ideas. It's certainly a great relief to get your particular anxieties off your chest.

So you may be interested to read the view of one man who has been about the country forming his ideas of how one great bogey of parting could be banished. It's only one man's view—but an interesting one—and you'll probably find it food for discussion at home.

EDITOR.

RECENTLY, in the North, I met a number of highly skilled war workers and their young wives, and I'm inclined to warn Mr. Bevin that his conscription scheme for young married women is causing uneasiness which could be avoided.

These young wives without children are ready to work, eager to help the war effort; many are frankly bored killing time in lodgings while their men are at the factory. But they want, if possible, to be with, or at least near, their husbands; their husbands view with alarm the possibility of enforced separation.

The point is that many of them are not satisfied that separation is always necessary.

One man in an important aircraft key job told me: "If they try to take my wife from me and send her to some distant job there's going to be a shindy. I work hard and I need her with me. It's asking for trouble separating wives and husbands in that way. It's going to break up a lot of marriages and I don't want mine broken up."

They were sensible and could not blind themselves to possibilities, whatever their ideas about fidelity. Far apart, they might be thrown into circumstances, temptations, which would not count in the ordinary way. Something might happen which would cut across their happiness. It was easy to say these things shouldn't occur, but sometimes they did. But the chief consideration was: they were happy together, and would miss terribly each other's companionship. They hadn't been married long; were they now to be dragged apart when, *with a little forethought*, they might work happily together for the war?

Here, I could see, was a craftsman doing a vital, specialized war job on which victory depends. Mr. Bevin would be wise to keep him, and others like him, happy at their work and not lonely and disgruntled.

I was told of men working drills in this same factory who should be at their machines all the time in the interests of output. But precious time was wasted every day while they went to a store for block and other material, waited for their turn to be attended to, signed chits and so forth.

This could easily be done by a boy or woman. Why should not this and similar accessory jobs be done by these young wives working beside their husbands as "mates" instead of being drafted miles away to work in separation, loneliness, and possibly—why shut one's eyes to the fact?—moral danger? That was his view.

A big tank factory in the Midlands has already set an example. Husbands and wives work there side-by-side, and the employers say that this "family co-operation" idea has proved a great success: the wives learn technical processes quickly by watching and helping their husbands as "mates"; it is team-work which helps output.

Most war factories, it is assumed, could employ a number of young wives in this way, and they would be of greater value to the war effort, in the long run, than separated from their husbands and dumped anywhere.

If there must be mobile woman-power ready to go anywhere, irrespective of ties, let it be recruited from the single women. Uprooting usually means less to them, and they may find fun in the adventure.

Wives of Service men, we know, have to endure separation when their husbands join up, and they may ask: "If we manage, why shouldn't the wives of factory workers?" But the parallel doesn't quite hold. Wives cannot usually be with their husbands in military camps or on active service; they can, much more easily, in war factories.

My talks with these war workers convince me that Mr. Bevin would be wise to give them the chance wherever it is humanly possible. Happy, married workers mean maximum output.

No place like home . . .

but, to the serving man, the next best thing is Naafi. He can always depend on it. In peace or in war, in the long, slow periods of waiting and between fast, fierce battles Naafi canteens provide him not only with good food and hot drinks but also with the hundred and one small extra comforts that take the edge off the hardships of Service life. Like home . . . Naafi is always there. To keep up this high standard of service to the Forces Naafi must have a steady flow of recruits. A break in the supply of recruits means that fighting men go short of little luxuries, warmth and comfort. Manageresses, cooks and counter assistants are urgently needed *now*. For full details about pay, uniform and conditions of service apply to Navy, Army & Air Force Institutes, Imperial Court, Kennington Lane, London, S.E.11.

Serve with NAAFI

Woman's Illustrated shows NAAFI workers were never far behind the troops after the allies moved deep into Europe.

Domestic workers were an essential part of the war effort, since they were the first link in a work-chain at the end of which could be found the front-line troops and full-timers employed on vital war-work. We tend to think of women replacing men, so that the men could go off to fight. But just as important was the move to bring in women to do part-time, light or relatively unskilled domestic work, thereby releasing women for skilled or more arduous work. Such women were particularly needed both to help staff the nurseries set up for the children of war-workers and to keep the hospitals going at a time when they were under great pressure from dealing with bomb victims and the return of wounded troops.

The Women's Land Army (WLA) was brought in to help farmers at a time when Britain was obliged to produce as much of its own food as possible. The farmers could not do this alone, and the 'Land girls',

as everyone called them, put in long hours as farm-workers, foresters, and even as ratcatchers. This was rightly considered to be vital war-work.

The WLA had originally been formed during the First World War but, like the other women's organisations, had been disbanded when peace came. It was reformed in June 1939 and had 20,000 volunteers by the autumn of 1941, when it was recognized that:

> 'Land Girls have done a fine job of work this year: ploughing, sowing, hoeing, harvesting our vital wartime crops, often working from dawn to dusk in all weathers. The vast majority work in complete obscurity, without many home comforts. All the more honour to them!' (Woman's Own, 26th September 1941)

Not only were their hours long, but they were often lodged in miserable conditions and sometimes looked down upon by the farm people for whom they worked and with whom most of them lived. The best magazines in which to find out about the life of Land Girls are those written specifically for country women, notably *The Farmer's Home* (Supplement to *The Farmer and Stock Breeder*) and *Home and Country*, the official journal of the Women's Institutes. An article in the latter refers to the prejudice against women farm workers and urges farmers' wives to be more welcoming to the Land Girls, the importance of whose work the writer underlines.

We cannot leave a chapter on women at work without mentioning the thousands of women who gave freely of their time, often under arduous and dangerous conditions, without payment. The best-known voluntary organisation was the Women's Voluntary Service (WVS) founded by the redoubtable Lady Reading in August 1938, originally to help with the ARP services. By early 1940 it had become a mammoth operation:

> 'The Women's Voluntary Services organisation has over 500,000 unpaid workers, 300 at the Westminster HQ. Lady Reading, chairman, says: "We have all types and ages. One fine thing is the way young women have sacrificed leisure or money to work for us. Only capability counts. A titled woman is subordinate to a typist if the typist is the better worker".' (Woman's Own, 24th February 1940)

It is difficult to imagine what official bodies could have done, either at national or local level, without the help of the WVS. They stepped in where local authorities were ill-prepared or under-staffed; there was no neighbourhood — in city or village — without its volunteers; and it was to the WVS that the authorities turned for help.

Angus Calder, rightly, pays tribute to the contributions made by the WVS. According to *The People's War* these women looked after bombed-out and orphaned children, ran mercy errands to blitzed homes, collected pots and pans during the great Alumimium Handover, distributed gift clothing from the United States and the Empire, and ran second-hand clothing exchanges. They also ran British Welcome Clubs for GIs, organised mobile canteens for

Dismantling and re=assembling a magneto.

LEARNING TO BE TRACTOR DRIVERS

Members of the Women's Land Army in Training—Theory and Practice

Centres have been opened all over the country to train women for work on the land. These pictures show them receiving instruction at one of the centres. They are proving most apt pupils, and their enthusiasm has aroused the admiration of their instructors.

Seeing how the engine works.

A real job of work with a cultivator and Fordson tractor.

Instruction in the theory of ploughing.

"Here is the very heart of the engine—the cylinders."

Urgently Required!

Are you one of those domesticated women who thoroughly enjoy looking after other people? Then here is just the job for you!

Urgently required—ten thousand women for domestic work in hospitals.

Ten thousand domestic workers, the situation desperate, hospitals with their grand record, their mighty responsibilities, in need. Clearly, one could not ignore the call to do something about it. One must go right away to the nearest hospital and find out exactly what sort of duties this term "domestic work" covers.

"Then," I said to myself, "I can tell Woman's Magazine readers all about it. Perhaps some of them will answer this emergency call."

A quick telephone appointment, and soon I am in the hospital asking to see the Matron. The porter, busy with switchboard and telephone, calls to an assistant to inform Matron of my arrival. Meanwhile, I wait in the clean, carbolic-scented corridor. Doors constantly open on either side as various members of the staff come and go. A white-coated house surgeon with stethoscope round his neck hurries to the lift. Blue-uniformed sisters and nurses pass me, intent on various duties. A woman nursing a baby enters and sits on a bench inside the door. At the far end of the corridor a kitchen door stands wide open, letting through an odour of hot soup in the making.

"Matron will see you in her office," says a voice at my elbow.

I find Matron, very business-like, at her desk. She gives a gesture of dismay at the very mention of domestic workers.

"Urgently needed? I should think so!" is her remark. "Here, in this comparatively small hospital, we employ thirty such on the staff in peace time. Now, with the wards overfull and very often the daily number of casualties almost doubled, we have only eleven. Cooks, kitchen-maids, dietitians, ward-maids, linen-room helpers, pantry-maids, and scrubbers—the hospitals in this country, without exception, are short of all these. How they carry on is a miracle."

We discussed difficulties generally. Then Matron told me how, instead of regular ward-maids, she is now engaging domesticated women to work in daily shifts. This enables those with family ties to return to their homes at tea-time.

The head cook is training her assistants and kitchen-maids—some of them educated women who have offered to take part in the war effort, but who have never before done a hand's turn. These are daily workers, too, who return home when off duty.

As we talked a V.A.D. nurse came in to collect hymn books from a cupboard on the wall.

"That means it is nearly five o'clock," Matron said. "The Chaplain is holding a service which I must attend. But before I go I will introduce you to our Millie. She is a good example of the sort of young women we want to come and help us through these difficult times—as paid workers, of course, and often with a meal and overalls included."

Millie was in uniform, trim and attractive, wearing an armbadge to show she is engaged on National Service. She is young, educated, married, without children. Her husband is away at sea. She lives in, making other arrangements when her husband is home on leave.

Protesting that it was all "terribly ordinary", Millie drew a brief sketch of the daily round. Four house surgeons and Matron are in her special care. She is up early, gets tea, sees to breakfast, makes the beds, tidies and cleans certain rooms. In the afternoon she is off duty for two hours, time enough, occasionally, to run round to her own little home—let to evacuees—and see that everything is going as it should.

Back and on duty in time to take round the teas, Millie gets busy again. Work slackens down gradually till nine o'clock strikes, with the call to hospital prayers. And so to bed. . . .

"I was always domesticated," Millie tells me. "I like looking after people and making them happy and comfortable. And I just *love* working in a hospital."

Ten thousand domesticated women urgently needed! Come along, Millies! There must be many of you who would like to help. Write to the Matron of your nearest hospital. Ask if she can utilize your services—and God bless you and your efforts.

---

firemen, helped with ARP at local level, as well as preparing tea and sandwiches for the troops landing from Dunkirk, and carrying refreshments to the engineers working on the caissons for the D-Day landings (while swearing not to breathe a word of what they had seen). They were even asked by the Government to organise the evacuation of the under-fives.

Until 1943 all civil defence was on a voluntary basis, and a quarter of all workers, some 375,000, were women. These included members of the Auxiliary Fire Service — both full- and part-time — and of the air-raid ambulance service; indeed the majority of ambulance drivers were women. Many such volunteers worked in conditions of considerable risk, and not only did they get no reward, but they were at first entitled (as we shall see in the next chapter) to lower rates of injury compensation than men.

Despite the long hours and possible hazards there seems never to have been a shortage of volunteers for the WVS, and other voluntary organisations. Perhaps this was because there had always been a solid tradition of British women — particularly of the middle and upper class — giving of their time to help with 'good works'. Add to that the stimulus of danger, even of possible invasion, and they flocked to volunteer in their hundreds of thousands. In *One Family's War*, Lady Mayhew — at that time President of the Norwich Division of the Red Cross — wrote in 1940:

> *'I must confess I find "the present situation" quietly but deeply exhilarating, but it's probably a female (and British female at that) sort of feeling which no male could begin to understand. When other people have always done your fighting for you it's an incredible relief to feel you've come to a time when that blessed Ministry of Information poster has some meaning for you at last. . . . here and now I wouldn't change places with anyone in history.'*

This may help to explain why the magazines rarely referred to the voluntary organisations. Certainly there was no need to write lengthy, fulsome articles in order to boost recruitment. Their activities, however demanding, or even dangerous, were judged to be respectable enough. Certainly no husbands or parents seem to have tried to prevent their wives and daughters from taking part in them. The British versions of Rosie the Riveter might have had problems with their menfolk; the Mrs Minivers less so.

[Photo: "The Times"

These girls are enjoying life in the W.A.A.F.

We have seen how the war caused women to take over many tasks and responsibilities traditionally reserved for men. Married women left at home were obliged to take all the decisions. Many of them found themselves earning good money, perhaps for the first time in their lives, and they were in charge of how it should be spent.

It is not surprising, therefore, that much was written about the roles of men and women. And there was considerable speculation about the ways in which these seemed to be changing.

Many of the men writing for the magazines seemed worried about any permanent shift in the balance of power between the sexes. A month before the outbreak of war Trevor Allen suggested that a woman could be the greatest help to her man '*just by being there*':

> '*Is that something the extreme feminist often forgets — that a sympathetic woman can give a man help and inspiration merely "being there"? That she need not be a tornado of "emancipated" activity to be of real use in the world?*' (*Woman's Own*, 11th March 1939)

And by November 1940, despite 14 months of war, the message had hardly changed. James Wedgwood Drawbell could still write in *Mother and Home* that:

> '*We men aren't everything. Without you women, with your understanding, and your patience, with your courageous smile, and your way of making the best of everything; with your quiet determination and your loyal comradeship — we'd be a pretty poor lot at any time. At the present time we'd be lost without you.*'

Women, meanwhile, had their own ideas on what their roles were to be. One point frequently made was that there might never have been a war in the first place if women had had more power to influence events. In *Woman's Own* of the 21st October 1939, a month or so after the war started, the editor asked her readers:

> '*Do you think that the most important work a woman can do is to fight the terrifying selfishness which, without feminine influence, can produce dictators, brutality — all that we associate with the horrors of modern warfare? And how best can women's influence be felt — in normal times? Do we do more by mingling as much as possible in the world of business, or in running our homes?*'

What was clear was that, in those most abnormal of times, women were eager to play an active role — '*Women want to be partners in the nation's war effort*' — the title of a *Woman's Magazine* article stated in November 1940. But being partners implied equality, and in many areas the obvious lack of equality created an increasing atmosphere of resentment:

In the home

> '*Would your husband think he was losing caste if he helped with the housework or the shopping? Most still think so, especially in the industrial North, but they must change their views now the wives are on war-work.*' (*Woman's Own*, 9th February 1942)

Many women, exhausted from war work and shopping, still found that they were expected to take sole responsibility for the housework. But they could not be certain of finding automatic sympathy from the magazines, as can be seen from the following letters and their replies by Leonora Eyles:

Next leave

> '*My husband has just been on leave; for 5 months I have had baby tying me hand and foot. Now my husband has gone back bad friends with me because I told him he ought to get up and light the fire; he even asked me to clean his army boots for him, which is a job no woman should be asked to do. He will be home again in 3 months; how can I make him see his duty?*'

> '*How can I make you see yours? How are you, in comparative peace and comfort, wanting him to wait on you hand and foot when he gets a much needed rest! You ought to be ashamed of yourself, my dear. Next leave, show how pleased you are to have him home again. It would be nice if you gave him his breakfast in bed. Make every moment one of gladness that he can look back on happily for months to come.*' (*Woman's Own*, 4th January 1941).

Soldier on leave

> '*I don't agree with you sympathising with a soldier on leave whose wife would not clean his shoes for him. Women are having as hard a time in this war as men, even harder; and they never made the war in any case. It is women like you, putting up with men's tyranny, who make wars.*'

> '*Or perhaps women like you, who preach such violent differences between the sexes, and who seem to me singularly lacking in the gentle spirit of love and service! ... I quite agree that women have the heavy end of the stick, and I believe that a world with more women in power would*'

THIS EQUAL PAY BUSINESS

"Equal Pay for Equal Work" is a slogan of the day. In a few years' time it may well be as dead as "Votes for Women." If it is, it will be because "the rate for the job" has become the accepted order in industry.

But before that day dawns "Equal Pay" is a cry that will ring through Parliament, figure on conference agendas and disturb the peace of many a breakfast-table!

Because, while it is being considered by a Royal Commission men and women all over the country, from Cabinet Ministers to people like you and me, are going to discuss equal pay, it's worth while considering some of the deeper implications behind these two words. There is more in it than eager anticipation of a heavier pay-packet!

RIGHTLY OR WRONGLY, wages in this country are in the main, paid on the principle that a woman is a single individual; man the supporter of a family. He is paid more money, not because he does a better job, but because it is assumed that he has to provide for more than one person.

If equal pay for women becomes the rule, this principle will go. The sole standard for wages will be competency at a given job.

Will women, apart from the cash, win or lose by this new method? Let's take a look at the debits and credits.

Some professional women—doctors, architects, solicitors—already get equal pay. No one suggests that they should deduct 25 per cent. from their fees because they wear skirts.

The claim to equal pay of women teachers who are paid less than their male colleagues who are doing identical jobs is equally strong, and they are the spearhead of this fight. If they win their battle, then undoubtedly the cry will be caught up by Civil Servants, bank clerks, clerical workers and women in factories.

It is at this stage that the armchair economists begin to get alarmed. They predict that such a step would result in economic and domestic chaos. "Men," they say, "have heavier responsibilities." This is partly, but not wholly, true.

The curious fallacy still exists that the single woman is unburdened with responsibilities. In fact, young women are quite as conscientious over their home responsibilities as young men. A large proportion of them contribute to the upkeep of parents or other dependents.

Many women do marry, but there still remain many who, from choice or necessity, stay single. It is an ugly fact, but nevertheless a true one, that their numbers are swollen by war. These women devote themselves as steadfastly and single-heartedly to a career as any man, and they deserve the same reward.

A married man with a family naturally needs a larger income than a single young woman—even if she supports a widowed mother. This difference in the outgoings of the two incomes must be—and there is reason to hope it will be—largely made good after the war by Family Allowances and tax remissions. Free secondary schools, a free-for-all Health Service which figure in post-war plans, will play their part in levelling out these differences.

But would married women resent the fact that single women received the same salaries as their husbands? Would Mrs. A complain because Miss B, who lives across the street and shares a flat with Miss C, earns as much money as her own husband?

REMEMBER that no one is suggesting that men should be penalized financially because women get equal pay. The Civil Servant will be neither better nor worse off in his own home because his girl colleague at the office draws the same salary as he does.

There is, I feel, one important psychological feature that has been ignored. It is the dread which haunts so many women in jobs that carry no pension—what will become of them when they are considered too old for the job? This may sound like a side-tracking of the main issue, but I am convinced that this is a very real fear that dominates the lives of many women, so that they skimp and save from incomes barely sufficient to provide for their everyday needs. Higher pay would lighten their anxieties.

OPPONENTS of equal pay argue that women earning high salaries will be reluctant to give up their jobs and have children. This is utter nonsense. Higher salaries will have no effect one way or the other on whether or not women have children. Equal pay is not a scheme to bribe women to leave their homes and go into offices, shops and schools. It is a measure to ensure that those who do—by choice or necessity—get a fair reward for their work.

So far, we've been looking at the credit side. Now for the disadvantages.

If equal pay becomes the rule, women will have to adjust some of their ideas. Complete equality of pay is going to bring in its train equal responsibility. On the material side that is going to mean that saving up for a home will become a joint affair in almost every case. Women will have to take it for granted that they pay their own bus fares and buy their own cinema tickets.

Far more important, to my mind, is the psychological aspect. As equals in offices, shops and factories, women are going to find competition fiercer, and "chivalry" rarer, and men's attitude towards them a little harder and less accommodating.

Do you think we should have equal pay? I do. I think it is a status that women should be proud of attaining—provided they are willing to adjust themselves socially and economically to the changes it will inevitably bring with it.

Don't for one moment think that it's coming "cost free."

MARGARET SUMMERTON.

---

be better. But they must be women who know the power of love, my dear, not the power of bullying.' (*Woman's Own*, 5th April, 1941)

Leonora Eyles, in fact, though possibly the most sensible and warmhearted of all the agony aunts, was still very rigid in her views on what constituted wifely duty. Her reply to the following letter can hardly have been of much consolation to the unhappy writer:

Discontented wife
'My husband retired 2 years ago, and I don't see why I should go on slaving. I have told him that he must take a share of the housework and cooking, but now all my married children are terribly disapproving.'

'Women can't retire, my dear; and if you looked on your home as your pleasure and enjoyed serving your husband you would not want to retire. He has worked hard all his life, and work for an employer is quite different from work in the home where one is free. Life is very short; why not be kind and loving and spoil your man a bit? Think of all those years of work he has done for you and the children.' (*Woman's Own*, 12th July, 1941)

Pay and conditions

But of course it was not only men who were putting in the hard work. And the most obvious cause of resentment was in the area of pay and working conditions, where unfair practices were blatant.

When the war started the great majority of working women received less than half the male rate. They were for the most part not allowed to work nights, Sundays, or for more than 48 hours per week, all of which cut down the chances of overtime.

By the spring of 1940 certain areas of employment had been so successfully invaded by women that concessions on fair treatment were allowed. In April an industrial court ruled that women transport workers aged over 21 (notably the bus conductresses, or 'clippies', that were suddenly to be seen everywhere) were to be allowed equal pay after six months.

The few women union officials were attempting to remedy the situation in the factories, as well as on government schemes where female trainees were paid a third less than their male counterparts. A victory was won in the summer of 1940 when employers in the engineering industry agreed to pay women the full rate after 32 weeks provided that they were engaged on work previously done by men. Over the next two years similar agreements came into force in other industries.

But such agreements could often be circumvented; it didn't take much, after all, to make a minor change in a job and then claim that it had never been done by men. And outside industry there were still whole areas of work — most notoriously the teaching profession — where women were undoubtedly doing identical work to men without receiving the same money.

. In other areas, too, women were shabbily treated. The editor of *The Lady* wrote in February 1941 that:

'Women have quietly swallowed a great many grievances since the war began and brought with it a revival of sex prejudice in matters of pay, promotion and responsibility; but there is widely expressed indignation that the War Injuries Compensation Scheme should provide smaller grants for women than for men. Indeed, the assumption that disablement is less costly or less important for women than for men is fantastic. There is no special rate for women in hospitals; their nurses and doctors charge them on exactly the same scale as men; their landlords charge the same house-room; the activities for which their injuries debar them are just as important to them as a man's are to him.

The unjust differentiation is probably based on the ideas that all men and no women have dependents — an assumption which has been repeatedly shown to be false. It is to be hoped that some revision of the Compensation Scheme will be made before its present unfairness breeds an ugly bitterness among women who are at least as eager as men to serve their country, and as ready to suffer for it.'

Although the war brought about certain permanent improvements in the financial position of women — notably the introduction of family allowances — the impression still remains that much was grudgingly given. It took four petitions to Parliament before the injury compensation rate was made the same for both sexes. And as late as the summer of 1943 women at the Rolls Royce factory at Hillington had to go on strike before they secured equal pay.

Such reluctance came from the top. Indeed, the most blatant example is that of Churchill who, in the spring of 1944, called for a vote of confidence rather than let Butler's new Education Bill include an amendment calling for equal pay for women teachers.

Changes

With such attitudes to be found at the highest levels, it is not surprising that throughout the land there was resistance on the part of many men to any changes in the *status quo*.

Such changes put the relationships between men and women under strain. But they also affected young women who were still living at home.

Before the war most young middle-class girls would have stayed at home, or been allowed to take up a limited number of jobs. These would, for the most part, have brought them into contact with few people outside their own class. As the war went on, however, women from all backgrounds found themselves working, sometimes living, together. Who knows what these well-brought-up girls might not pick up from the riff-raff they were forced to associate with! That parents often felt such alarm was clear from the letters sent to Leonora Eyles.

Some were from the parents themselves:

Daughter out late
'I have 2 daughters and a son married, and I have always brought them up strictly and made them mind me. But my daughter of 16, who has just started in business, won't come in at night. Often she is out till 11.00 and as there are lot of soldiers about, this worries me.' (Women's Own, 13th April, 1940)

Hard to handle
'I am so worried about my daughter of 16; she has started to make up to look much over 20 and stay out till after midnight. She is often a little the worse for drink when she comes home. She was a nice girl till she started to work in a factory, but now I don't know how to manage her. Her father is overseas.' (Woman's Own, 16th June, 1944)

Others were from daughters:

So depressed
'Ever since I had to register I have longed to belong to one of the many organisations in our town; I have a job on essential war-work but have to get home every evening straight from work, and if I work overtime Father phones the firm to make sure it is true. This shames me before others, and I am so depressed and fed up. (Woman's Own, 5th May, 1944)

There was also much debate about how much young girls should know about the 'facts of life'. When young women wrote to Leonora Eyles, revealing their ignorance, she used to send them some information. This didn't always please the girls' mothers:

Shocked
'I am very shocked at your advocating telling girls the facts of life before they get married. It is too soon enough then for them to find out the dreadful lot of women.' (Woman's Own, 20th March, 1942)

Protest
'I am very indignant. My daughter of 18 wrote to you asking the facts about sex, marriage and babies; and a letter and a booklet came to the house which I burned immediately. I think young people should be protected from people who take away their innocence this way.' (Woman's Own, 23rd October, 1942)

Leonora Eyles sympathised with worried parents, but suggested they make their homes most welcoming for their older children. She encouraged the children

How much freedom should a daughter have?

This is a constant bone of contention in many families. In publishing this sincere cry from a young girl to her mother we give the first word to the younger generation . . . but in fairness we publish her mother's reply.

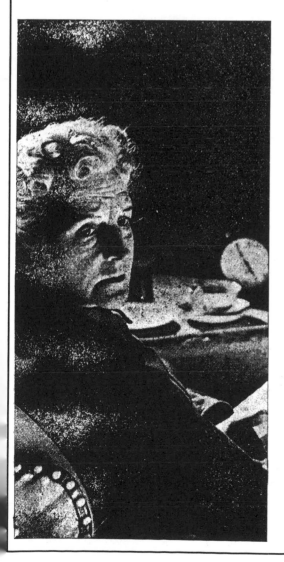

CASE FOR MOTHER

Dear Jenny,

I am glad you wrote me that letter, because it has given me a chance to see your point of view dispassionately, and unfortunately when you have come in later than usual and I have been terribly worried by an anxious period of waiting, I say things I do not really mean, and so do you. We are both worked up and inclined to be unjust about the other person.

Because, you see, dear, I don't want to be stuffy. And honestly, the last thing I want is to prevent your enjoying your evenings out. You are young and I want you to enjoy life all you can under the present limitations. I keep wishing it could be perfect for you, and wishing also that you will get the best from life. I would do anything in my power to give it to you, and I know you deserve it.

But I also know other things. I was eighteen once, too, and I haven't forgotten. It is not a time when one is worried by the mechanics of living. There is your home behind you, and unconsciously it is your security, as I want it to be. I don't suppose you think about it—you just accept it. But so much has gone into its making that you will never know about, and in the end it has nearly all been done for *you*. Because you mean so much to Daddy and myself, and because above everyything we want to see you happy.

The world is so very far from the one we would have chosen for you in your nineteenth year. It has never been so rough and tumble; perhaps it has never been so easy for young people to make mistakes. Life is quick and dangerous and emotional and sudden, and all the time I am terrified for you of the pitfalls and dangers that are covered up by the ideals of youth and the excitement of living. I am terrified of your being hurt, assaulted, frightened—so many things that I really didn't believe in at eighteen, but which I know now are so bitterly possible. Not just for any girl. For *you*, because you are young and gay and pretty, and most of all because you are my daughter and I love you.

All those things which can hurt you and endanger you I want to spare you. But I do realise that you will have to deal with them sooner or later, and this is sooner. Will you please try to realise that the rules I make are only made so that you will not have to deal with all those problems at once, but gradually find your own feet and the measure of people? Particularly young men.

I DON'T SUPPOSE a mother exists who is not afraid of the young men who take her daughter out. She knows that most girls are romantic and idealistic, and that the majority of young men are on the whole realistic. They are living as best they can with very abnormal strain and for the day, because they dare not plan slowly and for to-morrow. And she is so terribly afraid that love, which is violent and all embracing when it first comes, may destroy her daughter unless she is sufficiently armed and secure so that its wonderful force may be the making of her. It can so easily bring danger and heartache and disillusion.

That is why I am so frightened for you—perhaps more frightened than I need to be. Because I know your character and your integrity, and because I do trust you. The knowledge of good comes young, but the knowledge of evil can only come later, and almost against one's will. And there isn't a parent in the world who would not do anything to protect a child against it as far as she can.

You see, when you came in so late last night I was very tired, and I had sat there imagining the things that might be happening to keep you. I saw you under a bus. I saw you attacked in the dark. I saw you lightheartedly going off on a jaunt that you hadn't planned before—a party with people I didn't know and wouldn't trust. Because you don't know yet who is to be trusted. That is a knowledge born only of long experience and sad trial and error. You were only an hour late, but it was dark, and quiet, and it seemed a much longer time to me.

Perhaps I have too much imagination, but in that lonely, anxious hour, I imagined everything, and the minutes crept by. I was listening every minute for your step. I couldn't help it. And when you appeared, careless and nonchalant—and looking so lovely and defenceless—the breaking of the suspense was too sudden, and out it all came. I said too much, simply because I was so relieved.

Come with me, Jenny, twenty years on. You have your own front door, and now it looks quite different to you. *You* are sitting in cold terror upstairs at eleven-thirty, listening. There is a sick, cold fear in your heart. *Can anything have happened to her?* He seemed a nice enough young man who took her out, at 6 p.m., but now, approaching midnight, he is positively sprouting horns.

You can't go to bed. You couldn't sleep. It is your house, Jenny, and you don't like to leave the door unfastened. Moreover, you don't like to fasten it because, knowing what she is, she may easily have lost her key. You are tired after the day's hard work. Things look worse, bogies loom larger, when one is tired and it is so cold and dark.

The little chit of a girl who will probably be rude to you when she does return, Jenny, or else do the Tragedy Queen next-time-I-shall-stay-out-all-night act on you, is *YOUR* daughter. You are the one who is now translated into the unpalatable role of the unreasonable, anxious mother. Then you will realise that it isn't so much that we don't trust our children as we dread what life, if we don't take care of them, may do to them.

I know I shouldn't worry. But you do worry when you love a person. You simply can't help it. You worry every moment, and young as you are I think you may be able to understand this a bit, because I think you are a little in love with John. That is part of the worry. He is very attractive, and—it takes so little to destroy so much. I know. It nearly happened to me. In any case, the fact that you haven't unlimited freedom, that you are looked after, that you must be home on time, is going to do you no harm, Jenny, in the right man's eyes.

I know you are high-spirited and want your head. I want to give it you, within limits. But you must, while you live at home and under my roof, try to observe and understand those limits. You will have years of your life without any limits, with continual responsibility, and it will come soon enough. Maybe then you will look back and be grateful for the security we gave you in spite of yourself, although I don't expect you to believe it. No girl of eighteen ever does!

As long as I know with whom you are out, and when you will return or telephone me when prevented, I want you to go out and enjoy every minute. I don't want it spoiled by the thought that I am sitting up worrying about you. I won't if you will promise me this, and try to understand a little bit of what I have written, now I am no longer angry and worried.

I mean all this, Jenny. Will you try to understand, and will you agree? If I loved you less I would let you go your own way, and then perhaps you would come back after life had hurt you badly and say, 'Mother, why didn't you stop me? You knew . . .'

Yes, I know. That is the reason, Jenny dear.
MOTHER.

to stand up for their rights to 'friendship and brightness'.

But she had no time for those who would hide from the realities of life. To the mother who destroyed her daughter's booklet she thundered:

'Have you any idea of the dangers of the world in which your young people are living today? Unless they know the things I try to teach them, they may form friendships which will ruin them for life. Ignorance is not innocence; innocence is - knowledge protected by a good code of behaviour.'

And the dangers were very real. By early 1943 there had been a spectacular increase in pre- and extra-marital sex, and in its consequences of illegitimacy and the spread of venereal disease. Magazine articles warned that it was not only girls of 'a certain class' who were affected: the mixing of young people from all backgrounds spread both knowledge and temptation, and a mother's first duty to her daughter was to tell her the facts of life before she went out into the world.

Some men, affected by the rumour-mongering of 1941, worried about what might happen to their girlfriends or fiancees in the women's services. One wrote to Leonora Eyles in March 1942 saying:

'I and my girl have been keeping company for 4 years now. I expect to be sent abroad very shortly and I look forward to the day when I shall come home and we shall be able to marry. What worries me — and I cannot bring myself to discuss it with her — is the fact that she is going to join one of the services soon. She will be meeting all kinds of men, perhaps getting in with the wrong kinds of girls. How can I be sure she will be true?'

In her reply Leonora Eyles referred disparagingly to the *'grossly exaggerated talk about so-called "immorality" in the women's service'* and wished the two of them luck. But what she failed to mention was that such women were likely to be in greater 'moral danger' from their boyfriends or fiances than from casual acquaintances.

War appears to bring with it an inevitable loosening of sexual restraint, and many servicemen, knowing that they were going off to possible death, brought pressure on their women to give them a special memory to take away with them. Some women wondered if they should do so.

Trial weekend
'I am in love with a man — we have known each other for 4 years — but there is no hope of getting married as he has only just qualified as an architect; and now he is being called up. He wants me to go away with him for his last weekend and I long to go, but somehow I don't think it's right. Yet, why should we be penalised because we can't afford to get married? ... And am I, like hundreds of other women, to spend perhaps the rest of my life regretting what might have been?' (*Woman's Own*, 19th September, 1940*)*

And others regretted that they hadn't given in:

famous as traveller, explorer and writer, says in this challenging article: Happiness is YOURS—any day, every day—if you know it when you see it.

Rosita Forbes remarks this week: "Girls come and go in men's lives, but wives remain."

ROSITA FORBES
Speaking

To those wives who find themselves fighting the hardest home front battle of all

HOW often have you heard a person say: "Something cracked inside me." Perhaps you, yourself, have felt it. I daresay we all of us get a bit chipped as life goes on.

Beside me there is a letter from a young woman who is evidently very intelligent. She speaks several foreign languages and runs a section of the censorship at one of our great ports, But she isn't very clever about her husband. His engineering job keeps him miles away from her, at a factory where nearly 1,000 girls are employed. He fell for a nineteen-year-old, how seriously I don't know. The wife writes: "It's over now. We're happy enough. But something has cracked. I can't feel the same, and it's so difficult not letting him see . . ."

Well, I must say that I think it's poor stuff that cracks under the decidedly temporary impact of the inevitable girl. There is no reason why the girl should be anything but temporary, if the wife keeps her commonsense and her sense of humour. I'm thinking of the factory hostel I saw recently—a fairly typical one, I imagine. Eighteen of its new, modern blocks housed girls of all shapes and sizes. The remaining dozen or so are all full of men, nearly all of them married and just upon middle age.

The hostel is a good many miles from a town, and, I rather think, twenty minutes' walk from the nearest pub. Men and girls share their spare time in and out of doors, at swimming-pool and sports-ground, in the games room, "tea-bars" and dance hall. All of them are cut off—perhaps for the duration—from their usual friends and occupations.

Flirtations may, or may not, grow out of unaccustomed loneliness. Girls straight from home, still dependent on their mothers for comfort and advice, don't think clearly and with wise foresight. The future to them is a vague term. They want to be happy to-day. There may be girls who go "all out" for married men. But there are, surely, far more who just like to go about with a man after long, hard hours of work, and who, when they first make friends with a neighbour in factory, or hostel or farm or office, don't bother about whether he is married or not.

I think, perhaps, that wives should remember that being married doesn't give total rights to somebody else's mind. A husband is still a separate individual, maybe with entirely different tastes and ideas! Marriage needs more tolerance than any other partnership that I have ever heard of!

Men don't necessarily want to smash their marriage just because they find someone amusing and interesting to go about with after work. Very few of us are "in love" only once in a life-time. Let's face that fact. But there is a difference between being lightly "in love" (which passing condition depends on mood and circumstance, and LOVING). Generally a man loves the woman he marries, and she has every chance to keep that love. It is the strongest of all bands, made up of sorrow and failure and disappointment shared, of illness and weary vigils, of parenthood and its responsibilities, of thrift and sacrifice and backache when something goes wrong with the kitchen flue!—as well as of success and joy and laughter.

That enduring band is part of marriage. It has nothing to do with being "in love." A husband can fall in and out of love as easily as a bachelor. There is no reason why things should be "different" afterwards. Wives must keep a sense of proportion, and not think too much about temporary lapses. They don't crack under the strain of full-time war-work with a house and family to look after as well. They must bring the same unconquerable courage to the problem of husbands. Our weapons are courage, kindness and faith. With these, wives have nothing enduring to fear. Girls come and girls go in every man's life. But wives, "uncracked," wives sensible and cheerful and companionable and not at all fuss-making—these remain.

His ideal

'Some months ago my boyfriend asked me to do wrong, but I would not. He then said he was only testing me to see if I was worth fighting for. Now I have had news that he is missing and I am heartbroken because I think that I ought to have given him what he wanted.' (Woman's Own, 30th June, 1944)

Leonora Eyles consoled the second writer with the thought that she had '*sent that boy to his duty with a clear and lovely vision of a girl he loved and felt was worth all he could give or do*'. And to the first she simply said, '*But why not get married, my dear … If you are sure of your love for each other, then that is the only answer.*'

But it was far from certain that such wartime marriages would survive into peacetime. As the war went on, the average age of brides dropped. *Woman's Own* reported in August 1941 that, according to the Rector of St Andrews, Mottingham, '*in 24 weddings, 17 brides were 21 or under, one was 17, two were 18. The tendency for girls to be married so young is lamentable.*'

It wasn't just that they were young; people who hardly knew each other were getting married. Lengthy courtships and engagements were becoming things of the past. As *Woman's Journal* said in May 1943:

'No one would begrudge the youngsters their hour of happiness or their dreams, but there will be many bitter awakenings when they go back to civil life and find they are from different backgrounds.'

And the war meant that for many couples the opportunities to get to know each other were rare. A man back on leave would be unlikely to want to hear about his wife's problems, and would probably expect to assume the role of head of the family as a matter of right. Small wonder, then, that such leave time was not always happy. One woman wrote that:

'We were married at the beginning of the war and have scarcely been together. Every time my husband comes home on leave I am terribly thrilled, and he writes me lovely letters beforehand. But when we meet it is nothing but silly little squabbles. After his last leave we thought we had better part and get a divorce; yet I love him very much and I know he loves me.' (Woman's Own, 16th June, 1944)

Leonora Eyles counselled patience and the need to keep faith. It was just '*one of those unfortunate things brought about by the awful conditions of wartime life*'.

But wartime marriages were often under strain even when the husband was in a reserved occupation:

War strain

'I am so unhappy; my husband was so much in love with me for the first three years of our married life but lately … he never seems to want to make love to me. I worry in case he is in love with another woman, though how he can spend any time with her I don't know, as he is working all day and doing Home Guard duty two nights a week. Is there something wrong with me?' (Woman's Own, 7th July, 1944)

Leonora considered that in such cases the strain of war, added to heavy work, was to blame, not another woman.

But in many cases, there was 'another woman' involved; or, increasingly, 'another man'.

Jealousy

'My wife is working on a farm, and I am in the Army. Each time I come home I see her being very friendly with the farm men, taking tea out to them and so on; and people tell me she always does this. Last time I came home unexpectedly she said she could not get off, as they were harvesting, and I ordered her home. I feel angry and suspicious.'

'Dear, dear! Fighting to end tyranny — and having a spot of it in your own home! Don't be so silly, my friend. It is your wife's job to take tea out to the men and be friendly with them; a smile and a bit of friendliness are worth a lot nowadays. Stop ordering your wife about; and do be loyal to her. Next time someone tells tales on her, I hope you will stick up for her and tell them to mind their own business.' (*Woman's Own*, 14th September, 1940*)*

Jealousy could work both ways, and was equally reprehensible when unfounded:

'My husband is doing work on a farm at present, and I can't help feeling a bit jealous of the land girls there — one in particular is most attractive, and all the men admire her. We have only been married such a short while and are so happy, that I would hate anything to come between us.'

'And I feel certain that nothing will. The right answer to your problem, my dear, is trust. If you love your husband (as you do), you will trust him, and not allow any feeling of jealousy to cloud your feelings for each other. Above all, don't permit any hint of suspicion to creep into your manner to him, just be your usual sweet, nice self. Knowing you believe in him, he will not let you down.' (*Mother and Home*, November 1940*)*

But the problems of infidelity were not evenly balanced between the sexes. Men away in training camp or overseas could be as unfaithful as they wished and no word of it would get back to their wives. It was only if they volunteered information, or left evidence about, that wives would become suspicious. Many women wrote of their suspicions to magazines, requesting advice. The typical reply stressed the need not to make a fuss, not to do anything to disturb the husband's leave, and suggested that friendships with other women — if they existed at all — were natural, and likely to be innocent.

Even when infidelity on the part of the man was admitted, there was a tendency to go easy on him. In March 1940 Leonora Eyles chose this as *Woman's Own* 'Problem of the week':

'A wife of 29 had to leave her husband at the outbreak of the war and settle the two children with her mother, as this was a danger area. While there her mother was taken ill and she had to stay

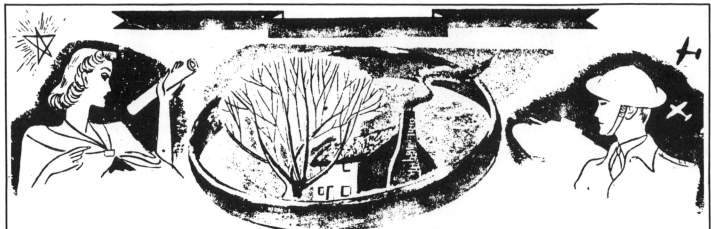

Rebuilding Marriages

The woman who is letting her husband down... Here the problem is frankly discussed by Leonora Eyles, who comes across her too often

MANY years of being involved in the troubles of other people have taught me some basic facts about them—and I, for that matter, have my own many and various troubles and I believe that lack of responsibility is to blame for more troubles than anything else. Lack of responsibility for one's own life, lack of responsibility towards those linked with us in various ways, and lack of responsibility towards the community.

To-day, for instance, there are numbers of young wives with an appalling burden to carry, the terrible feeling that they have lowered themselves, lost their heads, let down a man who loved and trusted them, and, perhaps, worst of all, have involved a helpless child in the smash. Think of the young girls who married during the first year of the war; many of them are working on war work, doing everything they possibly can to hasten the end of the war if only by one minute. Has it ever occurred to you, by the way, that you can, by your work, say "I ran the war for one minute"? All honour to these girls—they are going to be happy when the boys come home; they'll have a clear conscience and, too, some very useful money in the bank to help buy the home they hadn't a chance to make.

But the others? Plunged into married life for a few hectic days, then into loneliness; back home with Mother, with only the Service pay to live on; too often they do no useful work, in fact some husbands are so prehistoric, so ignorant of human nature, that they simply forbid their wives to work. (Funny to think of a modern girl being "forbidden" to be useful by a man, but some still put up with that sort of thing and seem to like it!) Is it any wonder they get lonely and lost? Can you imagine what your life would be with no work to go to, no home to care for, no definite responsibility of any sort? Is it any wonder some of them get into terrible tangles?

For a few days, or weeks, perhaps, the loneliness and slackness give place to hectic excitement when "He" has leave. Yet boys who came back from Dunkirk by the most wonderful miracle in our history, and spent a week's leave with the strange girl they had married, have told me they wondered why they had ever married her—she seemed so silly, so selfish, so narrow to the man who had done deeds of heroism and feats of endurance almost unbelievable. Some of the boys have told me that the girl seemed to suffocate them—they were glad to get back to the company of men with a job to do. And the girl must feel the difference.

Is that why some of them have turned to another man, a man on the spot who has some money to spend, who brings excitement and life for a time into the monotony? Yet, you know, a man who will make love to another man's wife isn't much good, is he? No sense of comradeship, no responsibility. You may be thrilled with him, he may give you a good time. But you wouldn't like to spend your life with a man who could do something so messy, would you?

Yet to-day, with husbands fighting in all the heat and horror of Egypt, hungry, thirsty, sometimes wounded, ill and worn, some girls are throwing themselves away on other men; to-day, with husbands enduring the agony and loneliness of a prison camp, some girls are being unfaithful with chance acquaintances, boys out for a good time, boys who, later on, will be enduring what the husband is going through, boys who will look back on these girls at home who went half-way to meet them on the path of dishonour, with a sort of loathing and horror.

I KNOW some of these young wives; I have every pity for them, every sympathy for their loneliness. But it is difficult to pity a girl who lets herself go so badly that she has to face the future with a baby not belonging to her husband. Every girl in this country to-day has been given enough moral training to realize that, no matter what the temptation, one doesn't kick over the traces while one's man is risking his life, while, perhaps, he is a prisoner behind barbed wire, under Nazi guards. "I know now that I love my husband best," these girls say when, with a baby coming, they wake up to find that the playmate of the lonely hours has vanished. Then they begin to feel too ashamed to face the future.

There is one way out for the lonely girl who is afraid she can't stand it. That way out is an old, old way, the way God ordained when man first became conscious of himself; the way of work. Work till you are too tired to mope; work till you win the comradeship of the other workers round you; work till you forget how much you long for "Him" to kiss you and put his arms round you. Work to help him come home again. And if you are one of the silly little ninnies who have lost your head, don't moan and say you can't face it. You made yourself responsible for your husband's happiness and honour and you've let them down. You've let down the spirit of British women, perhaps, to Dominion or foreign soldiers. You've made yourself responsible for a child. You can't let that down.

There are homes that will help you, I know. But why should they? Why should someone else support your child? Work for it yourself and in working for it, find your salvation. Don't throw the burden of your trouble on your fighting or imprisoned husband; it isn't fair. Suffer yourself, as much as needs be—but take care that you are the only one who does suffer. You'll find a way to hang on to your baby if you want to—plenty of people are only too ready to help you. Let the future take care of itself. Some husbands, of course, will not forgive a wife who presents him, after the war, with a baby of another man's, but many out of the charity and understanding of pain and danger, will; we are getting more civilized about babies, realizing that they, at least, must not suffer, whatever their parents did. Step from day to day, not looking too far ahead—and out of your silliness, your pain and your courage you will build up a personality that can cope with your husband's reactions.

BUT it all comes down to responsibility; you have a duty to your country to work when it has its back against the wall; you have a duty not to let the many foreigners here to-day find British girls poor, weak stuff; you owe it to your husband to pull your weight and, if you have made a fool of yourself, not to sit down and cry but to stand up and fight. There isn't much a British girl can't do if she tries. You try it and see—whether it is enduring the horrible separation, fighting the cheap temptation, or getting up after a nasty fall.

for six weeks and nurse her. On her return home her husband had been unfaithful and admitted it. He said he had been lonely. She feels she cannot forgive him such disloyalty, although he now says he is very sorry.'

'Well this seems to be a case where tolerance and understanding are the only way to save the situation. It *was* lonely, and many people at the beginning of the war felt very distressed and off their balance. Even if she doesn't forgive him, what can she gain except the ruin of her married life? I would forgive him and never mention it again. He will be so grateful and so full of admiration for his wife's loving understanding that probably they will be happier than they ever were.'

In August 1941 an infuriated reader accused her of showing too much sympathy to men who strayed, but she defended herself on the grounds that '*one isolated mistake*' should be forgiven while '*it is obviously impossible to make a life*' with a man who is '*persistently unfaithful and extravagant*'. Despite this rebuttal, a great degree of tolerance towards errant husbands was preached in the magazines. But when it came to wives being unfaithful then the words could be somewhat harsher, the condemnation more forceful.

Women and fidelity

Among the most moving of letters were those from young women struggling to remain faithful to fiances or husbands whom they had not seen for years. And these received for the most part, particularly tender replies:

Keeping faith
'Please help me, you can't imagine my trouble. My boy has been a prisoner in Japan for three years and I can't go out with other boys when I think of what he may be suffering. All my girl friends are courting now and I am so lonely I don't know what to do.'

'Poor little girl, it is terrible that this, which should be your happiest time, should be so clouded. But I am glad that you are keeping faith with your boy. ... Isn't there a youth club you could join and make new friends? Or how about volunteering at any local canteen several nights a week? ' (*Women's Own*, 7th July, 1944)

And where the man was missing, perhaps dead, the problems of loyalty were even greater. Evelyn Home of *Woman* chose such a case in June 1944:

'Separation has immensely increased the problems of human relationships. I have a letter from a girl whose fiance has been reported missing at sea. This happened some months ago, since when no further news has been received of him, and the girl has been approached by another young man who wants to marry her. The girl tells me that she is still in love with the man who is missing and she feels that she will never love anyone else. Would it then be wrong for her to marry the second man — and devote her life to trying to make him happy?'

'Personally, I don't think this girl has waited long enough, either to know whether her fiance is truly gone beyond recall or whether she is really ready for marriage with another man ... I advise this girl to wait another 6 months at least before she makes up her mind. She may find that there is no need to make up her mind — circumstances and people may have changed in the meanwhile, and her problem may have vanished.'

But on occasion women were told that they *could* go out with other men, provided that they knew where to draw the line. They should remain scrupulously faithful, not even allowing a kiss. And most 'decent' women were considered to be loyal and true by nature. A single case of infidelity on the part of a woman was not necessarily seen as the end of a marriage:

Soldier's wife unfaithful
'I am a soldier and recently got 48 hours unexpected leave. I went home feeling on top of the world but I found that my wife had been associating with another man. I have every reason to believe she has been unfaithful. What ought I to do about it?'

'Everything depends on how things were before you went away; were you both happy and in love? Is this — if your suspicions are correct — likely to have been a temporary lapse? Talk the matter over now the first shock has worn off — perhaps she could come to where you are stationed. Give her another chance if you feel she has learned her lesson; but, if not, go to your chaplain; he will tell you what legal steps to take, if any.' (*Woman's Own*, 27th March, 1942)

But confessions of persistent infidelity received little sympathy from the agony aunts.

Shall I tell my husband?
'I have been married for 5 years, and 6 months ago my husband went overseas. Just recently I have met a young man   and we find we are falling in love with each other. He wants me to write and tell my husband this and ask him to give me my freedom when he comes home so that we can get married. I have no children to consider. Do you think I should tell my husband of this affair now, or wait until he comes back?'

'I am going to speak plainly to you, partly because I think that you, and others like you, who seem to have a very sketchy idea of loyalty, need to face facts. Your husband has gone overseas. Do you realise what this means — danger, privation, loneliness, possibly pain and death? Do you realise that he and all those with him are facing all this cheerfully and for your sake so that you, and all of us here at home, can live in safety and comfort? So that we can go out and about freely and safely — so that we may have enough to eat, and so that our homes shall remain homes, and not targets for an invading enemy? Do you think you are worth it? Can you believe that you, and others like you, who have no idea of remaining loyal to their marriage vows, who talk lightly of "being in love" with another man, are worth the lives of all our gallant men? I strongly advise you to sit down and do some hard thinking about this. Cut out this affair; give up seeing this man; avoid him as you would the plague, and you will soon get over it. You certainly should not say anything to your husband about it; you don't want to add to his hardships.' (*Woman's Weekly*, 24th July, 1943)

Almost without exception the columnists were insistent that a husband should not be told of his wife's infidelity while serving abroad. But when the man was due to return home to find that his wife had borne a child to someone else, they usually suggested how the news could be broken as gently as possible:

Don't tell yet

'My husband is a prisoner of war, and I was dreadfully depressed and lonely until I met two allied officers who were very sweet to me. Now I realise that I am going to have a baby, and I don't know which is the father. My husband is shortly to be repatriated, and I don't know how to tell him.'

'It is very difficult for me to advise you. I appreciate the loneliness and depression you were suffering, but that you could do such a thing — and with two men — passes my comprehension. But now the main thing to do is to avoid hurting him, isn't it? I advise you, as soon as you know he has reached the country, to write to the matron of the hospital, or the commander of the next camp to which he is sent, tell them the whole truth, and ask them how you can arrange some way of not seeing him until your condition is not apparent. Wait until his health is better before you tell him the truth. It might be the finish of everything for him if he knew it now.' (*Woman's Own*, 10th December, 1943)

Some readers questioned whether the truth should be withheld from a man serving abroad, and to one of these Leonora replied:

'Try to see his point of view; he is, perhaps, thousands of miles away, fighting for his life and thinking of home and wife. Surely it is unfair to let him have such a ghastly shock when he can do nothing about it? I am appalled at the infidelity of a serving soldier's wife, my dear, but I cannot see that the situation is improved by his suffering. Let her wait till he comes home and can face the position with his time and mind at his own disposal, not taken up by the business of fighting for life.' (Woman's Own, 27th August, 1943*)*

But it was a man, Stephen Francis, writing in *Woman and Beauty* in November 1943, who produced the fiercest condemnation of such would-be confessions — *'what untold harm a foolish, unthinking woman can do with a scrap of paper, a pen and ink'.* He described as *'fifth columnists'* those wives *'who are unfaithful and want to ease their conscience with confessions'.* He quoted a war correspondent as asking:

'Are half the wives in Britain demented? Won't they realise the men out here have a job on that's more important than the heart-burnings and soul-searchings of all the silly females who have nothing better to do than pour out on paper their wretched "confessions"? Don't they know what they're doing to the morale of the men?'

And he went on to say that he knew that kind of letter well:

'It begins … with some such stock phrase as "I don't know how to write this to you …" Well, why write the cursed thing? Keep it. Tear it up. Wait till the war's over — you may have learned more sense by then. Or, if not, perhaps he'll have died happy.
Cruel? Possibly. But not so cruel as the pen of a thoughtless woman. The amount of damage to morale and to the war effort that some thoughtless women are doing daily in their letters to their men in the Services is probably greater than that done by the whole of Dr Goebbels' propaganda machine … I accuse all such women of activities dangerous to the prosecution of the war. I suggest they think twice before they dip their pens in this poison and ask themselves: Do I write this because I love him or because I love myself? Is it devotion or downright selfishness? Am I being forthright or fifth column? Their husband's happiness — perhaps his life — depends on their answer.'

Pregnancy

Today it is difficult to understand how narrow the choices were at this time for a woman who wanted to avoid having children. The contraceptive pill had not been invented; abortion was strictly illegal, and only carried out, for the most part, by back-street practitioners whose medical training was usually minimal. And a woman could not even offer a baby for adoption, since this needed the consent of her husband, whether he was the father or not.

Many women in such positions wrote to the magazines for help and advice, but little could be said other than *'tell him the truth and ask his forgiveness'.* A lot of men would not forgive. The divorce rate rose from 10,000 in 1938 to 25,000 in 1945, most proceedings being brought by husbands and usually on grounds of adultery. Some men accepted the new child; others were prepared to resume their marriage on condition the child was put out for adoption. And the 'Homes', as Leonora told one distraught women in 1944 *'will take a baby on condition the marriage is not broken'.*

Venereal disease

An unwanted pregnancy was not the only possible consequence of freer sexual behaviour. Between September 1939 and the middle of 1941 the venereal disease rate increased by some 70 per cent; and the arrival of several hundred thousand Americans in 1942 sent the figures spiralling upwards. In October of that year the Minister of Health launched a campaign to inform the public about the causes and treatment of venereal diseases. A series of notices appeared in all the women's magazines. They made readers very aware of the dangers of casual sex, and in response some wrote in to ask how they could know whether or not they had caught VD. Their letters revealed a general ignorance about sex, and the answers to them sought to inform and reassure.

From a doctor's DIARY

"Is V.D. treatment something new, doctor?"

No, not at all. Free Treatment Centres for V.D. were started many years ago — in 1916 in fact. More than a hundred were opened to cope with the increase in V.D. during the last War when the problem was more serious than it is now.

By 1920 there were over two hundred treatment centres in Great Britain and hundreds of doctors, nurses and laboratory workers had been trained specially for V.D. work. By 1939 the number of early syphilis cases coming for treatment had dropped to one-third of the 1920 figure. We were making steady progress year by year.

Then came the present War — and, as always happens in wars, V.D. again began to increase. So the Government strengthened its free treatment services to help win back the ground that had been lost. And the Government also did something

just as important. It tore away the curtain of secrecy that had surrounded V.D. Nowadays we talk more openly about these diseases because we recognise that the more publicity is given to their causes and terrible effects, the more likely are we to reduce and conquer them.

Today 278 free treatment centres — often called V.D. Clinics — are available. In addition 182 specially trained doctors in various towns and villages give free treatment in their own surgeries.

The most important thing about V.D. is to avoid the loose behaviour which spreads disease. And anyone who has reason to suspect infection should seek advice at a clinic without delay. Some people just "put off" going. They say they are nervous about going to a clinic. But they should be much more afraid of the awful consequences of neglected V.D.

Clean Living is the Real Safeguard

FREE CONFIDENTIAL ADVICE AND TREATMENT are available at clinics set up by County and County Borough Councils. (The addresses are on local posters.) Further information can be obtained IN CONFIDENCE from the Health Department at your local ... the Medical Adviser, ... Square, W.C.1.

VD Shadow on HEALTH

Under war conditions, the number of cases of venereal disease in Britain has risen every year, and this increase is one of the few "black spots" on the nation's wartime health record. A very important cause of the spread of venereal diseases is ignorance. The object of these advertisements is to provide information of their prevalence; how they are contracted; and how they may be cured by early treatment.

What are the Venereal Diseases? There are a number of them, but the main ones are **syphilis** and **gonorrhœa**, two very different diseases caused by different germs.

What is Syphilis? Syphilis is a dangerous, a killing disease. If not treated early, skilfully and completely, it can cause death or total disablement in early middle life. Unless an infected mother is given skilled treatment early in pregnancy, she can pass on syphilis to her unborn child.

What is Gonorrhœa? Gonorrhœa, though not so dangerous as syphilis, is a serious disease and is one of the causes — not, of course, the only one — of chronic ill-health and inability to have children.

What are the signs of V.D.? The first sign of syphilis is a small ulcer on or near the sex organs; it appears from 10-90 days — usually three or four weeks after infection. Gonorrhœa usually shows itself first between two and ten days after infection, as a discharge from the s x organs.

How are Venereal Diseases caught? In

adults, almost always through sexual intercourse with a person who has already got the disease. The passing of the disease in any other way is so uncommon that it need not be feared.

How can they be avoided? These germs cannot appear in the body of their own accord. Nor can they be carried through the air like the germs of colds or measles; but any man or woman, boy or girl, who has sexual relations with a casual acquaintance risks picking up syphilis or gonorrhœa. Clean living is the real safeguard.

How and where can V.D. be cured? Venereal diseases can be cured if treated early by a specialist doctor; self-treatment is useless and may be disastrous. A specialist's advice, and treatment if necessary, are given FREE at any V.D. clinic; the addresses of local clinics and the times of opening may be found on local posters. Treatment is **absolutely confidential.** Anyone who has the slightest reason to suspect V.D. should seek skilled medical treatment AT ONCE.

FURTHER INFORMATION IN CONFIDENCE can be obtained from your local Council's Health Department, or by writing to the Medical Adviser, Central Council for Health Education, Tavistock Square, W.C.1 enclosing stamped addressed envelope.

Issued by Ministry of Health and Central Council for Health Education.

(V.D.37-7)

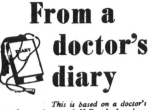

From a doctor's diary

This is based on a doctor's experience of cases of V.D. It has been carefully edited so that the people concerned shall not be recognised.

"'I don't believe it, doctor'

a friend said to me the other day. He did not believe what he'd read about the effect of untreated V.D., so I told him about a man I had seen recently in a mental hospital.

The man is now 36. When he was 18 he left home and got mixed up with a bad crowd with far too much drinking and loose behaviour. As so often happens when people let themselves go like this, he contracted syphilis, but because he didn't dare to tell his doctor about it he went to a quack. The quack treated him and, after a time, told him he was cured. Four years later he got married. Now, when he should be in the prime of life, he is in a mental home. His syphilis has developed into what is called General Paralysis of the Insane. He has been treated for this, but as sometimes happens at this very late stage, the treatment has failed to cure him and he is a hopeless insane invalid for life. He has infected his wife and she is now ill. They have spent their savings and she is left with heavy debts to pay off. What will happen to her I don't know.

I know that this is a terrible story, but I'm afraid it isn't uncommon. How I wish parents wouldn't allow their sons and daughters to go into the world without any real knowledge of the things they ought to know!"

FREE CONFIDENTIAL ADVICE AND TREATMENT are available at clinics set up by County and County Borough Councils. Any doctor will give the address. Further information can be obtained IN CONFIDENCE from the Health Department at your local Council's offices, or by writing to the Medical Adviser, Central Council for Health Education, Tavistock House, Tavistock Square, London, W.C.1. Please send stamped addressed envelope.

Issued by the Ministry of Health, and Central Council for Health Education.

Venereal VD Diseases

This is an extract from one of the many letters received and permission has been given by the writer to use this extract.

"Are you ever properly cured?"

"Just after he had gone back I received a letter ... saying that he was ... suffering from gonorrhœa ... After a test I was told that I also was suffering from it ... could you tell me if this disease can at any time come back in the way of a relapse as I have heard people say it can, that you are never properly cured, but don't you think I stand a good chance with going to the clinic in the early stages? ..."

The Doctor replies:

"You need not worry. The doctors can cure Venereal Diseases completely if they are given a fair chance. All you must be sure to do is to continue going to the clinic as you so sensibly did in the early stages. If you do this and continue until the doctor treating you says you are cured, you need not fear a return of the disease after cure. But you will realise that you can catch the disease again even after your present infection has been cured. That means that your husband must also get completely cured. The Army specialist who is treating him will tell him when he is cured."

FREE CONFIDENTIAL ADVICE AND TREATMENT are available at clinics set up by County and County Borough Councils. Any doctor will give the address. Further information can be obtained IN CONFIDENCE from the Health Department at your local Council's offices, or by writing to the Medical Adviser, Central Council for Health Education, Dept. M-9 WM, Tavistock Square, London, W.C.1. All replies are sent in plain envelopes.

Issued by the Ministry of Health, and Central Council for Health Education.

Traditional values

From all this it might be inferred that the vast majority of women in wartime Britain were having a wild time with their fiances or husbands away. And it is true that traditional values were severely shaken. But the majority just struggled on, though few people wrote about them. One such woman wrote to *Woman's Own* in March 1945 to say that:

'One hears so much these days about broken marriages due to the separations brought about by the war, that it sometimes comforts me to consider the cases of my friends. There are about half a dozen who spring to mind at once. All have been married for 4 years or longer; some have children, some not; one has unfortunately lost her husband in this war; another's husband has been a prisoner in Japanese hands since the loss of Singapore. For those of us still fortunate enough to have our men within letter distance, our greatest pleasure is in writing to and hearing from them, and we all long eagerly for their return. Surely there must be thousands like us in England — faithful, loving wives? But one reads so much of the others that the fact that there are many happy marriages in spite of war difficulties is apt to be overlooked.'

And of course she was right. There *were* thousands like her. But, sadly, for many of them, their menfolk would come back broken in mind or body; if, indeed, they came back at all.

Some men feared that they would never come back or, if they did, would be a burden on their wives. And this caused many of them to wish to put off marriage until the danger was over. One woman who wrote to *My Home* in April 1940 complaining of her fiance's reluctance to marry was told:

'You are up against a very big obstacle — a man's sense of honour. He is certainly thinking along these lines: "Marriage means undertaking the responsibility of a girl's future, of guarding and protecting her, as well as giving her companionship and support. And to do this I must be able to count on a reasonable amount of security in our joint lives. War makes all this impossible, as well as bringing inevitable risks for myself of being maimed or even killed. Risks which I would face alone, but to which I cannot subject the woman I love."

'That is the way he is reasoning, and a very manly way, too. But he leaves out one important factor, the kind of love you have for him … In a true woman's heart there is a passion for giving. Giving all sorts of lovely things. Things like patience, self-devotion, sympathy and inspiration … But in order to give them fully to the man she loves she must belong to him, and have the proud name of wife. Can you make him understand this? Make him see how empty the months and years will be for you and how, if the worst comes to the worst, the great consolation for you would be to have been his?'

To a similar letter, from a woman whose fiance was worried about being killed, Leonora Eyles gave a more laconic reply:

'If you are sure he is sincere and really loves you, try to chaff him out of his depression. But are you sure? He may be trying gracefully to break an engagement he has grown tired of. Get him down to brass tacks and, if you feel he is not being sincere, give him up. I'm afraid it is the only thing to do, my dear.' (Woman's Own, 5th July, 1940)

But such worries were not without foundation. People *were* killed and injured. Towards the end of the war, the letters came steadily in from women seeking advice on coping with maimed and injured loved ones, or in facing life alone, having lost fiances and husbands.

A disturbing letter was sent to Leonora Eyles in early 1943 by a wounded air gunner, sent home on sick leave, who wrote that his wife:

'… who has been everything to me for 6 years says that the sight of me makes her sick because I have murdered innocent people. She has fallen for a civilian, and wants to leave me and take the child. Is this what we are fighting for?'

And perhaps the saddest she received was:

'Three of us have lost our fiances in the war and look like being spinsters. A friend has told me that spinsters deteriorate mentally and physically. Another friend says that spinsters should learn to sublimate. What does this mean?'

Leonora Eyles, and her counterparts in the other magazines, did what they could to advise, console and, where necessary, admonish the thousands who wrote to them. Nearly 50 years on some of what they wrote may seem quaint, old-fashioned and occasionally misleading. But at a time when people were more reluctant than nowadays to talk about their deepest worries, the agony aunts were perhaps the only escape-valve for many of the women of Britain.

HIS COURAGE

will help you face the first hard days if he comes home wounded. From her own memories Ursula Bloom gives you a personal message of hope to help you if this ordeal is ever yours

"YOU see," she said, "I don't quite know what it will be like to meet a man with one leg. He'll be awfully miserable, and that worries me."

I smiled wanly. Such a lot of women have got the wrong ideas about the men who are coming back to them. In the last war I worked at a Hospital Convalescent Home by the sea for men who had been badly wounded.

NO GLOOM, NO SELF-PITY

I went on duty the first time sure that I'd feel sick at the sight of their misery. Being wounded—I mean being wounded in such a way that there is no hope of full recovery seems such a dreadful thing. Ten minutes in that Home taught me two things. First, to be terrified of the Sisters. Second, to adore all the patients. The first man I ever nursed had lost an arm and both legs; he would never get up again except into a wheel chair, and, as far as I could see, he had got very little left to live for. Was he sorry for himself? Not a bit. He was extremely jolly. I shall never forget his sense of humour, or the way he could laugh and, heaven knows, I should have thought that he had precious little to laugh at. But he did make a success of his life, for he married from the Home, and was amazingly happy.

I also had the idea that in the Home everybody would be miserable and depressed, that the one-legged men would totter about, and the armless men would have to be fed and waited on hand and foot. It wasn't so. The patients' one idea was to re-learn everything they could manage in the shortest possible time. We taught them to walk, and there were even some reckless ones who would bicycle when our backs were turned. It made your blood run cold at times! I remember seeing three of my patients with only two legs to the lot of them insisting on playing tennis!

And we had the greatest difficulty in keeping them in. On summer evenings when Sister used to inquire if all the patients were safely indoors, and we used to say they were, it was horrifying to find that two or three of them, with half their rightful number of limbs, had purloined a wheel chair or two, and had gone off to the local pub!

"I'm sure I don't know what you nurses do, but you certainly never mind your patients," Sister would complain.

The wounded men who are coming back will be brave. They made the best of having to go out to fight a war that nobody wanted, and they'll make the best of their handicaps now. Much can be done to help them. It needs a war to send surgery spurting forward with wonderful new inventions. Have you ever met a man from St. Dunstan's? No? Then you have no idea how well they "see."

IT'S UP TO YOU

I'm not pretending that one can ever make up to the badly maimed for what they have lost; no one in their senses would imagine that. What I am saying is that the woman who is frightened of the injured husband she may meet, need not be. She will find he is the same man who left her, but with an added courage. He won't sit down and cry over the past; he'll want to learn the best way of living the future. And it is up to his wife to help him.

It is something to have him back with you, and to know that, even if he is maimed, there are some wives who have not even got a maimed husband. Think of it that way and remember what an immense amount you have to be thankful for.

Meet him with a smile. He'll be a bit scared that you'll burst into tears, and say "Darling, how awful for you!" Your attitude must be "Darling, isn't it wonderful to have you back?" Give him that lead, and you'll find that he'll take it.

I know life is going to be a bit different and difficult at first, because all new things are hard until we get used to them.

> "To look at everything always as though you were seeing it either for the first or last time: thus is your time on earth filled with glory."—Betty Smith, "The Tree in the Yard."
>
> "A gentleman is one who expects much from himself but little from others."
>
> Confucius.

Forget the past and go forward bravely into the future. He never lacked courage, and I'm sure you won't when you meet him. You're going to have a surprise, the same surprise that I had when I put on my blue frock and fastened my white belt about me. But then life is surprising, you know.

BUILDING ON EXPERIENCE

Experience gained in the last war has been of immense value in helping the wounded in this war, but since then tremendous strides have been made in the treatment of men who are badly disabled. You would be amazed at the miracles that are accomplished to-day under the dull names of "Rehabilitation" and "Occupational Therapy."

In the 200 or so Red Cross and St. John Convalescent Homes throughout the country, convalescence is no longer looked upon as a period of passive invalidism, but a time during which everything is done to help the patient readjust himself to civilian life. "Rehabilitation" teaches him not only to face life again with the loss of a limb, but to enjoy a happy and satisfying life.

"Occupational Therapy" is the name of a system that teaches men to do all kinds of handicrafts involving close concentration and the manipulation of new muscles. In Convalescent Homes you'll see men who have lost limbs learning to weave, make gloves, toys, rugs and a dozen other things. The training is useful, but it is the effect it has on the mind of the patient that is most important. He forgets his disabilities and loses any tendency he may have towards invalidism. To use an old-fashioned phrase, "it takes him out of himself."

In the limb-fitting centres the disabled man receives training in recovering the use of the neglected muscles, and in using the intricate mechanical limbs which modern scientific research has provided.

He learns to walk, run and work until these activities come naturally and without strain. He learns to take up again many of the activities which he probably thought he would have to forgo for ever.

*And even while he is in hospital the Ministry of Labour officers get in touch with him and his doctors to see if it would be wise for him to be trained at a special training centre for a new trade, so that he may be restored to a secure place in society, and to the happiness and independence which only a worthwhile job can bring. The Government rightly feel that there is nothing more important than the happy resettlement in civil life of disabled men—*EDITOR.

Beauty

Wars are no respecters of time, persons or pretty faces, and at the start of the war, the magazines' first requirement was to ask women to be confident and cheerful in their appearance, ready to meet the day ... or anything. Worry was considered by *Woman's Magazine* to be the main cause of an unsightly appearance. In November 1939, the editor pointed out that:

'Anxiety is a dreadful ravager of loveliness, and no man wants to come home to a wife or a sweetheart who shows in her face how much she has worried about him.'

However, some people were just lazy. There was no excuse for a woman to get slack just because her man was away. Ursula Bloom warned:

'Have you thought what it will be like if, after the war, men came home to wives and sweethearts who have let themselves go? If you let go now, you may not get the chance to pull up afterwards. Stay lovely.' (Woman's Own, 8th February, 1941)

Beauty was not necessarily obtained through the use of lavish cosmetics ... *'All it need take was ten minutes really well spent with a mirror, an old lipstick, a jar of face cream and a few face tissues'*, said *Woman's Sphere*. But this was not always possible when there were air raids at night. There just wasn't time to go in for the skin hygiene usually practised before bed. Besides, who would want to go down to the shelter looking a mess of nourishing cream and hair nets? Ursula Bloom gave some useful tips to stay beautiful in the shelter:

'First invest in a warm dressing gown with large pockets to keep your air raid beauty make-up in. Some little refreshers for cleansing of any surplus grease (they'll cost 6d), a tube of powder cream, which, in an instant takes off all the shine and leaves you matt and composed (6d again), a handkerchief-puff well-filled with powder, and a tiny mirror. If you're fussy, have a lipstick, but it isn't necessary. In the second pocket put a small comb, a bottle of smelling salts, a flask with something in it to keep cold out and your favourite tablets to quieten the nerves. You may need them. Add some cotton wool to ram in your ears if the world gets too noisy. There are special 'silencers' which you can use ... and they shut out all that very demoralizing din which is one of the most unpleasant parts of an air raid.' (Woman's Own, 10th November, 1940)

But beauty preparations of all kinds were already in short supply. The best way to cope with this was to make absolutely sure that the 'foundations' — figures, hands, feet, hair, eyes and skin were all in tip top condition. Even if clothes and accessories were shabby, hair should be shining. Skin should be fed if it was to stay young and unwrinkled; no-one could afford to do without face-cream. Eyes, after feeling the strain of dim lights and black-outs, should be bathed every day. Hands, too, should not be neglected — even if your hands were rarely out of water, and your house full of evacuees:

'Do remember that when HE comes back he will want to kiss the hands that have worked for him. It will be easy enough to bleach them with a lemon and magnesia face pack the night before he gets home.' (Woman's Own, 7th March, 1940)

Good grooming was the most essential attribute to beauty throughout the war. If you neglected yourself because there was a war on you would feel the worse for it. It had already become a prerequisite for women in the services. They looked trim and tidy in their well-kept uniforms, and their posture was erect. Many had cut their hair or they wore it up beneath the uniform cap. Make-up was the only problem in the forces. Which lipstick would go with khaki? *Woman's Journal* in December 1939 discovered one brand that would do the trick:

'If you have to stay in khaki, don't despair — there is a new lovely make-up for you, especially created for this rather trying colour. Its name is "Burnt Sugar". It is a warm glowing shade that goes beautifully.'

WHAT THEY DO AND WHAT THEY WEAR ...

WOMEN'S AUXILIARY AIR FORCE

The Women's Auxiliary Air Force was formed in 1939. Before that members did duty with the Royal Air Force Companies of the A.T.S., formed in 1938. But experience of the specialised nature of their duties resulted in the formation of a separate organisation. Now the W.A.A.F. is an integral part of the Royal Air Force. At the outbreak of the war there were five trades in which women could enrol. Now there are over sixty! The attractive uniform is air force blue, and badges of rank are identical with those of the R.A.F. showing close association with the fighting service.

JOBS in or out of uniform make us value the healthy freshness that enables us to do them well and enjoy our leisure too! Happily we can all renew that splendid feeling of Personal Freshness daily by using ...

LIFEBUOY TOILET SOAP

LEVER BROTHERS, PORT SUNLIGHT, LTD.   LBT 586A-630

Don't get Slack!

"It is every woman's job to wear her gayest clothes—and a smile!" says the actress RUBY MILLER—reminding us that cheerfulness is war work.

WOMEN in wartime should not relax their efforts to look attractive. I went through the last war, so I speak from experience.

It is easy to look smart in a uniform, but after a tiring spell of duty, one doesn't feel inclined to trouble much about one's hair, skin and nails, and still less about mufti.

That I believe to be a mistake.

Your menfolk who may be serving at the front or in camp, left you looking your usual charming selves. It means a great deal to them, when they return on leave, to find you still as attractive.

Don't get slack. A woman who is unkempt and ill-dressed soon loses her *morale*. I know it takes courage to carry on as though nothing out of the ordinary were happening, but that is the kind of courage women must have if we are to keep alive the vital thing Hitler has menaced—civilization.

Some places of amusement have opened again, others will no doubt follow, and once more we may see our restaurants and dance floors crowded by men in uniform accompanied by *soignée*, tastefully gowned women. Social relaxation is as necessary in war as in peace if we are to keep cheerful and fit, and the women of my generation know how much our appearance meant to men on active service. It was a tonic.

In the first dark days the thought of dress and beauty treatment may seem irrelevant. We think: "Oh, what does anything matter?" Later we realize that such apparently trivial things matter a great deal.

For one thing, men always look smarter in uniform than in mufti, so we start with a handicap, since we do not wear uniform off-duty as they do.

In the last war I knew V.A.D.'s, W.A.A.C.'s, W.R.E.N.S.'s, and W.A.T.'s who started off with that "What does it matter?" attitude but changed their tune when they found themselves left out in the cold.

Attractive clothes and beauty aids are much cheaper than they were in the last war; and yet my generation contrived to keep up to the mark. We wore charming pyjama suits and boudoir caps during air-raids—though the latter *would* look a little comic crowning a gas-mask, I admit!

BUT one generation is very much like another, and the god of love wins most of the victories—in war as well as peace. Many romances may have their beginning

The wise woman realises what a tonic she can be to men on active service —and so she looks her best

in air-raid shelters, with sparkling eyes looking through cellophane. . . .

It is our job to bring colour and cheerfulness to the grim business of war. Before we know where we are, charity fêtes and flag-days may be upon us, and all available women will be called upon to help. That's the time you will find how much your appearance counts—in hard cash—for a deserving cause.

We shall soon become rather bored with Fritz and his threats, and spend our leisure thinking out ways and means of giving "the boys" a good time and helping them to forget for a spell the horrors of war. Don't be an added horror!

Wear light-coloured clothes. Not only will they have a cheering effect —they will minimize the danger of being run over during these long evenings when the lighting restrictions are in force.

Freedom in dress is one of the charms of democracy, so we shouldn't stint ourselves if we want to "do our bit" apart from actual war work.

When a woman feels her best she is usually wearing a new dress, hat, or make-up. She is smiling and joyous, and those are two unbeatable assets. We have to show Hitler how little he can scare British women with his Big Bad Wolf methods.

Be as attractive as you can at work and in leisure hours, and you'll soon discover what a delightful impression you make on friends and how formidable you can be—indirectly—to foes!

Incidentally, you will be helping British industry, especially textiles, to carry on and maintain that financial stability without which wars cannot be won.

Be as attractive as you can at work and in leisure hours

The Liberty Cut

by Mary Embrey

This new style of hairdressing meets war-time needs, and allows the hair to be arranged according to individual taste

WHEN the B.B.C. programme "Women at War" was launched at the beginning of the year I gave the first two talks on good grooming. The "high-ups" of each of the three Services—the W.R.N.S., A.T.S. and W.A.A.F.—had their own ideas of the points most in need of emphasis.

But all were agreed on one point. They were anxious to impress on women the unsuitability of a long bob when the wearer was in uniform. I was only too glad to have the opportunity of supporting their arguments. They regarded the hair-on-the-shoulders fashion as unsuitable because it looked untidy under a service cap, because it was unhygienic, and because it obviously detracted from the smartness of a girl's appearance.

It might be pretty and becoming for many young girls in peace-time conditions and with constant attention, and in the hands of a skilful hairdresser it could be adapted to suit tailored clothes, but for women at war it was neither pretty nor suitable.

Looking at the argument with an eye trained to see hairdressing from the fashion angle, I agreed entirely. Fashion is essentially ruled by one axiom—"to be suitably dressed is to be well dressed". You would not consider any woman well dressed if she did her shopping in a dance-dress, no matter how perfect the dress might be, or if she wore the finest fur coat over a cotton frock. The same rule applies to the hair. From the fashion angle it is well dressed only if it is *suitably* dressed.

Shorter Hair

The fashion rule for tailored clothes insists that the hair should be worn so that it does not touch the collar of the jacket. It may be the "three-inch-long" style advocated by Elizabeth Arden, in which the hair is brushed to form a halo-like roll.

Equally attractive, especially for the older woman, is the revival of the semi-shingle. In this case the hair is tapered at the back with one side left slightly longer than the other to allow for waving across the back of the head. Either suggestion permits for variations from the front view. The parting may be centre, side or non-existent. The hair can be brushed up in front in waves with curled ends or in a simple roll.

The new "Liberty" cut recently launched by the Guild of Hairdressers allows the hair to be dressed in any one of a number of styles which can be chosen to become the individual. But each style obeys the fashion dictum, that hair is invariably dressed well above the collar-line when simple tailored clothes—uniform or civilian—are worn.

The "Liberty" cut has other advantages. After the initial visit to the hairdresser for the essential cutting and tapering, the expense in money and time of further visits is reduced to a minimum. The hair will need to be re-cut at about three-monthly intervals. In between it can easily be washed and dressed at home. Brushing and combing,

One of the many charming hair styles which can be based on the Liberty Cut

far from upsetting the waves or curls, will actually improve their set, and it goes without saying that this fact will greatly add to the health and beauty of the hair itself.

Everybody's Hair-style

The older woman, especially the woman with white hair, should welcome the innovation quite as heartily as her daughter will greet it. It is one of the few hairdressing suggestions I have ever encountered which can be adapted with equal ease to emphasize the charm of youth and to give poise and sophistication to the mature.

But you cannot expect—whether you are young or not-so-young—to get good results unless your hair itself is in good condition. Far too many women have given up brushing and massaging because they have feared to upset their curls and waves.

The result is a deterioration in the health of the scalp and consequently in the appearance of the hair. It lacks sheen and burnish, and, lacking stimulation also, becomes too dry or too greasy according to its type.

Before you have the new cut—and you will have no difficulty about this, for hairdressers all over the country are sponsoring it—give yourself ten days' intensive treatment.

For a start shampoo your hair. Then each morning and evening massage the scalp well for two minutes. You can use a simple tonic if the hair is lank, or a little coco-nut oil if it is too dry. Finish each massage with a good brushing, and finally comb the hair in every direction—up and down and round about.

At the end of the ten days' treatment visit your hairdresser and ask for a shampoo and the new "Liberty" cut, followed by a lesson in dressing the hair in the way most likely to be attractive for your individual self.

In early 1941, cosmetics and hair preparations were rationed. Although the Board of Trade was fighting to maintain a supply to boost feminine morale, the chemicals needed to make cosmetics were required for munitions and in extremely short supply. Mary Embrey, beauty expert for *Woman's Magazine*, tried to put a brave face on it in April 1941 by saying:

'I am inclined to think rationing will be an excellent thing for faces! I suppose most of us felt a little dismayed when we heard that cosmetics were to be rationed down to a quarter of the amount usually available, but we have been extravagant in the past ... very often using far too much and thus doing more harm than good.'

There were other shortages too. Hats practically vanished, making hair all the more important. But hairpins had disappeared as well, and there were reports in 1941 from factories that workers were disfigured for life when their hair caught in machines. The answer was, of course, simply to shorten the hair and a national campaign to do so was put into effect. *Woman's Own* took up the challenge. In January, 1942, it said:

'We've watched since the war began for shorter hair to come in. You still see plenty of shoulder-brushing manes about. But there is a steady trend towards the neater, more patriotic style ... and mannish? No, not a bit of it.'

In May, Ursula Bloom said:

'Shorter hair means fewer hairdresser's bills, cleaner and healthier scalps. It means ... goodbye to the Greta Garbo raggle-taggle locks to the shoulder. They never did make you look your best. There is today a new cut called "The Liberty Cut". It thins the crown and makes the hair much easier to manage so that you can set it yourself far more. Don't be afraid to show your ears. Ears are coming back into fashion, and personally I think they look charming.' (*Woman's Own*, 29th May, 1942*)*

The new Liberty cut saved hairpins, was more hygienic and less trouble. Once the initial cut and perm had been given, hair could be attended to at home.

By 1944, most women had shorter hair or at least they wore their long hair up. Many took to rolling their hair up in one sweep, using a hair ribbon or scarf, maybe broken with curls in a 'cockscomb' in front. This style needed few or no combs and pins to keep in place. Combs were also in short supply.

Meanwhile, the shortages of cosmetics had, during the second half of 1942, forced The Board of Trade to urge women to reduce their cosmetic buying still further. *My Home* suggested getting all the old lipsticks out of their cases and melting them down over a gentle heat. A little of this lipstick mixed with a spot of cold cream would expand its spreading power and could be used for rouge as well. Bright nail varnishes were dying rapidly — duty in canteens, hospitals or in munitions called for capable hands, not *'pale hands pink-topped'*.

The glamour girl was now a thing of the past. Maybe high heels and glamour could bring a note of

Mansel Beaufort's Page

BEAUTY IN MINIATURE

CONSPICUOUS make-up has gone with the wind and pre-war glamour. To celebrate this back-to-nature move I have arranged for you to have the special little set of make-up shown below. The :ample includes cream rouge, powder rouge, lipstick and face powder. Each enhances your own colouring instead of adding an artificial shade. SIXPENCE is the price complete. Write to Mansel Beaufort, address above, enclosing 6d. in stamps. Mark your envelope Miniature Make-up.

'gay relief' to those magic hours of leisure, but generally speaking, it was *'desperately old-fashioned'* to be glamorous. Hard work and wartime duty had caused the vampish woman to change. *Woman and Beauty* in April 1943 thought:

'The jealousy-provoking kind of coquetry now seems cheap. Flirts have reformed. Character has broken through mask veneer, serenity has won over studied smoothness. There is a special kind of beauty preparation. It can't be brought at a single shop in the world, because you must manufacture it yourself. It's a product of spirit, heart and simple courage, and you make it fresh for each day and as each need arises.'

Dora Shakell from *Woman's Own* thought that an occasional abstinence from beauty preparations altogether worked wonders to the skin. Instead, there was that new knowledge, gained from wartime health propaganda, which told a woman it was what she ate that really made her beautiful:

'You've got to look lovely for his leave. First of all, do eat for beauty. Liver is your meat. It is not rationed either.' (Woman's Own, 16th March, 1941)

By 1943, the fuel shortage had necessitated the cutting down of baths. Deodorants were the obvious answer. But it seemed that many women were still apprehensive about their use. *The Lady* in May 1943 tried to reassure the uninitiated by saying:

'You need a good deodorant, you know. Some people are still nervous of deodorants, thinking they are harmful. Of course they are not. They are a vital necessity for your friend's sake as well as your own.'

The girls in the forces, at least, kept their figures trim with their physical training. Many girls, because their work was sedentary, had, what *Woman's Magazine* called '*that tendency towards wider measurements which used to be termed "middle age spread"*'. *Good Housekeeping* had reports of telephone operators getting huge across the back of the hips. To help control this position, the magazines recommended various exercises.

By the end of the war, exhaustion was the main mar to beauty. Jean Cleland suggested, in *Woman's Magazine*, that relaxation and a sound healthy sleep were the cure. First, you should have a warm bath followed by a hot drink before going to bed. Only the women in the armed forces seemed to take it all in their stride. Rosita Forbes summed up the picture of healthy wartime beauty in an article, on the ATS (Auxiliary Territorial Service):

'They swing along straight-backed, their heads look small, instead of resembling a birds nest ... Tidiness is far more attractive than any amount of artificial glamour ... I don't believe we need nearly as much colour on our faces as we imagined. I believe the new young, up-to-date attraction depends on being extremely well-washed and brushed and darned and ironed. No more violent lipstick ... heels comfortable and low. This "neatness first" attractiveness goes for all of us — wherever our warwork takes us — or if it keeps us in our own homes.'

Fashion

When they went out to dine on an August evening in 1939, women were wearing richly-textured sweeping gowns in soft black morocain, patterned in silver or red and green lamé stripes, showing a good deal of glamorous back décolletage. By November they were sitting at home in the blackout making a siren suit for the kids or a pair of good strong dungarees for themselves. It was the women's magazines which came forward with new patterns and new ideas to beat the rising cost of materials and the rocketing price of new clothes. *Woman's Own* in November 1940 said:

'In these days our Pattern Service is being appreciated more than ever by the woman who is able to be her own and her children's dressmaker ... Any woman who has a sewing machine and an iron can make her own frocks.'

The new wartime fashion in 1939, was to have a '*waist like a stem*', accentuated by a gushing front, gathered pleats, belts and ties and an interesting neckline with maybe a yoke. It was money well spent if a new foundation garment was purchased, as the small waist and rounded hips were here to stay.

The first wartime winter was freezing. Swagger coats acquired huge hoods and large pockets, feet snuggled into over-boots of waterproof velvet or gaberdine with fur round the ankles, and the handbag now incorporated a handy gas mask container. If you were unable to afford a new coat, the magazines told you how to cut the collar off an old coat and buy a short length of the fashionably-cheerful plaid with which to make a new hood and a pair of plaid cuffs to match. If you were clever with the needles, had some wool, a few black-out evenings and a knitting-pattern from the magazines, you could knit a warm practical lumber-jacket or warm undies for the winter.

For Christmas, the women turned their hands to knitting delightful snoods in bright coloured chenilles, threading them with ribbons to match their frocks. And when they went out, they wore a luminous brooch which gave off a glow that could be seen for fifteen feet in the blackout night.

HE war can take you two ways—both unpleasant ! Predicament one is that you are not getting the exercise you were brought up to expect. Skating, riding, dancing, games are interfered with by black-outs and budgets and general busy-ness. Your health and figure are suffering, and you still wake up tired. Here is a trio of morning exercises to make good some of the exercise you are missing. ONE is done while you still cannot bear the thought of getting out of bed. Throw out the pillows, lie flat on the back. Swing both legs up and towards wall behind the head. Swing them down again as body comes up to a sitting position. Bend down to touch the toes. Do it in one continuous swing and repeat three times. TWO is done standing and is specially for hips and bust. Face the wall, hands against it. Fling each leg up and out behind, from the hips, bending the knee at the last minute, throwing back the head. Repeat ten times. THREE is for loosening up the legs, increasing the spring of the whole body. Feet together, arms out. Raise and lower heels rhythmically, working up to a little springing jump, counting to 20.

1.

2.

3.

Morning and Night

PAULA CATOR brings you to life at the beginning of the day, relaxes you at the end

REDICAMENT two is that war work and worry and inconveniences leave you all in at the day's end, too tired to enjoy yourself or even to rest. These three exercises are for general let-out, easy ways of untying the tension. ONE : Lift eyes and hands to the skies in protest, breathing deeply in as you raise the arms to circle loosely over the head. Let the arms fall as the body droops forward and the knees sag and the head hangs. Breathe out through this collapse. Three times. TWO is done lying on the back with knees crooked. Bring the knees alternately to the chest, bringing each foot back to the floor with a stamp. It relieves congestion in the lower back, relaxes the lower part of the spine. Repeat 20 times. THREE is done face downwards on bed or couch. Raise head and waist, relax forward on to the bed. Repeat six times, ending in complete relaxation. It counteracts stoop and droop of head and shoulders.

To give women an appearance of strength during 1940, all the smartest suits and coats were cut on military lines, with broad padded shoulders, straight fronts, and moderately flared skirts which had a well placed pleat at the back. The knitted jumpers followed suite with square shoulders 'smart as a soldier'. Someone ingenious had written to the magazines suggesting that your old silk stockings, if folded over and tacked on, would make ideal shoulder pads. Grey was the favourite shade for the main outfit, as it would match most accessories already owned, making a different looking outfit every time.

A printed woollen dress was the most popular formal day wear for every occasion throughout the war, especially if it was made in the American shirtwaist style. As men left for war and the women filled their jobs, they increasingly took to slacks and trousers, and these, worn with a hip-length jumper, became a common outfit. The magazines bemoaned the masculine style which was pushing its way into the woman's wardrobe. Wynne Tate wrote in *Woman's Own* in April 1940:

'Having with the best intentions in the world, clothed ourselves as nearly as our lords and masters, what must we do but imitate their other privileges too. We prop up bars and we tell stories. We hide our femininity under a cloak of masculine headiness. We must try hard not to let our new-found bravery make us tough.'

Even James Laver, the authority on fashion and keeper of costume at the Victoria and Albert Museum said:

'War leads women to straight lines and lack of femininity instead of lovely natural curves. We must strive to keep the colours up, the line more interesting.' (Woman's Own, May 1940)

The magazines gave tips on how to look demure without having to spend money. You could add a sweet little frilly collar to your frock, hand embroider a yoke of gaily coloured silks, or maybe manufacture a big organdie flower — using a packet of white pipe cleaners for the stalk. A new hat was the best tonic and this could easily be made at home.

'... one blackout evening dedicated to a simple bit of millinery will repay you in soaring spirits next time you go up the street.' (Woman's Own, November 1939)

Many of the younger girls were earning wages for the first time and could afford to buy new. Once out of their uniform or overalls they sparkled in sequins for the evening. Some of the older women who had been told 'Never buy new where old will do', felt bitter.

Many women were making no effort at all to look trim. These were duly admonished by Ursula Bloom:

'It's economy time, but that doesn't mean that you need look shabby and down at the heels. Not many clothes around this autumn, I know, but there's no earthly reason why you shouldn't give your old ones that "flip" which makes them look new and gives you the feeling of appearing at your best. It is your duty to make yourself look your best.' (Woman's Own, October 1940)

PRACTICAL IDEAS FOR AUTUMN

Popular Shirt Blouse. No. 782.
Here is a smart interpretation of the ever-popular shirt blouse. The front and back are gathered on to a yoke, or fine tucks can be used. Sleeves are finished at the wrist with plain cuffs, and the front buttons through a straight strap. 'Celanese' crêpe-de-chine would be a good choice of material, of which you will need 2¼ yards, 36 inches wide, for each size. Patterns supplied for 34, 36, 40 or 42-inch bust, price 10d. each post free.

A Cosy Dressing-Gown. No. 783.
This dressing-gown has been specially chosen for its snug-fitting hood, useful in time of emergency. For cosiness make it in flannel or molleton. Material required, 36 inches wide : 4 yards for each size. Patterns supplied for 34, 36, 40 and 42-inch bust, price 10d: each post free.

Coat for Girls of 8 to 16 years. No. 784.
This collarless coat is ideal to slip on over a summer frock. It fastens

Simple Frock. No. 785.
Stitching or braid on the bodice of this frock makes it most attractive. There is a seam down the centre front of the skirt, and the back is quite plain. The sleeves are cut full length and tucked or gathered into the armholes. Material required, 36 inches wide: 3⅜ to 3⅝ yards, according to size. Patterns supplied for 34, 36, 40 and 42-inch busts, price 10d. each post free.

Smart Autumn Coat. No. 786.
Choose a soft woollen material for this smart autumn coat, which is extremely simple to make. There is no collar, the fronts turn back to form wide revers, and seams are made from armholes to hem both front and back. Material required, 54 inches wide: 3 to 3¼ yards, according to size. Patterns supplied for 34, 36, 40 and 42-inch busts, price 10d. each post free.

Up-to-the-Minute Frock. No. 787.
The bodice buttons from neck to

782
783
784
FROCK 785
COAT 786
787

with two or three buttons at the neck, and there is a yoke at the back only from which the coat falls in a slight flare. Tweed or flannel would be suitable materials to use. You will require 1½ to 2¼ yards, 54 inches wide, according to size. Patterns supplied for 8 to 10, 10 to 12, 12 to 14 or 14 to 16 years, price 10d. each post free.

waist, where it is finished with a buckled belt coming from the shaped side-pieces. The back of the dress is cut on the same lines, but without gathers. Suitable materials are fine wool jersey or silk crêpe, of which you will require from 3¼ to 3¾ yards, 36 inches wide, according to size. Patterns supplied for 34, 36, 40 or 42-inch bust, price 10d. each post free. '

Woman's Magazine in November 1940 noticed a laxity in dress among younger girls who were not, it seemed, hiding enough. They were deliberately going round without a corset and with very large feet:

'How many young girls of seventeen one sees at a dance with shapeless figures, the lack of control echoed in over large feet and bad posture. The well-corsetted girl has a figure which will last her for life, a good carriage and feet many times smaller than those of the uncontrolled.'

Dress manufacturers were now not making so many sizes. Many women took to buying their dance dresses with laces under the arms and on the hips which would adjust to different measurements, and the favourite day dress was a pinafore dress which wrapped around a figure of any size. By the end of 1940, due to the shortage of dyestuffs, shops were selling garments in a limited choice of colours. Trimmings, too, were disappearing fast, so that the new summer clothes had button-on pockets and collars.

Now home dress-making was more important than ever. *Woman's Home Companion* in November 1940 said:

'With the cost of ready-made clothing rising considerably, it becomes more and more of an advantage for every woman to do her own dressmaking. In that way she can get not only the style but also the material that she wants at about half the cost. AND she can be sure that her clothes REALLY FIT and wear longer.'

In 1941, the second freezing winter of the war, the knitters turned their skills towards making warm shawls, hats, pullovers and entire suits, in addition to garments for the forces. The wool manufacturers had been forced to restrict variety in yarns, but they still managed to supply the demand, though finer two and three ply qualities were the result. These, however, made lovely openwork patterns and girls could make themselves lacy blouses and maybe sew on some sequins. And there was a report from the Palace that the two Princesses were knitting for the troops and getting most proficient with the needles.

Knee-length stockings in bright colours were the latest things to knit. These were considered more cheerful to wear than the compulsory brown lisle stockings which had become the only hosiery available since the banning of silk stockings in December 1940. Through 1940 there had been a shortage of silk which was needed elsewhere, to make things like parachutes. The magazines produced tips on how to prolong the life of the silk pairs of stockings that remained. You had to rinse them through in methylated spirits before wearing them; you had to draw a line in colourless nail varnish just under the suspender top and over the toe joint (the two most vulnerable places) and while you were wearing them, you could put inside little homemade cloth toe-caps for further protection. The few pairs cherished for that precious off-duty date, should be kept in an air-tight jar so that they would keep for ages. In the warmer summer weather many women wore:

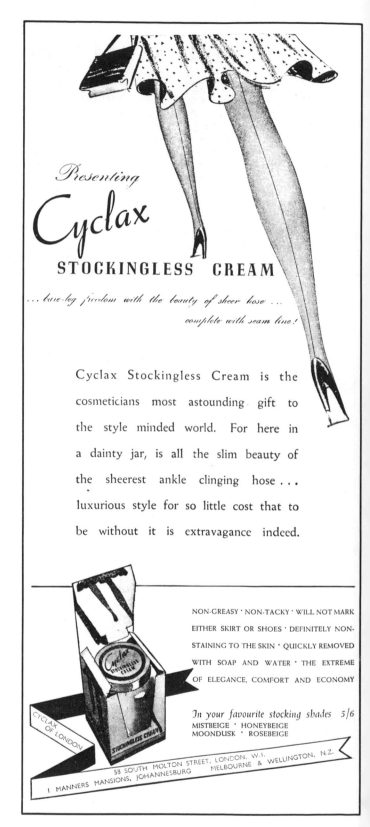
'Those exciting new stockings which come out of a bottle. You can buy this leg make-up in two stockings shades. Grape Mist and Gold Mist, the latter being perfect with suntan make-up and you can pour out about 8 pairs of stockings from the 1/3d size bottle. Apply it with a large pad of cotton wool, stroking it on rapidly, then draw in the seam with a brown eye-brow pencil. It won't rub off or smear your skirt, and it's waterproof, a soap-and-water scrub being necessary to remove it.' (Mother and Home, July 1940)

MAKE-DO and MEND

UNPICK UNWEARABLE GARMENTS COMPLETELY To Salvage every inch!

Advice centres and classes provide an opportunity for every women to help or be helped!

Make-do and mend is an everyday phrase just now, and we are all striving to make our clothes and household goods last as long as possible, and to turn items we don't want into something we do.

Now just sitting at home and wrestling with our own clothes problems is a very boring job, especially if we need a bit of help or advice. We get much better results, and much more enjoyment, by working in a group, or sharing our

There are thousands of useful unofficial make-do and mend groups among friends and neighbours

problems with an expert needlewoman.

It was for this reason that the Board of Trade launched the Make-do and Mend campaign two years ago. Since then, many local education authorities and women's organizations, supervised by the Board of Education and assisted by the Board of Trade, have honeycombed England, Scotland and Wales with a

series of classes and advice centres where women can get help on all clothes and household mending problems.

There are more than 20,000 official make-do and mend classes, and quite as many more unofficial ones among groups of friends and neighbours. Some 150 advice centres are now at work, and many more are planned. As well as having advice centres in factories, there are sometimes classes as well. These are held after working hours in the works canteen or the factory's social club.

What the classes do

Primarily, they aim at solving as many individual problems as possible. You take along the ancient winter coat which might be made into a jacket, or old shirts to make into frocks for baby, or clothes the children have grown out of, or your own frock which is out of date or doesn't fit you any more.

Because many women's problems are the same, you will get class help on such problems as drafting a basic paper pattern to fit your own figure, altering an existing pattern to fit yourself, unpicking and cutting out, making openings and plackets, and finishing hems and edges. In addition, you will get individual help with your own job, and assistance in cutting out, fitting and finishing.

One specially good point about the classes is that you see how other women's problems are solved, and that gives you ideas. Another point is the social side of the classes; you will get as much fun as work out of your weekly class.

Make-do and mend advice centres

Many women have no time to attend regular classes, and for these the advice centres have been started. They are held for two or three periods each week. Sometimes a shop or room is taken specially for the purpose, or shared with the Ministry of Food for the purpose of giving food advice. In some towns the gas or electricity showrooms will house the centre, or a retail departmental store may provide space.

Advice centres are also held during the lunch-break in factory and works canteens. Here the full-time woman worker can get help, both with general clothes problems and those connected with the repair and maintenance of industrial clothing such as overalls and caps.

Each centre is staffed by experts, supplied from local technical schools, assisted in some cases by qualified members of local women's organizations, and

you can consult them on any problem concerning clothes or household goods.

They will tell you the best way to mend a carpet or clean a mackintosh, how to darn a tablecloth or patch a hole, suggest ways of "letting out" frocks and blouses, give you ideas for using up remnants of material. They will also show you renovated garments to give you further ideas, and in some cases will hold demonstrations on such subjects as making slippers and refooting stockings.

You will not, of course, expect the staff to do the work for you, but they will willingly help you when you get stuck. There is no charge for the advice given, and no obligation—except that of saying thank you.

Starting a class or advice centre

If you would like to make use of a class or advice centre, ask about it at your local Citizen's Advice Bureau. If there isn't a class near you, why not get one started? Wherever there are twelve or more women anxious for a make-do and mend class, they can approach the director of education for their county or county borough and enquire whether a teacher can be made available for them. They can also suggest that an advice centre be started, if the local population is of a size to warrant it.

Every woman can help the success of the campaign by using as regularly as possible all the facilities provided, and encouraging her friends to do the same.

Also, capable teachers and assistants are often difficult to find, and if you are a practical needlewoman with years of experience of family and home clothes problems, and can spare a few hours a

by RUBY M. EVANS

MAKE UP TOGETHER ONLY MATERIALS THAT REQUIRE THE SAME CLEANING or WASHING!

The shortages continued until, early in June 1941, the Government at last introduced the 'points rationing' scheme to clothing. It had managed to preserve secrecy to prevent a run on the shops. Now everyone was restricted to having just 66 coupons for a year. Most women were relieved. The wise ones chose to use their coupons on a suit that was good looking, hard wearing, cosy and comfortable for duty 24 hours a day. Some brought a dress that they wouldn't get tired of, and made it play a different part for each occasion with artfully contrived changes.

They raided the cheap trays at the haberdashery, painted their own buttons with coloured enamels or found that an appliquéd design, added to their old office dress, would transform it fit for a date. With it they wore the new wedge shoes which were more practical than high heels, and, as scarves were on coupons, did miraculous manipulations with a hat. Even the Queen confessed that she'd had '*an old hat turned inside out, remade, and it looked like new*'.

Following the Austerity Regulations of spring 1942,

Utility Cloth[es]

Many of the well-known fashion houses are now making, to Government specifications, Utility clothes, putting into them the best materials and workmanship

A Harella coat and a Wolsey jersey two-piece, both good examples of the moderate-priced garments that are now obtainable

IT is now obvious to us all that whatever dress purchases we are fortunate enough to make must last us longer than clothes have lasted since the early days of the century. They have to be loved and admired . . . or they have to be endured and regretted. How is it possible to ensure that every purchase made belongs to the former class?

Just as the toilet preparations which you buy now give you no assurance or satisfaction when they have to be bought with strange names on them in place of the famous names which you trusted, when you go dress buying look for the labels. The famous dress houses are still making grand clothes as heretofore: look for their name inside the garment as an assurance that you are getting good fabric, good cut and good wear, with style.

Names You Know

Can you be sure to get names that you trust and that are familiar to you? In some ways we are in a better position there than we have ever been, because many of the high-class houses, whose price ranges might be outside our purses in the ordinary way, are, for patriotic purposes, making Utility clothes to the Government specifications at prices for modest purses.

More than that: many of them were so anxious to step forward and give the women of the country the best that was to be got, despite the restrictions on profit and price, that they put into these first Utility ranges the very best fabrics that they had, the best workmanship and the best styling, irrespective of the cost to them. So you can get coats or suits that ordinarily would cost you nine to twelve guineas for the under-five-guinea price of the Utility range.

That is general advice. Now for specific: what shall you look for? Only Utility clothes? No, far from that. There are old friends who may not be making Utility ranges at all, either because they are already doing their full quota for the Government in other ways, or because their prices have always been modest and their work sound and good.

Take an example: Wolsey models are models you trust for their really superb wool (the best made), for their cut and for their price, yet they are not Utility models while they come in the same price range as Utility. Why? Because their Government work is done in their stockings and their underwear. But you will get all the excellent finish and fabric and so forth laid down by the Government even though this is an uncontrolled range.

A Good Fit

"It is just as cheap to cut a garment perfectly as it is to cut a poor one," is what one of the heads of the Wolsey design department said recently at a conference. And that is true: labour is scarce now, and it is wise to have the very best cutters and fitters and designers when you have a name to uphold as to be a firm which thinks that inexpensive clothes should have poor design and cut and fit.

What ought you to be paying for your clothes to-day? Much depends on whether you are a suit woman or a dress-and-coat type. Suppose you are the latter: then make a compromise between that and wearing a suit (this is a suit year if ever there was one) by buying a jersey two-piece which is a soft wool suit buttoning right up to the throat and ending in a small turnover collar. This obviates the blouse and so saves you coupons and lets you have change-and-change-about schemes.

For a Wolsey model you would pay four and a half to five guineas, as you would for one of their take-to-pieces dresses—that is, a skirt with pockets, a shirt blouse (tuck stitched), and a detachable bib front which transforms it into a pinafore dress to make variation.

There is your compromise (in the jersey up-to-throat suit), and now you seek a coat to top it. Suppose you were to choose a Harella "year-round coat", for the same reason, that you know the reputation of their label and can trust line, cut and fabric.

You will pick their classic coat lines with that swing from the shoulders which speaks style. You can choose either the delightful pale summer colours or the workmanlike darker tones to see you the whole year through: which you choose depends on your purse and your coupons.

And here you can either buy a Utility coat in the Harella range, in the controlled price, under the five-pound limit, or buy a magnificent handwoven Harris (up to ten and a half guineas), a pussy-soft wool that yet has years of wear in it, or the mohair pile which women love so dearly.

Now, whether you have bought inside the Utility prices or outside them, you have got something which will never date, which will never bore you, in colours which are truly beautiful.

by Alison Settle

the Government not only cut the rations to 48 coupons a year, but felt obliged to restrict the number of pleats, seams, and trimmings. They cut the width of sleeves, hems and collars and sequins were banned. The women got round the regulations with their dress-making skills. They shortened skirts and nipped waists in a bit; they replaced sequins with metal studs; they even manufactured their own buttons by knitting squares of wool and fixing them over wooden button-formers, or sewing circles of felt together (using a penny as a pattern) stiffening it in between with cardboard. Spare parts were let in to old dresses; sometimes whole sides were taken out and replaced with a different material. Those who were hopeless dressmakers joined the Clothes-Pooling Clubs that had opened throughout the country, run by the WVS (Women's Voluntary Services). There they and their children could swap garments with others of their own size. Also in the spring of 1942, the GIs arrived in Britain. The lucky ladies dating them always looked better dressed and managed to procure pairs of those new nylon stockings.

In May, 1942, 'Utility Wear' was introduced by the Government. It wanted to ensure, through standardization, that enough good quality clothing could be manufactured to meet minimum requirements, and that even a working-class family could afford to buy it. Top designers in the country were asked to use their skills to design garments using only the best material and employing the finest workmanship. Eventually, Utility Wear accounted for four-fifths of all production.

In 1943, a woman might spend under £5 for a well designed Utility Suit, or eight guineas for one made from gentleman's suiting. She could get a coat for under the £5 limit, or a wool dress for under the £3 limit. The designs were smart, simple and plain and well fitted to the body to save on material. Handbags were scarce because they didn't come under the Utility scheme, so she would probably make her own from material or crocheted string. She need give only four coupons for one of the new crease-resistant blouses in a lovely fabric, made to look like flannel, linen or crepe-de-chine.

Her leather Utility shoes had low or medium heels and took five coupons to buy. There were some pretty designs, but she might have preferred to buy wooden shoes, which took two coupons less. *The Lady* in April 1943 instructed her on how to manage her new 'woodies':

'If you find yourself walking a bit duck-footed in the first few days, concentrate on placing your toes in a pigeon-toed position and you'll find your muscles will soon co-operate and you'll be walking the right way once more. If you get them wet, dry them on trees away from direct heat so the wood will not crack, or the leather uppers dry out.'

Her underwear was most reasonable. She could get Utility woven vests and knickers from around four shillings, nightgowns and slips from nine to sixteen shillings, pyjamas and combinations for half a guinea. Utility corsets and girdles cost under a pound, but because the materials to make them — whalebone, rayon, cotton, silk and rubber — were virtually

She chooses

DOLCIS... on or off duty as the perfect solution of her present day problems —comfort, long wear and good looks.

Dolcis

THERE IS A DOLCIS SHOE STORE IN EVERY LARGE TOWN

unobtainable, she might have to wait several months to get one on order. With the increase of starchy food in her diet, her larger figure would need one; or if not for herself, the magazines insisted that she should at least obtain one for her working daughter. Girls were getting so much bigger that the department stores were having to stock larger sizes. Alison Settle in *Woman's Magazine* in July 1943 wrote:

> *'I would counsel firmness, and that is where the corset belt is concerned. A girl may think she can save coupons and money by doing without a belt, that a younger figure does not demand one. But the young are doing more than nature intended them to do so early, and nothing so overcomes fatigue and bad posture as a first class belt. Buy the best you can for her, and in later years — not now — she will be thankful.'*

Many women spent their last coupons on a pair of slacks. When nearly everybody was working in 1943 and 1944, trousers had become an essential part of the wardrobe. A pair of 'Slimma' slacks could be purchased for £4, using eight coupons, and these, with a sweater, stout shoes, tweed coat and one of Montgomery's fashionable berets, became the sensible things to wear. Although slacks were worn universally now, some magazines still objected to women wearing trousers every day. *The Lady* in May 1943, for example, said:

> *'Undoubtedly slacks are here to stay and they feel comfortable and look very well when worn for the right sort of activity. Gardening, for instance, or fire-watching, or going for a country walk, but sloppy and unsuitable in towns and never for fat women, or with high heels, or brightly-coloured, or by mothers pushing prams, or long, floppy hair.'*

Many women had joined the Make Do and Mend Clubs which had sprung up everywhere and which were advertised in the magazines by the Board Of Trade. There you were taught to 'turn' a frock and sew it up again the other way round, or to darn, patch and strengthen before a hole appeared, using a length of fabric unwound from the seam. There, too, you might share the dwindling resources of needles, or learn how to clean your worthy suit (without the aid of petrol, turps, lemon, methylated spirits or other unavailable cleaning agents), by giving it a sponge over and a press under a damp cloth.

Wool was now rationed, and knitters who could not afford the coupons, unpicked their old jumpers, steamed the unravelled wool in a colander and wound them, after drying, into new balls. Small coloured oddments would do for a pretty Fair Isle or a horizontally striped jumper.

On D-Day (6th June, 1944), *The Lady* reported that in France:

> *'The girls had dressed themselves in full skirted, gaudy cottons, painted their bicycles in bright colours, done up their hair to ridiculous heights in order to look as unlike Frau Emmy Goering as possible.'*

Once again, a supply of new dyestuffs and a new trend in fashion appeared from Paris. It showed swinging

LET'S ASK THE MEN

Six men give Anne Edwards the masculine gen on these clothes

WHAT men have to say about women's clothes is usually interesting, aggravating, and surprisingly sound. So that once in a while it's a good idea to ask them what they think, even if you don't intend to take so very much notice of it!

I showed this picture of three smart girls—each in a typical wartime rigout to six different men and asked each of them what he thought of the clothes. The men's ages varied from twenty to sixty, their jobs from hairdressing to flying, and yet their instinctive criticisms were all on the same lines.

MR. SMITH, grey-haired and sixtyish, thought the nicest outfit was the one the girl on the left is wearing. He thought the girl on the right "quite nice," doesn't like hats on the back of the head because they "look silly," and abhors women in trousers. Pressed to give a reason for this, he just said it's not natural, and how would we women like to see men in skirts? But he did admit that in these days, and for some jobs it might be practical to wear slacks.

MR. BURNS, about thirty, a printer, also plumped for the girl on the left. He said: " She looks the most feminine." What appealed to him were the soft fullness of the coat with its swinging skirt, the warm, fluffy material, and the brimmed hat tilted across the forehead. His second choice was the girl in slacks, because they are well cut and she has the right sort of figure. Least of all he liked the suit girl whom he said " looked dull."

NIGEL, very sophisticated, and twenty-five, bracketed the girl on the left and the girl in slacks for first place. He said the girl in slacks was actually the smartest, but she lost marks because a town isn't the right place for them.

Anywhere else she'd have had top marks because the slacks are well cut, she has the right figure (which he specified as broad shoulders, narrow hips, long legs and sufficient bust to balance the length of line). She's wearing the right shirt and jacket. His only criticism was that the sleek hairstyle is far too groomed and glamorous for the informal outfit.

JOHN is only nineteen and his choice was the suit girl on the right. He liked it because it looks sensible and right for these times, he liked the wedge shoes because they're smart, and the back-of-the-head hat because it is gay and youthful. John was the only male too young to remember the pre-war clothes, and his tastes have been formed during wartime.

A/C PLONK, of the R.A.F., fell hard for the girl in slacks. He said he likes girls in slacks if they have the right figure (and this one has) and above all the right jacket. He said the slacks are well pressed, the jacket well cut and long like a man's, yet with a feminine curve. He thought, too, that she wears the right sort of shoes and shirt and considered the hairstyle simple and well cut.

Second place he gave to the girl in the coat, but criticized her thick-soled shoes because they make her feet look so big. He liked the suit-girl's wedges better because they make feet look smaller—but hankered after high heels.

ADRIAN, an artist in the office, was the last man to whom we showed our much criticized trio. His trained eye looked for line alone, and he gave the palm to the girl in the coat, liking the belted line and full swing of her skirt. Belts, he says, are always feminine because they outline small waists.

The trousered girl he disapproved of because her jacket is too tight and shows signs of strain, and " women aren't the right shape for trousers anyway—their waists are small and they have a sudden outward curve below." He thought the suit badly fitting round shoulders and bust, and the hat wrong for that suit. He doesn't like low heels but is getting used to them.

So there you are girls! Now you know that if you want to please your escort you'll have to put on your austerity shoes if he's under twenty—and your feminine high heels if he has nostalgic memories of pre-war days. Wear your slacks if he's sophisticated, but not if his father comes too. Remember men's eye for tailoring and valeting—that's where they're on their own ground.

Otherwise just go ahead and follow your own star—taking just as much or as little notice of their remarks as before!

---

dirndl skirts, draped and gathered bodices and plenty of feminine net in soft pastel shades; it revived romantic frocks with caped shoulders and lots of frill. But the Secretary of the Wholesale Textile Association told disappointed women that the shortage of materials would continue for at least a year after the war was over, and *Woman's Own* said in March 1945:

'Clothes are disappearing like autumn leaves, just at the time of year when we have a special longing to look at least presentable. The clothes situation isn't easy for anyone.'

The dressmakers were reduced to decorating their dresses with bits of cord or string bows, and the knitters had already turned their attentions to knitting for the liberated countries, about which *Home and Country* magazine said in December 1944 that 'The hardship and suffering is something which we, who have known shortages but no real privation, can hardly realise'.

It was *The Lady* which summed up people's feelings at the end of the war when it wrote in December 1945:

'How we have longed, during the shabby war years, for something new! What dreams we have made, while mending and making do, of bonfires of old clothes and the arrival of new dress boxes with lots of new tissue paper in them, of new paint and wallpaper, of new curtains and carpets, of new flower-beds and new cars, as soon as the war was over. As it happened war's end wasn't like that at all. We are still making do and ready to pull our belts and mend and make do for years to come rather than sell ourselves.'

Now more than ever

By October 1939, the first month after Britain entered the war, references to the war were already appearing in magazine advertising. With the slogan '*An active Britain needs BREAD FOR ENERGY*', one advertisement showed a smiling landgirl holding two huge shire horses, while the text read:

'Whatever your share in the National task, BREAD — the supreme source of vigour and activity — will help you tackle the task with unflagging energy. Now, more than ever, your diet must include sufficient Bread. Eat it at every meal.'

Thus one of the main wartime advertising themes had been born. There seemed to be no product, from underwear to cigarettes, from sewing machines to biscuits which was not needed '*more than ever*' before.

Certain manufacturers implied that under wartime conditions some of their competitors — unlike themselves — would be unable to keep up pre-war standards. Twixwol, '*The Quality Underwear*', informed readers that '*Surely now — more than ever — quality tells*':

'By wearing TWIXWOL Underwear this winter you are assured of bodily warmth and protection … Despite difficult war conditions the pre-war standards of TWIXWOL Underwear have been maintained.'

And Player's bearded sailor brandished the familiar packet above the slogan '*SOUND SECURITY*', while the text read:

'More important than ever to-day is the significance of the name 'Player' to cigarette smokers. It is a guarantee that quality and purity remain unchanged.'

At a penny cheaper than Player's for a packet of ten, De Reszke Minors preferred to ignore quality, claiming that they were '*Now more than ever, the best value on the market*'.

Value for money was stressed by the advertisers of Ryvita, who, with a picture of a smiling boy and girl, declared that '*NOW MORE THAN EVER this crunchy food should be the basis of your children's diet*'.

And, again emphasising the importance of children's health and fitness:

'Don't ration his VITAMINS — give him his daily Haliborange. NOW MORE THAN EVER it is all important to keep the youngsters thoroughly fit. Now more than ever we want them to carry their summer-time health right through the winter.'

An active Britain...

Whatever your share in the National task, BREAD — the supreme source of vigour and activity — will help you tackle the job with unflagging energy. Now, more than ever, your diet *must* include sufficient Bread. Eat it at every meal.

needs BREAD FOR ENERGY

C.F.H.595

Advertised Goods are Good Goods. 169

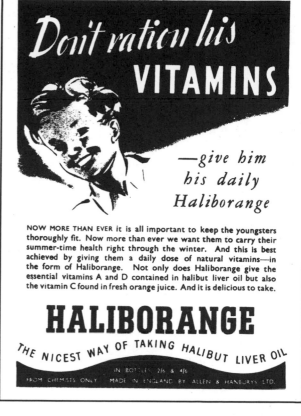

By November 1939, Singer was also using the slogan, concentrating on the economy angle. '*NOW! more than ever you need a SINGER sewing machine*', they claimed, explaining that:

> '*Now when you must economise a Singer Sewing Machine can save you pounds. You can make all your own garments and household requirements on a Singer ...*'

And within a few months the same slogan was being used to show how:

> '*The latest Electric Singer Sewing Machine with the Singerlight is ideal for making your own garments ... during the Blackout.*'

Stress and strain

The second major theme to emerge shortly after the start of the war was that of '*stress and strain*'. Once more, an astonishing range of products used this slogan, or some variation on it:

> '*In these trying times you need the extra nourishment OXO gives and you'll enjoy the extra richness and improved flavour.*'

> '*In these trying times skin infections are on the increase. The nervous strain causes rashes and irritation to appear. Unaccustomed work and strange surroundings bring about attacks of eczema, dermatitis, psoriasis, boils and other disfiguring ... skin disease. DDD Brand Prescription is an old and reliable remedy ...*'

> '*IN TIMES OF NERVOUS STRAIN "Guinness accomplishes marvels" — SAYS A DOCTOR. In these nerve-racking times, a glass of Guinness a day is a wonderful help and comfort to women. Guinness brings calm to tired nerves, new strength to tired limbs.*'

Even a Gor-ray skirt with permanent pleats was advertised as '*a real boon in these harassing days ... no matter how hurriedly and often it is slipped on*'; while '*Allenburys Diet*' was the thing to beat the '*Black-out Blues*':

> '*Black-outs may be fun to begin with, but the novelty soon wears off. The strain begins to tell. Only by getting the proper amount and proper sort of sleep can you ward off depression and keep yourself "fit for anything". Make sure of doing this by taking a nightly cup of Allenburys Diet ...*'

By February 1941, with Rommel arriving in North Africa and London being pounded nightly by bombs, Allenburys were justified in asking women readers '*Are your nerves feeling the stress and strain?*'. But now the slogan was '*WORK WELL — SLEEP WELL*' and under the heading '*Steady NERVES!*', a woman, helmeted and determined, sits at the wheel of a lorry.

In the following year Sanatogen ran a campaign showing a series of women in their civilian compared with their wartime jobs. One woman, for example, is shown first as a waitress, all starched collar and apron, then striding out in smart ATS uniform — '*From carrying trays ... To carry messages*':

TO KEEP YOU SMILING
in times like these

old friends are best

Wherever the principles of good health are appreciated, the value of Beechams Pills is unquestioned. They are regarded as an old, reliable friend—and this is the fourth generation of men and women to trust them.

Take Beechams Pills at bedtime and your body will act *as nature intended*. This is the secret of the clear healthy complexion, the slim active body, and perfect freedom from everyday ailments possessed by those who take Beechams Pills.

Obtainable everywhere

TAKE

Beechams *Pills*
BRAND

Worth a Guinea a Box

Hot Bovril - cheers!

A piping hot cup of Bovril puts you on top of your form. Instead of feeling cold - and - weary, Bovril makes you warm-and-cheery.

Be strong yourself and by your example comfort and cheer others around you.

GET IN A SUPPLY OF BOVRIL *NOW!*

'Out in all weathers ... tanned, healthy and enjoying life, instead of long, tiring, airless hours in a restaurant ... She's one of the people who may no longer need "SANATOGEN" NERVE-TONIC FOOD.'

The Sanatogen advertisements represented the positive, optimistic outlook that, fairly quickly, replaced the earlier 'stress and strain' theme. Determinedly grinning faces were common by the end of 1940, as in the Beechams Pills advertisement which assured millions of constipated readers that '*TO KEEP YOU SMILING in times like these ... old friends are best*'.

The Beechams model is out-grinned by a man sipping his cup of '*piping hot*' Bovril which:

"... *puts you on top of your form. Instead of feeling cold-and-weary, Bovril makes you warm-and-cheery ... Be strong yourself and by your example comfort and cheer others around you.*'

At such a time of national emergency, the women of Britain were duty-bound to keep smiling, to grit their teeth and carry on regardless. An advertisement for Benger's hot drinks appearing in October 1940 stated this bluntly, with a slogan that read, '*A National Duty — KEEP WELL*'.

And women had to keep well in the most trying of times, even when they had '*NO MAN TO LEAN ON*'. Wincarnis tonic wine used this slogan in November 1941, and went on:

'Do you sometimes long for your men-folk to be home again? Do you feel you just can't go on facing life alone? Do you feel you'd like to have a good cry on a khaki-clad shoulder? It's natural enough. But women can and will carry on like the heroines they are. But when you're feeling down there's nothing like a regular glass of Wincarnis ...'

And women could be heroines, even if they were just keeping the home fires burning. In November 1939 Sirdar Wools assured women readers that '*If you can KNIT you can "do your bit"*,' and, in another advertisement:

'Let YOUR National Service be knitting — it's important work which will bring warmth and comfort to those you know in the Fighting and ARP Services.'

Copley's knitting wools, the following month, claimed that '*England Expects every hand will do its Duty!*' and Secil Wools, in the same issue, urged women to '*Make this your WARmth EFFORT*', following this with some lines which have not, so far, figured in any of the anthologies of Second World War poetry:

'There's more that goes to win a war Than tanks and 'planes and guns! Than men prepared to do their best To overthrow the Huns.

The Home Front, too, must play its part And you can do YOUR bit To help our gallant fighting lads By starting NOW — to knit!

*You cannot knit too many things
To keep out wet and cold;
Like mittens, helmets, socks and scarves
GO TO IT — young and old! ...*

*A unique twist prevents this wool
From "bitting" ... "rubbing-up";
It isn't "ersatz" like the goods
Turned out by Messrs, Krupp!*

*So go ahead and do YOUR bit —
Order at your woolshop
These 3 and 4-ply Secil wools;
For value they're the top!*

*The Army, Navy, R.A.F.
Are counting on your aid;
Your ammunition — Secil wools,
Till Adolf's bill is paid ...'*

Beauty marches on

While women had a duty to be cheerful, whatever the circumstances, and they had to do their bit (even if their national service consisted of sitting at home knitting socks for the men at the front), they had another duty, too: it was their duty to be beautiful.

'*Beauty marches on*', declared the Elizabeth Arden advertisement in November 1939, and the message was that, whatever a woman might have to do during the trying times ahead, it was:

*'her duty to face the future calm and unruffled,
Beauty — like business — must go on.'*

In October 1940 *Good Housekeeping* was promoting their beauty leaflets under the heading, 'A Woman's Duty', while readers were told that:

A Woman's Duty . . .

More than ever it is a woman's prerogative, and her duty, to maintain health and beauty in these days of stress.

Miss Frances Loring, Director of Good Housekeeping Beauty Clinic, has written the following invaluable Leaflets with the object of achieving this aim :

1. Good Grooming and Cosmetic Harmonies.
2. Sane Slenderising—with Special Diet Chart.
3. Acne and Blemishes in Adolescence—with Skin-clearing Diet.
4. Problem of Superfluous Hair, Facially, and on Limbs.
5. Home Treatment for Eye Puffiness, Ageing Lines and Wrinkles.
6. Beauty and Health of the Hair.
7. Personal Charm in Pregnancy —with Calcium Diet.
8. Hand and Nail Beauty Routine.
9. Foot Comfort.
10. Complexion Beautifying.

They may be obtained, price Sixpence each, post free, from Good Housekeeping, 28 & 30, Grosvenor Gdns., London, S.W.1

But *Good Housekeeping* was only using a theme already familiar from a whole string of advertisements for various beauty products. In December 1939 the makers of Vinolia, '*The soap that refreshes you ... 6d A LARGE TABLET*', coyly suggested that:

'*Because many women are now in uniform, it doesn't mean that they should abandon their femininity and charm. On the contrary, men expect them to be just as attractive as ever ...'*

Sometimes men actually appeared in such advertisements. One of the series of 'Norma Knight's Wartime Beauty Hints' for Knight's Castile showed a woman, presumably a NAAFI worker, cheerfully drying some dishes while a couple of soldiers look on. Norma's hint for December 1940 starts:

'*Don't let it get you down. Keep smiling — and don't neglect your looks! It's your duty to others to keep looking your best.'*

Women in uniform should know

Because many women are now in uniform, it doesn't mean that they should abandon their femininity and charm. On the contrary, men expect them to be just as attractive as ever. But many women are finding that their service duties make the maintenance of their personal daintiness more difficult.

It is to these women that Vinolia Soap will prove especially useful. Vinolia was designed to impart a characteristic fragrance of freshness. No matter how strenuous a woman's duties may be, this air of freshness will never desert her if she washes with Vinolia as often as she is able. Vinolia is the most refreshing of all soaps for men, too.

VINOLIA

The soap that freshens you

6d A LARGE TABLET

Bath Tablet 10d.

The Vinolia Book Pack is a most ingenious Christmas Gift and contains four tablets of Vinolia Soap — 2/3. The Vinolia three-tablet carton is now available with a colourful Christmas Greeting wrapper — complete 1/6.

NV/217c/118

that reminds me

In war as in peace the theme is the same—Vinolia for Freshness. Freshness is the secret of the attractive woman. The daily bath with fragrant Vinolia is the wisest and most economical beauty hint of the times.

for Victory and

Vinolia

The soap that freshens you

VT/24?A/122

In the early months of 1940 Icilma Beauty Aids ran a series showing different women at work and then in each case, beautifully coiffed and gowned, dancing with a member of the armed forces. The January women was a nurse, later seen dancing with a moustached, brilliantined officer. *BEAUTY IS YOUR DUTY*, the headline goes, while the text runs:

> *'"How lovely you look!" It means a great deal these days when someone says that to you. For Beauty inspires happiness and cheerfulness both for yourself and others too. So remember your loveliness is important, and preserve it ...'*

The following month a factory worker was being told by her sergeant escort that there was 'no *restriction on loveliness*' and that '*nowadays beauty is a duty, since it cheers and inspires both yourself and others*'.

Increasingly, though, it was the woman herself who appeared in uniform. Sometimes this was the only difference from pre-war advertisements but more frequently the changing conditions of life were referred to in the text. Thus, in December 1940 an ATS private smiles out from an advertisement that reads:

> *'When change of air and food upset you ... take ENO'S "FRUIT SALT" first thing every morning.'*

By February 1941, however, the model looked solemn and determined, and the instruction to take ENO's was described as '*Your first orderly duty*'. Occasionally the text of an advertisement remained unchanged during the war years, while a woman soldier was substituted for a man. By February 1940 there was a woman in ATS uniform, carefully folding her things, next to the message, '*Mark your kit with JOHN BOND'S marking ink*'.

Other branches of the women's services appeared too. By November 1939 a model in WREN uniform was being used to promote Tangee lipstick '*for Beauty on Duty*', while WAAFs were soon to follow.

BEAUTY IS YOUR DUTY

" How lovely you look ! " It means a great deal these days when someone says that to you. For Beauty inspires happiness and cheerfulness both for yourself and others too. So remember your loveliness is important, and preserve it. Icilma have specially designed a range of Beauty aids with which you can look your most attractive self always, with little trouble and at trifling cost. Icilma is making it possible for thousands of women to do their essential duty of being beautiful.

BEAUTY IN A FEW MINUTES

CLEANSING. *Icilma CLEANSING COLD CREAM clears every speck of dirt, leaving your skin clean and soft— so use it each night. It's wonderful for hands that become rough or chapped. Tubes 6d. Jars 6d, 1/3.*

FOUNDATION. *To protect your skin in all weathers use Icilma FOUNDATION VANISHING CREAM, and you can always be sure of a clear skin. This is the ideal foundation for powder— and it has a most entrancing fragrance! Tubes 6d. Jars 6d, 1/3.*

POWDER. *Icilma BEAUTIFYING FACE POWDER gives that touch of perfection to your complexion. Lovely and velvety, it clings for hours. Boxes 6d and 1/3.*

ROUGE. *Icilma FLESH-TINTED ROUGE CREAM will give your cheeks a natural bloom that cannot be detected; it cannot go streaky or patchy. Tubes 6d. Jars 1/- and 1/9.*

5-MINUTE SHAMPOO. *Uniform Caps, and the strenuous, work of these days, often bring lifeless dull hair. But you can restore the full radiance and lustre of your hair in five minutes with Icilma Hair Powder. Sprinkle the powder in the hair and brush out. No Washing —No Drying—Only Brushing—and your hair is looking as pretty and well-groomed as ever. 3d a sachet.*

Icilma

BEAUTY AIDS

CLEANSING COLD CREAM . FOUNDATION VANISHING CREAM . SHAMPOO
BEAUTIFYING FACE POWDER . FLESH-TINTED ROUGE CREAM . HAIR POWDER

TANGEE LIPSTICK
for Beauty on Duty

All the nice girls love—TANGEE ! Orange in the stick, this unique, incomparable lipstick changes on the lips to the *exact* colour needed to make them look their loveliest. Blush rose, coral, carmine— whichever shade is called for, TANGEE gives it according to your type. By enhancing *natural* loveliness, TANGEE has banished that garish 'painted' look for ever—made 'beauty on duty' open to all.

Try TANGEE Theatrical for evening occasions when a brighter colour is required.

Tangee Lipstick for YOUR individual colour - - 1/9 and 4/6
Tangee Rouge to match. Compact - - 1/9 and 3/6, Crème 3/6
Tangee Face Powder, six shades - - - 2/6 and 4/6

6d. trial sizes obtainable everywhere.

When change of air and food upset you . . .

TAKE ENO'S "FRUIT SALT" first thing every morning

Doctors recommend Eno's!

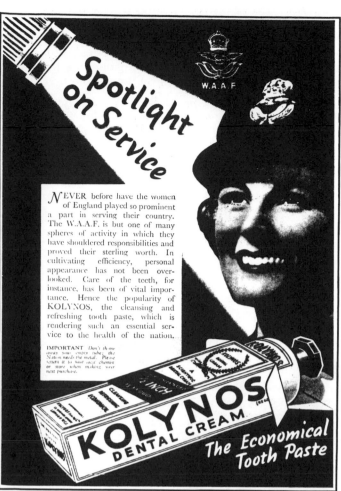

Uniforms

By 1940 it was sometimes difficult to find an advertisement in a woman's magazine which didn't feature a woman in uniform. And as the categories of jobs open to women increased, so did the range of uniforms or work-wear featured in the advertising.

Several manufacturers chose to feature a series of women in a variety of occupations. In early 1940 Regulo New World Gas Cookers were described as being perfect for 'WOMEN WHO WORK' and who therefore had less time to spend on preparing food. In March they claimed that:

'Air Raid Wardens appreciate the Super-Fast Burner ... which boils 1 pint of water in 125 secs!'

In the following month it was the turn of the Auxiliary Fire Service:

'The A.F.S. discovers the High-Speed Grill ... Toasting heat in just over a minute! What a blessing when quick meals are needed ...'

Just five minutes for tea and toast!

In just over 2 mins., with her Regulo New World Cooker, the kettle's boiling and in about 60 secs. the High Speed Griller is ready for toasting! Other refinements for better, quicker and more economical cooking appreciated by all women-folk, include two simmering burners; unique oven design with single burner; and, of course, the 'Regulo', which automatically saves gas, and enables a complete meal to be perfectly cooked in the oven, all at the same time.

OVER 2 MILLIONS IN DAILY USE

See the Cooking Number in the REGULO TRIANGLE ▲

REGULO NEW WORLD

GAS COOKERS

SEE THEM AT YOUR GAS SHOWROOMS

A Radiation product

Regulo used photographs which were either of genuine women at work or at least appeared to be authentic reconstructions. But most series used drawings of pretty young things. In some the frivolity of the drawings was matched by that of the text:

'A certain young girl in the WRENS is always one up on her FRENS, for to Wolsey she goes for frocks, undies and hose, which reflect the most up-to-date TRENS!'

'Said a sparkling young thing in the ATS, "Without Wolsey I think I'd go BATS. For their undies and stockings and marvellous frockings I give them my hearty CONGRATS!"'

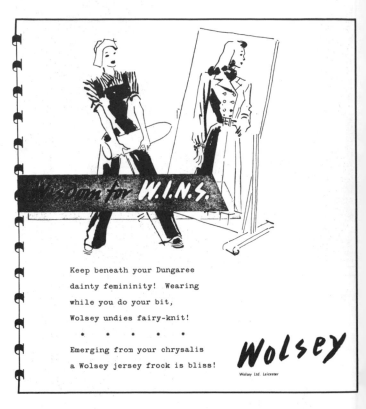

Keep beneath your Dungaree dainty femininity! Wearing while you do your bit, Wolsey undies fairy-knit!

* * * * *

Emerging from your chrysalis a Wolsey jersey frock is bliss!

Wolsey

Wolsey Ltd. Leicester

During 1942 and 1943 Yardley ran a similar campaign featuring drawings of individual servicewomen, looking pretty but determined. And this spirit of determination carries over into the text. In July 1942, when over 80 per cent of single women under 60 were either in the forces or in other forms of work, their advertisement read:

'No surrender ...
War gives us a chance to show our mettle. We wanted equal rights with men; they took us at our word. We are proud to work for victory beside them. And work is not our only task. We must triumph over routine; keep the spirit of light-heartedness. Our faces must never reflect personal troubles. We must achieve masculine efficiency without hardness. Above all, we must guard against surrender to personal carelessness. Never must we consider careful grooming a quisling gesture. With leisure and beauty-aids so rare, looking our best is specially creditable. Let us face the future bravely and honour the subtle bond between good looks and good morale.
PUT YOUR BEST FACE FORWARD ... Yardley.'

Said a sparkling young thing in the ATS,

"Without Wolsey I think I'd go BATS. For

their undies and stockings and marvellous

frockings I give them my hearty CONGRATS!"

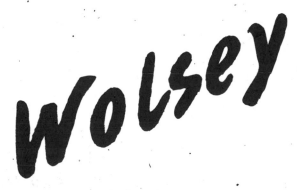

Coupons mean that what you buy must wear as ne'er before;

so wait for Wolsey (if you must), it's well worth waiting for!

No surrender...

War gives us a chance to show our mettle. We wanted equal rights with men; they took us at our word. We are proud to work for victory beside them. And work is not our only task. We must triumph over routine; keep the spirit of light-heartedness. Our faces must never reflect personal troubles. We must achieve masculine efficiency without hardness. Above all, we must guard against surrender to personal carelessness. Never must we consider careful grooming a quisling gesture. With leisure and beauty-aids so rare, looking our best is specially creditable. Let us face the future bravely and honour the subtle bond between good looks and good morale.

PUT YOUR BEST FACE FORWARD.. *Yardley*

Develop an " eagle eye " for Salvage.

Since women were doing men's jobs, they could no longer rely on traditional female excuses: '*War will not wait on woman's weakness*', proclaimed the makers of A-K pain-killing tablets in February 1940. '*Now she MUST carry on*'.

"**Now She MUST Carry On**"

War will not wait on woman's weakness, nor need any woman "go sick" on account of periodic pains and headaches. Just take one or two A-K Tablets and you will be able to carry on as usual.

If you suffer from regular pain you must try A-K Tablets. They cost so little and bring such comfort that you owe it to yourself. They relieve pain in a few minutes and their effect is lasting. Join the thousands of women who have found A-K a safe, sure method of relieving periodic pain. Don't suffer another month. Get A-K Tablets to-day, and enjoy this freedom from pain. *NOTE.—A-K is how thousands of women ask for Anti-Kamnia brand Analgesic Tablets, and if you say A-K your chemist will know. 1/5 a box (including Tax).*

A series exploiting this principle was that run by Tampax. In January 1940 their advertisement showed a box and two tampons, while a headline informed the reader, '*Now you can try Tampax FREE!*'. A long explanation of what the product was followed:

'*… the modern form of sanitary protection that is so dainty, convenient and comfortable in use that you are not even aware of its presence.*'

By the following month the main text was reduced to the words: '*What a blessing it is that Sanitary Protection is now worn internally!*' while the point was underlined by a drawing of three women in uniform standing together in conversation.

During 1941 Tampax ran a series of drawings of women doing jobs traditionally associated with men — a bus conductress, a soldier changing a tyre — each with the slogan: '*In a man's job, there's no time for "not so good days"*,' with text such as:

'*War work won't wait … a man's job doesn't allow for feminine disabilities. Tampax — sanitary protection worn internally — has come to the rescue of thousands of women on service. It gives new freedom; complete comfort …*'

By the end of 1941 Tampax had launched the slogan '*Women are winning the War — of Freedom*', with drawings of women making tanks, working at lathes, manning anti-aircraft guns, all contrasted with a logo showing a woman in crinoline and bonnet. The standard text read:

'*England has always been a "free country" but grandmother's mother would have been surprised at the spacious activities of girls in 1941. It was not*

Women are winning the War — of Freedom

England has always been a "free country" but grandmother's mother would have been surprised at the spacious activities of girls in 1941. It was not "polite" when she was young to do a man's job—and it was not possible. Women were still largely restricted by natural disabilities. Tampax—sanitary protection worn internally—has changed all that. In doing so it has liberated women of today for the strenuous struggle for freedom; the task that allows no time for "off-days".

TAMPAX

Regd. Trade Mark

worn internally

PRICES 7d. 1/2 & 1/9

NEW FAMILY PACK 40 FOR 6/-

Sold by BOOTS, TIMOTHY WHITES & TAYLORS, and other chemists, departmental stores, drapers, WOOLWORTH'S, MARKS & SPENCER LTD and THE N.A.A.F.I.

For further information regarding Tampax please write to The Nurse, Tampax Ltd., Belvue Rd., Northolt, Middlesex.

---

winning the war of freedom

Women's tasks today leave no room for disabilities. The active non-stop life of the war-worker demands freedom of action never before known. In this, Tampax—sanitary protection worn internally—is woman's best ally. Today it is used by thousands of workers in every field of service.

PRICES 7d. & 1/9.

Sold by BOOTS, TIMOTHY WHITES & TAYLORS, and other chemists, departmental stores, drapers. WOOLWORTH'S, MARKS & SPENCER LTD. and THE N.A.F.F.I.

For further information regarding Tampax please write to The Nurse, Tampax Ltd., Belvue Road, Northolt, Middlesex.

TAMPAX

REGD. TRADE MARK

Worn Internally

Women of the A.T.S are winning the war of Freedom

The new life of active service demands new freedom from feminine disabilities. Tampax —sanitary protection worn internally—is providing the convenient and effective answer for hundreds of women in the forces and the factories.

TAMPAX

REGD. TRADE MARK

Worn Internally

PRICES 7d. & 1/9

Sold by BOOTS, TIMOTHY WHITES & TAYLORS, and other chemists, departmental stores, Drapers, WOOLWORTH'S, MARKS & SPENCER LTD. and THE N.A.A.F.I.

For further information regarding Tampax please write to The Nurse, Tampax Ltd., Belvue Road, Northolt, Middlesex.

BERLEI BULLETIN Nº 2

Figure *Precautions*

It's bad for morale to let figures go—and it's bad for efficiency too. If you're feeling the strain of war-work you need a good modern foundation and the very best you can get is a Berlei—lovely, cool, feather-light, supple as youth and pliable as a second skin. A controlette costs you only four coupons—but production is strictly rationed, so you may have to search, and wait, and search again. So—good hunting —and good figures and good health for the lucky Berlei finders.

REPAIR SERVICE
If you already have a Berlei we can give it a new lease of life by expert repairing. Please ask your nearest Berlei stockist for details.

Berlei

FOUNDATION GARMENTS

MADE BY PEOPLE WHO BELIEVE IN *SERVICE*

"polite" when she was young to do a man's job — and it was not possible. Women were still largely restricted by natural disabilities. Tampax … has changed all that. In doing so it has liberated women of today for the strenuous task of freedom; the task that allows no time for "off-days".'

This was certainly one of the most successful advertising campaigns of the war. And, helped by the fact that women of different backgrounds discussed such matters freely in the Services and at their workplaces, it ensured that tampons were permanently to take over from *'the old clumsy and uncomfortable methods'*.

Clothes manufacturers, too, ran series advertisements, one of the best-known being the *'BERLEI BULLETINS'* of late 1941. In these a fully clothed working woman stood next to a ghostly outline of the same woman dressed only in a Berlei 'controlette' corset. The text against the drawing of an ARP warden (responsible for *fire* precautions) ran:

'Figure Precautions
It's bad for morale to let figures go — and it's bad for efficiency too. If you're feeling the strain of

war-work you need a good modern foundation and the very best you can get is a Berlei …'

In the advertisement illustrating a lathe-operator the text read:

'Secret Service
Her war service is helped by a secret service — the smooth, firm, supporting control of a Berlei. If you have to stand for long hours a Berlei, cut to your figure type, will correct your posture, lessen fatigue, give figure and clothes a lovely line … And a Berlei controlette, remember, needs only four coupons!'

But by 1944, with controlettes and 'fairy-knit' undies in increasingly short supply, more mundane advertisements were being aimed at women doing dirty jobs. One of the most straightforward showed unglamorised women getting on with the job, while the text read:

'Shift grease and dirt with ZIXT hand soap
4d per table
1 coupon
Makes hands clean — leaves them smooth.'

You need VIM—it does most of the household cleaning except washing clothes

6d—COUPON FREE

V 57A-9-55   LEVER BROTHERS, PORT SUNLIGHT, LIMITED

This may show that, after four or five years of war, some advertisement copywriters were beginning to realise that women were tired of frivolous copy, just as they were tired of long hours, shortages and worries for themselves and their loved ones. Throughout 1943 and 1944 advertisers clearly recognised women's efforts and vied with each other

BOVRIL "doffs the cap" to the splendid women of Britain . . .

The way in which women are tackling unaccustomed, strenuous and often dangerous war work, has won, and deserved, wide-spread admiration. As mechanics, as bus conductors, lorry drivers and porters, as W.R.N.S., A.T.S., W.A.A.F., land girls and nurses, their record of service is itself the most eloquent tribute to the women of Britain. Bovril acclaims their fine spirit, and makes a practical contribution to their supply of strength and energy.

HOT BOVRIL CHEERS!

* Exercise to keep fit—and warm.

to express their admiration for what women were doing. In January 1943, for example, 'BOVRIL "doffs the cap" to the splendid women of Britain ...':

'The way in which women are tackling unaccustomed, strenuous and often dangerous war work, has won, and deserved, wide-spread admiration. As mechanics, as bus conductors, lorry drivers and porters, as W.R.N.S., A.T.S., W.A.A.F., land girls and nurses, their record of service is itself the most eloquent tribute to the women of Britain. Bovril acclaims their fine spirit, and makes a practical contribution to their supply of strength and energy.'

Similarly, a Standard Motor Company advertisement of September 1943 shows a woman in full battle kit, hand raised high, under the words '*This composure*'. The main text runs:

'It is, perhaps, one of the most exciting moments of her life; but ... the signals from the command post must be accepted and transmitted — calmly, swiftly, efficiently.

It is, perhaps, one of the most exciting moments of her life ; but ... the signals from the command post must be accepted and transmitted—calmly, swiftly, efficiently

We can't all work on Anti-Aircraft instruments. But we can all cultivate *sang-froid* in times of danger and difficulty As Britishers we have a reputation for it ! ... This is the quality that will earn for us the admiration of our children and of our children's children. So that in the years to come they will ask themselves in wonder : " *But for their calmness in those dark and dangerous days ....?*"

The Standard Motor Company Ltd., Coventry

We can't all work on Anti-Aircraft instruments. But we can all cultivate "sang froid" in times of danger and difficulty. As Britishers we have a reputation for it! ... This is the quality that will earn for us the admiration of our children and of our children's children. So that in the years to come they will ask themselves in wonder: "But for their calmness in those dark and dangerous days ...?"'

And, in February 1944 Hoover showed a woman operating a massive crane, next to the label '*Housewife 1944*', with the text:

'The Hand that held the Hoover drives a Crane! Not many of our housewives are doing jobs of war work like this! The great majority of those in the factories and workshops are plugging away on far less spectacular tasks. But whatever the job, these "Housewives 1944" stick it, and run their homes as well! Many of them, now more than ever, must bless the day they bought a Hoover to save their sorely needed time and energy! We're proud to have helped them do a "double job" in war-time and in admiration say —
Salute! FROM HOOVER.'

In tiny letters at the bottom was added:

'Hoover users know best what improvements they would like in the post-war Hoover. Suggestions are welcome.'

The housewife of 1944 might be operating a crane, but Hoover — like all the other manufacturers — was looking ahead to the day when she would be safely back in the home again, surrounding herself with all the goodies she had done without for so many years.

HOUSEWIFE 1944

The Hand that held the Hoover drives a Crane!
Not many of our housewives are doing jobs of war work like this ! The great majority of those in the factories and workshops are plugging away on far less spectacular tasks. But whatever the job these "Housewives 1944" stick it, and run their homes as well ! Many of them, now more than ever, must bless the day they bought a Hoover to save their sorely needed time and energy ! We're proud to have helped them do a "double job" in war-time and in admiration say—

Salute! FROM HOOVER

Hoover users know best what improvements they would like in the post-war Hoover Suggestions are welcome.

BY APPOINTMENT TO H.M. KING GEORGE VI AND H.M. QUEEN MARY
HOOVER LIMITED PERIVALE · GREENFORD MIDDLESEX

Allies and Others

This chapter was originally to be called 'Allies and enemies', but, reading through thousands of issues of dozens of magazines, relatively little could be found about the 'enemies'. There was the odd article contrasting the amount of freedom in the Allied and Axis countries, but the number of column inches devoted to the Germans — let alone the Italians and Japanese — was surprisingly small.

It is as though the war itself was the enemy: '*Who, today, talks about the "bloody Boche" and the "damned Hun"*?', as Muriel King asked in *Woman's Own* in January 1941. There was little of the jingoism and sabre-rattling of the First World War, and the enemy — when they were mentioned at all — were used as reminders of a system that could still be imposed on Britain if the people flagged and failed to give of their utmost.

Our allies, on the other hand, were rarely absent from the pages of the magazines. And the great ally, at first, was France. Ironically, it was in June 1940, the month of Dunkirk and the defeat of France, that *Good Housekeeping* chose to publish a profile of General Gamelin, Commander-in-Chief of the Allied Forces. Gamelin came from a family of soldiers and had served with distinction in the First World War. His army was led by experienced officers and waited behind the impregnable Maginot Line for the Germans to make any foolhardy attempt to attack. How could Hitler, the 'guttersnipe' and failed house-painter, hope to beat the invincible French army lead by such a distinguished officer and gentlemen? History shows that it took no more than a week for the French front to be smashed, and three weeks for the entire army to be routed.

From then on we had no major ally, until Hitler turned his attention east and — on 22nd June 1941 — attacked the Soviet Union.

WOMEN OF RUSSIA

Russian Women play an important part in the difficult task of governing their country. They are able and willing to tackle any job—and make a success of it, as H. T. Shepstone tells you in his interesting article on page 50, "Women of Russia"

A collective-farmer's family at lunch in the Southern Ukraine

The steamroller in the foreground is driven by a woman

Girls applying for work at a factory at Ivanovo-Voznesensk

October the 25th Square, Leningrad, with the station on the right

Members of the village council—or Soviet as it is called—gathered for a meeting

Everything in Russia is rationed. These women are lining up for their allowance of cloth

Three happy young members of a Russian family

Mother and child from the Turkmen Soviet Socialist Republic

Russian girls marching through Red Square, Moscow, on International Youth Day

Leningrad's monument to Peter the Great, who founded St. Petersburg in 1703

A modern block of workers' dwellings in Moscow

Typical early morning scene at a tram stop in Leningrad

A Russian family at dinner in a communal restaurant

One of the wedding courts in Moscow

The Russians

For the next few months, with the Germans easing up their attacks on Britain, Russia bore the brunt of the fighting. The British people looked on in fascination and lapped up any information about this huge country. So little was actually known about it and so much was imagined. Women knitted comforts for the gallant Russians, while output soared in factories when it was announced that the tanks, waggons or other equipment in production were destined for the Red Army.

Articles on *'our Russian allies'* appeared in profusion in the magazines while stories and rumours about strange, unpleasant happenings in remote parts of that huge country no longer appeared. Only the positive aspects were mentioned. Joseph Stalin, leader of the Soviet Union, was described in *Woman's Own* in May 1942 as *'a family man — although one hears little about that side of him. His snow-haired mother once remarked that it was a mistake to regard her son as the iron-willed dictator, indifferent to human values. … His daughter Svetlana is the apple of his eye, and his great pleasure is to sit in the darkness and hear her playing Chopin.'*

A major article in *Good Housekeeping* in November 1941 praised the way the Soviet Union had changed swiftly from a basically agricultural country to one with the resources necessary to take on a highly mechanised and industrialised enemy. The writer noted in particular the part that women could play, in a system where they were guaranteed absolute equality with men.

In fact most articles on the Soviet Union concentrated on the role of women, and the equality of their position, whether in peace or in war. Typical was a two-page article that appeared in *Woman's Magazine* in January 1942, declaring:

'Women enjoy the same complete equality of status as men. There is no barrier shutting them out from participation in the social, economic and political, life of the country.

If the woman elects to continue work after marriage — and the greater majority do so — she recognises that both she and her offspring will be fully protected. Six weeks before and after childbirth she is entitled to a holiday from her work with full pay during this period and her job is kept open for her. She is also entitled to free medical advice and maternity services, and there are state nurseries where her child can be taken care of during the day once she has returned to work.'

And as the facts and statistics poured out — the number of Soviet women doctors, judges, ambassadors; the heroism of front-line nurses, even female fighter pilots — the implications became plain. If they can do this, why can't we? The government might be hoping that British women would be inspired by the Soviet example to flock to the factories and work ever longer hours; but they couldn't prevent these same women wondering why they were earning less than their menfolk, or why their civil rights should be less than those of their Russian sisters.

Five young Red Army nurses from Krivoi Rog who volunteered for front-line work

A field nurse gives first aid to a wounded sniper on the battlefield

NURSING WITH THE RED ARMY

OVER seventy per cent. of soldiers wounded in the Red Army return to the ranks. A great deal of the credit for this magnificent achievement is due to the heroic part played by the Soviet nurses, many thousands of whom are working under fire on the battlefield and in military hospitals behind the lines.

Theirs is indeed a proud record. There is no place too dangerous, no place too distant for them to reach. When the snow is too thick for ordinary transport they advance on skis. They allow no weather, no natural barrier to defeat them.

A FRONT LINE JOB

Clad in crash helmets, thick padded uniforms with white armbands, they descend by parachute into the thick of the battlefield, carrying with them medical supplies so that they can give instant first aid to wounded men in the front line.

Some of the nurses have astonishing records of the number of men they have rescued under fire. One nurse has carried a hundred wounded men from the battlefield. In another instance, a Red Army field nurse saved the lives of fifteen seriously wounded soldiers by dragging them out of a burning house. These nurses penetrate into the machine-gun nests and give first aid to wounded gunners; they are on constant duty in the advanced first-aid dressing stations.

To be fitted for their great task the nurses of the U.S.S.R. have to undergo a rigorous training. They must be self-reliant, resourceful, and equal to any emergency that may arise.

When they are qualified they can administer surgical first-aid, inject anti-tetanus and anti-gangrene serum. They know all about blood transfusion, which plays such an important part in modern battlefield medicine, and the very latest method of setting fractures and bones.

It goes without saying that the Nursing Services of the U.S.S.R. have had to be enormously expanded. Before the Revolution there were under 10,000 Red Cross Nurses. In 1940 the Soviet Nursing Schools passed out 39,000 women for medical institutions and children's nurses. To-day that number is greatly increased.

TWO-YEAR TRAINING

And the standard of the training has been raised. Before she is able to enter a Nursing School, a student must have graduated from a secondary school.

The training, which is a practical one, takes two years, during which time students receive free board and lodging and a salary.

Many nurses, working at front-line posts, or in military hospitals far behind the lines have been decorated for gallantry and distinguished service.

They are doing a grand job.

IT'S EASIER FOR US!

Co-operation—that's the story behind the Russian women's fight for equality, says LEN CHALONER

"ISN'T Ludmilla Pavlichenko wonderful?" (She is, admittedly.) "Just think of being an officer in the Red Army! But there—women in Russia have absolute equality. It's easier for them."

It's certainly easy to say things like that when you think of the problems of our women in the Home Guard, who aren't even allowed to train in the use of firearms; or if you think of the constant problem of unequal pay for equal work, or the marriage-bar difficulties in professional careers, and half a dozen other die-hard traditions. You decide, *yes*, it's easier for women in Russia.

It may be true—to-day, in one sense, but it has been far, far harder, only a few years since. Do you realize that only twenty-five years ago—after the last war in fact—brave women pioneers, the mothers of countless Ludmillas, suffered the most appalling things in their efforts simply to bring into ordinary village life the Soviet Law which gave them liberty and equality as citizens? Kerosene was poured over one pioneer in an isolated district, and set alight! One, who did nothing more than run away from an elderly husband to whom she had been married under duress, was caught and brought back and tortured; her health ruined for life. Others were knifed, or chained, or beaten up. But still the struggle went forward. The Soviet Union is made up of vast territories stretching right away across to China, and embracing many peoples with their own customs and religions and traditions. In some of the Eastern districts women, right up to 1925 and onwards, wore veils and were kept in the most utter subjection.

Can you imagine what it meant when the Soviet Constitution ordained freedom for them and equality with men citizens throughout the country? You can guess how the ignorant male peasants hated and resented and obstructed it. It was difficult even for the women themselves to understand their liberation in the eyes of the law, for few of them could even read at all. Under the old regime they were debarred from all higher education, even the rudiments seldom came their way.

Picture, too, how difficult it was to get changes in such a vast country, where the distances were so immense and isolation so great in many parts. Women pioneers, Genotdel, as they were called—a little like the girls trained under Madame Chiang's New Life movement—courageously went out to these far districts, trying to bring understanding of what the new freedom meant to women and to arouse their interest to struggle and make it a reality. The Genotdel started by teaching them hygiene, child care and allied subjects, and founded women's clubs in the villages, where the women could meet and talk, and hear lectures, and learn to read, so that they could know and understand what the new Soviet law and progress could mean to them as citizens.

Little by little the women became interested, and the secret in each district was to gather together two or three brave spirits to be leaders and help the others wholeheartedly, to develop the new knowledge and activities, and to show men that given the chance in open competition, they were capable of doing the same work for which they claimed equal pay—just as well as the men.

Gradually the men began to see reason and prejudices began to fade. But even so, it was not until 1928, fifteen years ago only, in the Red Square of Moscow, on Women's Day, March 8th, that a great pile of veils, the symbol of the slavery of women in Eastern Russia, was burnt in public demonstration of women's right to freedom and equality. And after that there was still an immense amount of pioneer work to be accomplished.

True, the women of Russia had the Soviet Government right behind them in their struggle, but look at the huge advances they had to make to reach even the most Victorian standards of freedom. Moreover, real though this Government backing was in the sense of its sincerity, it must be remembered that the Government itself had its hands more than full with other vast problems.

The women of Russia had therefore largely to help themselves. The secret of their success has been co-operation among themselves. They learned to work together, to give and take with each other's individuality in order to make the most of each other's gifts in the service of the great cause. This is how they finally convinced their menfolk that they are in fact—different maybe, but equals nevertheless. It has been the lack of real co-operation on a big scale among women in this country that has held up their progress far more than masculine opposition has prevented it.

It has become a tendency in our admiration for the heroic struggle of Russian arms to underrate or be a little destructive towards our own efforts in almost every theatre, not forgetting the feminine ones. The answer is that running ourselves down won't achieve anything. But work will! What really happened to us in the pre-war days was that having won the vote, we thought that everything else would follow quite simply. We forgot that it's how you use your vote that matters; the demands you make on your Member of Parliament before he is elected; the amount you have concerned yourself with organizations working for the reforms you want, who can, in turn, bring pressure on parliamentary circles to achieve them.

If you want training in firearms for women in the Home Guard, or equal work, or family allowances, or the abolition of the marriage bar, or anything else you are keen about, there are constitutional ways of putting them forward. We have to learn to co-operate with other women in getting the woman's viewpoint heard.

To-day we know that a country can only progress if its women, as well as its men, progress, for women are not only half of the community, but always the mothers of the next generation. Somewhere behind all this great struggle for a New World lies the knowledge that we have to harness ourselves to concepts of doing something not for personal gain; "of doing"—in Sir William Beveridge's words: "Something of service which is done consciously, because one is a member of a nation, or of a brotherhood of humanity." It was with something of this ideal that the Russian women struggled in those early days for the sisterhood of women—only no one will pour kerosene over us. It's certainly easier for us.

The Americans

The outburst of articles on the Soviet Union and its people dated from after the German invasion. But references to Americans were fairly frequent, even before December 1941, the month America entered the war.

In the autumn of 1940 *Woman's Magazine* ran a sympathetic series on the life of the President of the USA, Franklin D. Roosevelt, with special reference to the active role of his wife Eleanor in his campaigning and his presidency. And the dominating position of women in American society provided the material for a number of articles in various magazines. Articles on American women drew attention to their work opportunities and to the fact that they succeeded as women, without disguising femininity or attractiveness.

Other articles referred with gratitude to the support given by the USA to the British cause. It was pointed out that America was sympathetic to the British position long before this took the form of Lend-lease supplies. American families had taken in refugee children from Britain, and women's groups were active in organising help for the mother country, most notably the English-Speaking Union's War Relief, which provided comforts for bombed-out British families.

Many such articles, however, contained the implied message that we were waiting for the Americans to take the final step, and come in on our side. '*The wide Atlantic has narrowed so much in these months of trial*', wrote Stanley Jackson in *Woman's Own* in August 1941:

> '*The Statue of Liberty is on our doorstep, reminding us that the blackout will not last forever and that we have good neighbours over the garden wall.*'

But it took the Japanese attack on the Pearl Harbour naval base to make them decide to join us on our side of the wall. On 26th January 1942 some 3,000 GIs landed in Belfast. By D-Day Americans formed the bulk of the 1,421,000 Allied, Dominion and Colonial troops stationed in the United Kingdom. And their presence did not pass unnoticed, especially by the women of Britain.

When You Meet the Americans

We have had so many inquiries about the difficulties of recognizing the various ranks of American soldiers that we have had this little chart made for you. You might like to stick it up in your canteen or club kitchen.

GENERAL – SILVER STARS
LIEUT. GEN. – SILVER STARS
MAJ. GEN. – SILVER STARS
BRIG. GEN. – SILVER STAR
COLONEL – SILVER EAGLE

LIEUT. COL. – SILVER LEAF
MAJOR – GOLD LEAF
CAPTAIN – SILVER BARS
1ST. LIEUT. – SILVER BAR
2 ND. LIEUT. – GOLD BAR

COMMISSIONED WORN ON SHOULDERS

MASTER SERGT.
TECHNICAL SERGT.
SERGEANT
PRIVATE 1ST CLASS

1 ST. SERGT.
STAFF SERGT.
CORPORAL
SERVICE STRIPE

NON-COMMISSIONED WORN ON BOTH SLEEVES

WOMEN OF THE U.S.A.

by Mary Dell

Here is a picture of the average middle-class American woman—the way she looks, the way she thinks, the way she lives

American women's activities are varied, and they do everything whole-heartedly and with enthusiam

(Wide World photos)

Mrs. Virginia L. Pfuderer, of Illinois, who is seventy-four, is the oldest woman to make a round-the-world flight

Mrs. Blanche R. Green, who began as a saleswoman and worked her way up to become President of the Spencer Corset Company

(Wide World photo)

These girls are members of the Women Flyers of America, ready to serve their country in an emergency

(Wide World photo)

Mrs. Franklin D. Roosevelt watches blind Helena Klein operating a loom at an annual sale of articles made by the blind, work in which she takes sympathetic and practical interest

(Wide World photo)

Sorting metal and rubber materials collected by American women to make armaments for the British war effort

(Wide World photo)

American girls about to fly to winter sports resorts in Idaho and Colorado

(Keystone photo)

Thousands of women in the U.S.A. are making munitions to aid Britain

MEET a bright, swift-talking sales-promotion manager in Los Angeles and you think: "This is the typical American woman. Charming, efficient."

Meet a smooth, easy-moving owner of a New York beauty salon, and you think again: "This is the typical American woman—so well groomed, so poised."

Meet a small-town wife who can cope briskly with the minutes of her Women's Club one half-hour and dimple over her baby the next—and you start thinking "typical" all over again.

Bewildering, but true. Because the American woman has a lot of energy, a lot of ability and the will to make the best of both.

Do you know what strikes me most about American women? They will never admit that there is any such time of life as middle age.

There's a reason for it. America has a youth complex. It is such a young country that its tradition goes back only a very short time compared with ours. And its people feel, perhaps unconsciously, that out of loyalty they must worship youth. They admire age and antiquity in other countries, but they themselves are always striving to be young.

This goes particularly for the women. You never find dresses in the shops specially labelled O.S. or "For the matron". The O.S. woman or the matron wears exactly the same kind of dress as the youngster, only on a slightly larger scale.

You seldom find a woman who thinks that an excuse for being a bit fat is that, at any rate, you look " comfortable and homely".

Mrs. or Miss America is immediately afraid it makes her look old, and is quite willing almost to starve and to go through all sorts of painfully energetic exercises to get back her youthful figure.

The American mother never thinks of the years after the children are grown up and off her hands as a time for settling down and growing old gracefully and quietly. It's her chance for taking up something she always wanted to, but missed when she was younger—it's a fresh beginning.

Terrific, never-failing energy—that's what you get in the average American woman. And I do admire her for that, because I do like "live" people.

LET'S look at the middle-class American woman from the outside before looking at her world through her eyes.

Long-legged, slim, with fine hair and a complexion that is lovely but "assisted" . . . that is the young American woman. She grows up much more quickly than our women, and starts having "perms" and visiting beauty parlours much younger. She has a weakness for uniforms—not on others, but on herself, I mean.

The American college girl doesn't *have* to wear a uniform, but she wears one all the same. A flared skirt, a wide-shouldered campus coat, knee-length stockings, flat-heeled shoes and a "beanie"—a small round cap stuck on the back of her head—she'd just die of shame if these didn't have their place in her college wardrobe, because all the other girls wear them.

In summer—for young and older women, too—the uniform is a white dress. You see them everywhere with satchel bags slung over one shoulder.

The latest uniform craze is "mother and daughter twins". For mother and small child to go out dressed exactly alike in every detail except, perhaps, shoes—why, that's just cute.

THE American woman looks—and is—healthy. She takes her duty to her looks more seriously than we do—and her duty to her body.

Say to her, "I must go to the dentist—I have toothache," and she will be horrified.

Her way is not to wait until she's in pain before consulting dentist or doctor, but to go to both at regular intervals for a thorough overhaul. She doesn't suffer constantly from headaches and think, "Why bother? It can't be anything serious." She makes quite sure it isn't by getting vetted right away. Which is, of course, the proper thing to do.

She's usually well-dressed, although the business girl's office dress isn't what you and I would go to work in. It's gayer, fussier—probably because she thinks it's more important to look feminine than business-like.

There's a reason for this, too. You see, in America it is an accepted thing that women should work in whatever capacity they choose. There isn't a profession or a business in which women can't rise to big positions if they have the ability and want to. They don't have to pretend *not* to be women to get on; they don't have to disguise their attractiveness or have their efficiency mistrusted.

They can succeed *as* women—not in spite of the fact that they *are* women. And that's why they're often so much more poised and self-confident than we are.

They're certainly more candid. If they think a thing, they will say it, and if it's something you're not too keen on hearing, well, that's just too bad, but you've got to take it. Because—if you deserve them—you get bouquets as well as criticism, just as freely, just as sincerely.

They're very honest, the American women, and some people think they're brusque. I don't, because I know from experience of the very warm friendliness and hospitality that lie behind their first appraising inspection of you.

They're easy to work with in business because they like getting down to the job without a lot of fuss and bother.

And you seldom find in an American woman executive the aggressiveness that, too often, you find in her English equivalent. That's because she hasn't had to fight for her "rights". She has grown up with them—they're accepted by the men as well—so what is there to be aggressive about?

THAT'S how the American woman looks and talks. How does she feel and think?

Well, her heart is subject to the same kind of flutters as ours; but her mind runs in a different groove.

Sadie wakes up one morning to the sound of mom calling out something about her being late if she doesn't get up this instant.

It's a grand October morning with a bite of frost behind the sunshine. But there's nothing to tell her that this is going to be a special day.

She goes to her clothes closet and decides that she'll wear the green dress and the short fur coat that pop gave her for her last birthday. She leaves the house at a run and gets to the office two minutes after time. And falls in love at half-past twelve!

It's been coming on for some time, of course, but she's never admitted anything even to herself about it because, so far, the new young man with the serious eyes in the Publicity Department has never shown anything more than an ordinary polite interest in her existence.

But to-day, at half-past twelve, he stops by her desk and dithers around talking nothings, while she tries to look busy and interested at the same time.

And then he says what about lunch, and she says that *would* be nice with such fervour you'd think most days she never had any lunch at all, and off they go to the café on the corner where they look much more than they say, and eat very little.

And that is the beginning of Sadie's big romance.

The end is a slap-up wedding with Sadie looking pink and adorable, very much like one of our own girls, Bill looking palish and handsome . . . and before you can turn round, Sadie is a Mrs. with a man and a home to look after instead of just herself and her job.

She doesn't look any different—a little more complacent maybe—and she doesn't think any differently. She still looks upon life as a kindly god-father who is going to hand her all sorts of good things—happiness included—wrapped up in neat parcels.

She gets much of her food in cans

all ready to eat without a lot of worry on her part; she gets her clothes ready made, and, because of mass-production, she gets all sorts of labour-saving luxuries very cheaply.

Bill spoils her. It's no fable about American men spoiling their women if they have the means. The American husband gives his wife everything she wants in reason and sometimes out of it, and in return she runs his home and children charmingly and competently.

But she still has energy left to do plenty more. And that's where her clubs come in. American women go in for clubs and communal "do's" much more than we do. They don't seem to depend on men to give a lift to their shows; they enjoy being just a crowd of women together, doing what they want without having to bother about whether the men are happy.

And they take much more trouble over their appearance when it's an all-woman party. Unlike us, they don't fall back on that "She's only another woman—so it doesn't matter how I look" excuse for laziness.

They are always curious, always rest-less-minded, always wanting to be doing and learning. That's why you get so many visiting lecturers at their clubs throughout the country.

They love listening to lectures, ab-sorbing new ideas and knowledge, and discussing it among themselves after-wards. It is their way of acquiring "culture".

But it is also a way of acquiring mass-produced minds. If you read the same things that everyone else is reading, listen to the same things, talk about the same things . . . you're going to think the same things.

THE American woman has courage.

If her marriage has gone irretriev-ably wrong, she has the courage to cut her losses and try again. Or, if there is still some hope, she will admit there are difficulties and go to a Psycho-logical Clinic to try and get them straightened out.

She has the courage to try new things when she is old—to take up an entirely new career if need be.

She has the courage—just as we have—to turn out and be the bread-winner if things are really bad.

She has the courage to fight for what she wants—man or job. You'll seldom hear her say, "Oh, what's the use?"

She knows she has what it takes; she knows there's a place for her in her country. And she means to fill it well.

Entertaining the Allies

'If, as part of your war effort, you have decided to help entertain some of our allies during their leaves, you will probably find them interesting and charming, but sometimes baffling, too.' (Woman and Beauty, November 1943)

With troops from so many countries stationed in Britain, the magazines saw it as their duty to advise women on how to make them feel welcome. This article in *Woman and Beauty* pointed out that women should not be offended if Allied troops talked about how much better things were in their own countries:

'… remember how homesick they are. This sort of remark is really made less to impress you than to give them the pleasure of recalling the good things of their own country.'

And forget your British reserve — be prepared to ask them questions:

'… it's only the English who find personal questions, even if they're not particularly intimate, rude. Continental people will like it, if you ask questions. They feel it's an indication of your interest.'

But do make an effort to find out something about their countries:

'It's a help, of course when talking to foreigners, to know a little geography. "Where exactly is Czecho-Slovakia?" is not a promising start to a conversation.'

And make a particular effort when talking to people from 'the Dominions':

'We may be excused from knowing about Central Europe, but we really ought to know about our Empire.'

Remember also that Slavs are unpunctual, and all foreigners may write beautiful love letters on one hour's acquaintance and then forget to mention that they will be turning up for the weekend with two extra friends.

The fact of having a language in common did not necessarily make social relations with the Americans any easier. Robert Arbid, an American soldier, explained this for *Woman's Journal* in March 1944:

'It was no surprise to us to find that what we had been speaking all these years was not English after all! But it was a distinct shock to find that almost no one in Britain spoke the language either.

We had seen so many films with English actors speaking in well-modulated tones … that we had the impression that all Britons spoke as do Herbert Marshall, Ronald Colman or Greer Garson … We were amazed to find that wherever we went in England the people used their own peculiar language, something akin to English, but entirely new to our ears.'

And British women were warned not to make fun of the way the Americans spoke. A *Good Housekeeping* article from October 1944, 'The funny thing is US', pointed out the tactlessness of the English who referred to American accents as difficult to understand, and suggested how useful it would be to learn the most common differences between 'British' and 'American' English.

An article in *Good Taste* in December 1942, 'A Dough Boy goes visiting', contrasted the reception 'dough boys', or GIs, had in two different English homes. In the first the English host and hostess prattled on about Niagara Falls (despite the fact that one GI was from Texas and the other from Florida), and then they commented on such controversial American topics as the colour bar, lynchings and gangsterism. In the second home, however, the Americans found their hosts genuinely interested in their respective backgrounds; they let them pitch in and help, and introduced them to friends with similar interests.

When reading through these and the many other similar articles it is easy to end up with the impression that the troops stationed in Britain were a bunch of lonely men, far from home, just looking for a chance to spend a friendly evening with a nice English family, drinking tea, playing cards or talking about life back in Wichita, Adelaide, Bratislava or wherever. But, on careful scrutiny, the magazines reveal that they were not unaware of the more intimate side of relationships between the rude soldiery and the local female population; the world of furtive encounters in the blackout, and of women who, for a taste of glamour or companionship, gave the troops a particularly warm welcome.

Love and the Allies

The most significant difference beween the British and their visitors from overseas, as the magazines saw it, was in their attitudes to relationships between men and women. In *Woman and Beauty* of November 1943, women were warned that:

'Misunderstanding, due to different customs, may arise in more serious ways. It's fairly safe to say that men usually assume women of a different nationality to have laxer morals than their own.'

Men from Catholic countries, it was said, might be misled by the early use of Christian names, and:

'You don't say "darling" unless you really feel affectionate; and you don't permit casual love-making as part of the evening's entertainment. If you do all these things it is assumed that you are prepared to embark on serious love-making, which the average English girl is not. This often leads to misunderstandings, and the idea that "foreigners are badly behaved" is held by both sides.'

Americans, on the other hand, were *more* likely to use terms of endearment and expect some show of affection early on. This prompted one English girl to contact Leonora Eyles for advice:

Goodnight kiss
'My friend and I go to dances where there are a lot of very nice Americans. They see us home and want to kiss me goodnight. We told them that girls here think it cheap to kiss on such a slight acquaintance, and they seem really hurt, saying that in the States boys always kiss girls goodnight. We don't want to hurt them, but what do we do?'

'Well, I think they should take your explanation, and will probably like and respect you all the more for your exclusiveness. If you liked to be kissed there is no harm in it, provided you don't let the boys get silly and excited about you.' (*Woman's Own*, 24th March, 1943)

But these differences, whatever form they took, seemed to fascinate the women of Britain. And, wherever they came from, the visitors seemed to pay more attention to them as women. By May 1942, according to *Woman's Own*, over 300 women from the Lowlands of Scotland had married Polish soldiers. One girl, engaged to a Polish armoured truck driver, told Rosita Forbes that they were '*so noticing*':

'"More than the Scots?", I asked. "Oh, yes!" she said. "They always notice what you're wearing, and how your hair is done. And they know an awful lot about food."'

The writer went on to say that:

'Our Allies, having "invaded" our country towns and villages, are setting a new standard, they appreciate what a girl makes of her appearance, and they consider it important. The Englishman's attitude so often is: "What does it matters how you look? You'll always be yourself, and nobody else matters to me."... Our men are used to taking their girls for granted. But the "oh you look all right" attitude hasn't a chance against the detailed and intelligently expressed appreciation of our Allies.' (Woman's Own, 29th May, 1942*)*

So the Allied troops were gallant and appreciative; they had the allure of the exotic and — in the case of the Americans, certainly — they seemed to have unlimited supplies of spending money. It is perhaps not surprising that they had immense success with local women. Nor is it surprising that this success led to resentment and jealousy on the part of many British people — the men who were being spurned or abandoned, and the women who thought that their sisters were making themselves cheap.

From early on in the war women were writing to Leonora Eyles to ask her advice about their relationships with the Allied troops. And it is clear from such letters that many were worried about what people might think:

Only friendship
'My two girlfriends and I met three Canadian soldiers recently. I'm afraid they said "hello", and we just picked them up; but they are extremely nice, respectful boys and want us to go down to their camp for a day soon, to see them. Is this making ourselves cheap? We feel they are lonely and we want to cheer them up.'

'There is no harm in it, as after all you are making up a party. Colonial soldiers are often lonely and enjoy the company of girls. But don't take them too seriously; they want friends and company, but probably have girls at home waiting for them. Don't let any romantic ideas cloud your judgement, and then the friendship should bring you nothing but happiness and interest.' (*Woman's Own*, 18th May, 1940)

And women who went out with Black soldiers — whether from the West Indies or the USA — discovered more distressing forms of disapproval:

Coloured soldiers
'There are a lot of coloured soldiers in our town and I feel so sorry for them. Only the cheap sort of girls speak to them, and they are so polite and friendly. Is it alright to be friends — and I mean friendly only — with them as they are fighting for us?'

'What a problem you have raised, my dear! Personally, I would be friendly with them, but I am a middle-aged, married woman. As you say, these men are not only fighting for us, they are, like all other Allied servicemen, strangers in a strange land. It would not be fair though, either to them or to you, to form such a close friendship as might lead to romance. It is by no means a question of them being "inferior", but *different*, and, certainly today, only in the very rarest cases do such marriages succeed.' (*Woman's Own*, 12th November, 1943)

And, of course, such friendships *did* often lead to declarations of love and proposals of marriage. Leonora was often asked what she thought of the prospect of marrying and moving overseas, and the degree of approval she gave depended on the extent of cultural and other differences between the couple. In the case of a Black soldier, predictably, she was very reluctant:

Jamaican

'I am 17 and have fallen in love with a Jamaican, who is one of the best men on earth. But every time we go out together people stare and pass rude remarks. I am afraid of my parents getting to know. If you could see how he and his Jamaican friends are treated here when they have come to fight for us your blood would boil. That was why I loved him at first. If we got married we would go back to Jamaica. What do you think?'

'I thoroughly approve of your ideas, my dear girl; you are chivalrous and sane; but friendship with a coloured man is very different from marriage. I dare say this man would be everything a husband should be, but the children might hate you for having brought them into the world. This colour problem is nothing in this country; we don't meet it; but abroad it is terrible. And you must study it, and think about it before you commit yourself to what might turn out to be a tragic unhappiness for both of you.' (*Woman's Own*, 5th December, 1941)

However, to a woman who was thinking of marrying a Maltese airman she replied:

'The Maltese are Europeans, and very fine and heroic ones; also, Malta is a British island. If the boy has everything in common with you, there is no reason why you should not be happily married to him.' (*Woman's Own*, 31st October, 1941)

Everything was different, the language, the countryside—even the little book we were given to help us didn't help

Whether it got as far as marriage or not, many thousands of British women became involved in one way or another with foreign servicemen. And the group that was written about more than any other in the magazines was the Americans. This was not surprising since for British women the arrival of American GIs offered them some new excitement after nearly three years of hardship and deprivations.

When it came to relationships with Americans there were two types of women about whom the magazines were particularly concerned: the first were the 'good-time girls', who were letting down the name of Birtish womanhood; the second were the innocent ones who were likely to end up hurt.

In *Woman's Own* in February 1944 Hugh Corbett launched what he called '*An Offensive*' against the first type of girl, describing her as '*cheap, unscrupulous, totally lacking in self-respect*'. These '*noisy, vulgar women*' give visiting soldiers '*a wholly wrong impression of Englishwomen*'. In a harsh indictment of straying women, he went on to say:

'The American soldiers, if you cheapen yourself, are going to make use of you, make a fool of you. They're not going to respect you or like you. As for anything more, you can count that right out. It's despicable to take advantage of a man's loneliness. It's like cheating money out of him …

For heaven's sake treat them decently. Show them you're women, not birds of prey … What have you gained when a man's wallet is empty and his mind is full of contempt?

Remember, once he's finished the job he came here to do, that's the end of him as far as you're concerned. If you're foolish, I've a shrewd idea it's also the end of you as far as other men are concerned.

You see, men are curiously fastidious about the things they intend to keep, though they spend a lot on junk they're going to throw away.'

In May the magazine published a selection of letters from readers, many of whom agreed that such behaviour was to be regretted. But the majority of correspondents pointed out that blame was not all on one side since the American GIs appeared to be more eager to consort with '*frivolous gold-diggers*' than '*decent girls*'.

In September 1944, with the Allies fighting their way towards Berlin, the magazines could '*foresee a lot of broken hearts*', as the war came to an end. They advised girls to look upon their wartime romances as '*sentimental interludes*' and to wave him goodbye '*with no tears and no regrets*'. But for many British women their wartime romance didn't end with a wave of a handkerchief at the quayside. About 100,000 married servicemen from Allied or Dominion countries, some 80,000 going to the United States as 'GI-brides'. It is tempting to imagine them, as the Statue of Liberty came into sight, taking a quick peek at their '*Bride's Guide to the USA*'; for, stalwart to the last, the magazines were ready with advice to help their readers cope with the new life ahead.

An American Good-bye

★ ★ ★ **A United States soldier tells you what knowing you has meant to him and his friends**

THIS is one person's "good-bye, and thank you." But as one person I think I speak for many Americans who have been with you these last few years.

I speak to you without a name, because my name wouldn't add anything to what I have to say. I'm a soldier, an American soldier, who came over here in 1942 as a G.I., and where I go from here—beyond going home for a short leave —I don't know. It is rather repeating what happened to so many of us when we left the United States years ago ; we did not know where we had to go to fight the war. But sail away we did—to your country, and stayed, and learned to fight. For that you are to be pitied, because war is a hard business to learn and you have had us for such a long time.

But, whatever you had to put up with in the job of winning the war—and we were not the smallest part of that "putting up with"—you did; and, together with others, we have all won the war—the fighting part. We leave you now with peace come to the world, and all that that means. Your soldiers will be coming home to you, just as we are going home from foreign lands to our homes and families. The fighting part of the war in the Pacific is over. It was won by so many soldiers on our side—yours and ours, with the Chinese and others. It has been one world, as a famous American said a few years ago. And now that the one war that was split into two parts is over, a peace for one world can be built by all of us.

It seems a lifetime ago since we sailed away from these shores, to Europe and its many countries and peoples. We saw a lot and learned some, but mostly we just passed through, spending a night or more with strangers. But, no matter how long we stayed in one place, the people always remained strangers to us, and we to them. And at the end, to get back to England, before going on to America, was like coming home to our own country, because you never made us feel like strangers here, even from the beginning.

For a day, for a month, or for years (as some of us know) you took us in and did the best that you could, which was more than you often did for yourselves. And in the first sixty days of being away from your country—the first sixty days after D-Day—we told you how we missed you, for 25 per cent of all the letters we Americans wrote came back to you here in the United Kingdom. We wrote home.

We have had your homes, your restaurants, your pubs, your cinemas, your cars, your sports, your schools, and particularly your taxis. "Taxi" will be a call that Londoners will long remember us for.

SOME of you did not like us, and some of us did not like you. But then lots of you don't like each other. I found that out when I first came, and was stationed in South Wales. I gathered that they did not like anyone in the British Isles. I am sure that some of you have heard how the Northern Californian feels about the people who live in Southern California, and how they call themselves native sons—when it can be proved by any one from Northern California that they all came from Iowa. I, by the way, was born in Northern California and will be glad to debate the 'native son' problem with any one who will send sixpence to the nearest Red Cross and St. John Prisoner-of-War Office.

We are taking back to America with us, as wives, many thousands of your young women. Thank you for letting them come ; we shall take the best care we can of them. Their road will not be too hard, but America is not made up of Hollywoods and New Yorks. They will be lonely and homesick for you and your land and customs, just as we have always been for ours. But I can only wish for them that America is as gracious and charming as most of you have been to us ; that they won't miss the fogs, the cold weather and rain that you have. We have that kind of weather in America, too, but not all in one place.

THAT is one reason why the G.I. has grumbled about your climate. He knows only one part of the United States, and compared what he found here with what he knew there.

Do not forget us, because we shall not forget you. Letters will be our bridge until something better comes along. We have learned in these many years of being away from home that mail from our families and friends is the thing that kept us going in spirit ; so write to us and we will answer. This will keep us together in the peace years that lie ahead.

They gave us soldiers—yours and ours— the job of winning the war, but the job we really would like to have is the keeping of the peace, as civilians. And the years we have spent with you here have taught us one way of keeping it. That is, knowing you and your way of life. Some of us will be back to live with you when we can bring our families. I hope that you will enjoy having us for good.

As an American soldier, I'd like to say, in saying good-bye to you, that the citizens of this country won the war with us. I know it and want to add, in all humility, bless you, and thank you for it.

F. H. P. C.

The magazines discouraged people from looking backwards. And on the rare occasions when they did refer to pre-war Britain there was little in the way of nostalgia. In May 1942, when *Good Housekeeping* invited readers to say what they had been doing three years previously, few spoke with regret of their peacetime existence. One woman had been living in a smart flat in Cairo, with a maid and servant boy to help her, but found more satisfaction working in a YMCA canteen; another, despite having lost her husband in 1940, declared that she was '*neither unhappy nor cast-down*', since she had '*every confidence in our splendid Forces*'.

As for the disappearance of pre-war treats, this was seen as a source of humour rather than of regret. In October 1940, A G Macdonnell wrote for *Good Housekeeping* about 'luxuries it is a pleasure to do without'. But attempts such as these to make women look positively — or at the worst, wryly — at the differences between the pre-war world and that of wartime were rare compared with those articles which looked ahead to the new day of peace:

'Looking back isn't only a silly waste of time now; it's a positive danger. Look forward with enormous hope to the future.' (Woman's Own,, 18th January 1941)

Discussion of the post-war world went on almost from the outbreak of the war. As early as November 1939 Pamela Frankau was urging readers of *Weldon's Ladies' Journal* to:

'... aim for the end of it! For the end of war ... Guess at the good things that will come after ... Say to yourself, "I intend to come out of this war a bigger, a better and a more useful person than I was when I went into it".'

So the themes of self-improvement and of a better life after the war were established early on. And as the war progressed space was increasingly given over to articles with titles such as 'And when it's over?', 'Tomorrow's Citizens', and 'Planning for the Future'. Nobody seemed to think that the pre-war world was worth recreating. '*The war cannot last forever*', said *Woman's Magazine* in April 1940:

'... it should be the duty of every responsible citizen to give some thought to the problem of reconstruction, otherwise we shall fall back into the "bad old days".'

This particular article had been prompted by the arrival of thousands of working class evacuee children whose pitiful appearance made their mostly middle class hosts aware of:

NOW AND THEN

Amusing Comparisons
BY GRETA LAMB

Your Hairdresser

THEN : ' Good-morning, madam—you forgot to make an appointment ? Never mind, we can fit you in. Come this way, please, madam. Now let me wrap you up in nice hot towels ; we've just had in dozens of these new peach ones —do you like them ? Now what friction would you like—they're all French ? We've got lots of new make-up in ; I'll bring you some to see. Here are all the latest magazines ; just call if you get too hot, and I'll bring you coffee presently.'

NOW! ' Have you brought your own towel, setting lotion and pins ? No ? Then I'm afraid it is quite impossible . . .'

Your Butcher

THEN : '' Ah, good-day, madam. No, don't get out of your car—let me come to you ! Sirloin ? Yes. Six kidneys, and a nice saddle of mutton for the week-end ? Before nine o'clock ? Right, I'll send the van up specially.'

NOW: ' No offal ! '

Your Stocking Counter

THEN : ' Good-afternoon, moddom. Stockings ? These are a very good line ; pure silk, fully fashioned, for three-and-eleven, in nutshell, blush tan, cokernut, plover, or smoke brown. Or would you prefer some of these finest crêpe ? They come in all sizes and shades at four-and-eleven. A dozen pairs of nine and a half ? Now, would you like them sent ?'

NOW : ' The only stocking we have in the place is this extra-coarse, ersatz, mud lisle. Eight-inch only.'

Your Chocolate Shop

THEN : ' Box ? Loose assorted, or slab ? Peppermint creams ? Nutty caramels ? Chocolate toffee ? Langues du chat ? Liqueurs ? Nougat Montelimar ? Edinburgh Rock ? Butterscotch Dragées ? Truffles ? Mixed candies ? Marzipan shapes ? Lemon and orange creams ? Toffee brazils ? Almond whirls ? A four-pound box of chocolates—and two pounds of candy. Thank you.'

NOW : ' Two ounces of Jelly Babies ? Have you brought your own bag ? Why, you've no coupons left . . .'

Your Pet Garage

THEN : ' We got your telephone message, and I've brought this car for you to have while I take yours away for the afternoon. Oiled and greased ? Yes, madam, and a wash and polish. Shall I fill her up with oil and petrol ? I'll bring her back by five.'

NOW : ' Fares, please ! '

'... the fact that many thousands of human beings lived in conditions which no self-respecting individual in more fortunate surroundings would tolerate for his dog and cat.'

People had been writing about such matters — and in similar words — since Victorian times; but it took the social mingling of war to bring the realities home to many people who were in a position to push for change.

Women realised, as never before, that they had a chance to make their views felt. And this growth of social consciousness manifested itself in the stream of articles and letters debating each aspect of life in post-war Britain. The proposals for legislation — particularly concerning social welfare and education — were examined, dissected and commented on. New towns were planned, new housing designed, new school curricula drawn up. So much space was devoted to these matters, indeed, that the editor of *The Lady* commented in February 1943 that:

THE TOWN OF THE FUTURE

■ There can be no doubt that our future towns will be as different from those we knew before the war as a radiogram is different from our first crystal set. And just as our admiration for the elegance and the greater efficiency of the modern does not in any way impair our affection for the old-fashioned, so we need have no regrets when we come to live in the town of the future.

Towns and cities damaged by the war are already considering their rebuilding plans. Residential districts, we are told, will be designed on the garden city principle of villas or semi-detached houses each with its own garden; or ten-storey blocks of flats surrounded by communal lawns, flower walks and rose arbours. It is gratifying to note that experts are planning for a ' green and pleasant land ' with plenty of space, light and fresh air. In the past, towns and cities have straggled and sprawled, capturing parts of the countryside with the same inevitable disappointment as the caging of a wild bird. The town of the future will be erect and compact, with the trees, the grass and the flowers of the country-side brought to its front doors. Schools and playgrounds for the children will be included as an integral part of the communal plan. These will be so positioned that children will not have to cross main roads on their way to school. The Shopping Centre, in view of its supreme importance to housewives, will receive very special attention. Architects, remembering the British climate, will develop the arcade principle for greater all-the-year-round convenience, specially appreciated on wet shopping days.

Ancient buildings will be restored and records and relics of a glorious past preserved. The town of the future will retain its cherished character, its unique individuality and its historical associations, yet it will sparkle and shine in its new pride.

New buildings, new services, new homes, rising up from the ruins of the old, will make for happier family life in Britain after the war. The better environment will invite us to make the most of our longer leisure and will encourage us to seek new interests within the pleasant, comfortable and healthy precincts of our new homes.

Pears

'There is something vaguely disturbing about this comprehensive planning for the future. How warmly the mind responds to something that has not been planned, but has simply grown, such as an old village street or market square.'

In no area was the debate more intense than in that dealing with the place of women themselves in the Brave New World. And one of the first questions was, what should be their role in the peace-making process.

Back in January 1940, in an article for *Good Housekeeping* called 'Making Peace', St. John Ervine stated that '*the day on which a war begins should also be the day when the peace terms are considered*'. And as the war went on the magazines began to demand that women be involved in the peace-making process. '*We women must be there when they make the peace this time*', wrote Storm Jameson for *Woman's Journal* in September 1943. While *The Lady* at the end of 1943 said that:

'All over this country women's organisations are determined to ensure that their sex shall get adequate representation on post-planning committees. They do not forget that women played a very small part in the peace proposals of the First World War, because they were then unenfranchised, but a quarter of a century's political experience has enabled them to contribute intelligent service to world affairs.'

In the same article it was reported that Anthony Eden had refused to allow any discussion of the right of women to enter the diplomatic and consular services until after the war, an act which the magazine described as '*an extraordinarily short-sighted policy, when women will be needed in those Services to help in international reconstruction*'.

It appeared, according to *The Lady*, that the Government was reluctant to give women an opportunity to speak their mind in public. By the autumn of 1943 there were nearly eight million women in the Services or paid employment (plus a further million working for the WVS) and, as a mark of appreciation, the Government invited:

'... over 6,000 selected members of women's organisations ... to a mass meeting in the Albert Hall. The Prime Minister was present, with members of the Cabinet. They addressed the meeting and questions were invited on paper! So far, the written replies to these have been disappointing.'

It is fascinating to speculate what kind of debate might have ensued in the Albert Hall if questions had been allowed from the floor and if Churchill and his ministers had been forced to respond to them. But such a forum was to be denied them. The women's magazines, in fact, provided practically the only outlet for such debate. How, then did they see the post-war roles of women?,

The standard view is that the Government geared its propaganda machine first, when the exigencies of war demanded it, to persuading women to go out to work, and then, with peace in sight, to encouraging women to step back into their traditional roles. In this

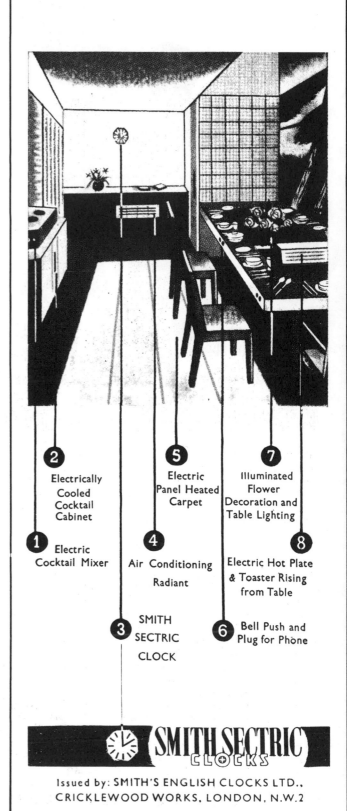

THE ALL ELECTRIC HOME OF THE FUTURE
No. 2 *THE DINING ROOM*

2 Electrically Cooled Cocktail Cabinet

5 Electric Panel Heated Carpet

7 Illuminated Flower Decoration and Table Lighting

1 Electric Cocktail Mixer

4 Air Conditioning Radiant

8 Electric Hot Plate & Toaster Rising from Table

3 SMITH SECTRIC CLOCK

6 Bell Push and Plug for Phone

SMITH SECTRIC CLOCKS

Issued by: SMITH'S ENGLISH CLOCKS LTD., CRICKLEWOOD WORKS, LONDON, N.W.2

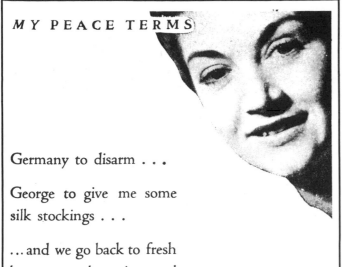
latter aim they were aided by the forces of big business, dangling the carrots of fitted kitchens, all washable tops and glistening striplighting, chock-a-block with the latest in refrigerators and washing-machines.

Following this line it is tempting to see the magazines as tools of the Government. After all, they did support the various official campaigns, they did chivvy women into doing their bit, and they only kept in business by selling advertising space both to Government departments and to the purveyors of the post-war Aladdin's cave of consumer goods.

The fact is that women were uncertain what their future roles should be, and this uncertainty was reflected in the magazines. Some magazines, it is true, were more conservative than others and tended to uphold the more traditional values. But even these wavered, no doubt reflecting the changing opinions and experiences both of their contributors and of their readers.

Good Housekeeping is the best example of a magazine which appeared to become more radical as the war went on. In 1942 it threw itself wholeheartedly into the campaign to persuade women to leave their homes and enter the Services and factories, but at the same time it made it clear that this would be for the

duration only. In an article it published that year, 'Finishing School 1942 Model', Mary Gray wrote of the way that war work would help women to be better housewives once peace had been restored:

'It'll teach them method and poise . . . After this war you're going to have far fewer women grumbling that they are run off their legs morning, noon and night in their own homes . . . They'll have a richer comradeship with their husbands because they'll really know what a man has been up against when he comes home and says "I've had a bad day".'

So women were not to get excited about earning their living. It would end when the men came home, and they'd be better chums because of the experience. And yet this same magazine, in August 1945, printed an article called 'When the Girls Come Home' in which Louise Morgan wrote that:

'Letters which reach me from Servicewomen have two things in common — an intense eagerness to be "back home", and a worried preoccupation with "getting a good civvy job". Girls who volunteered for the factories or were directed into them show much the same frame of mind . . . Whether on the uniformed or the overalled front, they won the war equally with men, serving their country as devotedly and dangerously, and they have earned their share of jobs.'

It is clear that many women disliked the idea of going back to whatever they had left, all those years before, whether this was to dependence on parents or on a husband. Some missed the camaraderie of a life which brought them into contact with other women. One wrote to *Woman's Own* in June 1944 to complain that:

'Coming back to civilian life after being in the ATS for 2 years — I had to leave owing to the birth of my baby — I notice a difference in people. In the Service, one finds comradeship and friendliness, which I am certain will stand for a lifetime. As a civilian, I am finding that queue-pushing, money-grabbing and self are the most important factors; while lots of girls try to shrink joining the Services, and try to obtain a nice, reserved job near mother. Little do they know what they are missing!'

And such letters also came from women whose work had not taken them away from home. One 19 year old firewoman told Leonora Eyles of *Woman's Own* in January 1945:

'I love the work and have put myself into it; although I long for the war to stop all the suffering, I dread it because it means my going back to the old emptiness of life. Can you help me to sort out my ideas so that I can do something of equal value afterwards?'

Little practical advice could be given to such readers, though the editor of *Woman's Own* in October 1945 suggested that women in this position should:

'Carry forward the grand things you have learned in your courageous war service and keep this new feeling of community living. Take it with you when the war is over to the building of a new world in

My Post-war Aims —

What are the Service girls thinking Below is a frank statement of the W.A.A.F. 897002 when she discards stripes, and lives her own and planning about the future? personal dreams and aspirations of her uniform, with its corporal's life as ELLA THOMPSON

W.A.A.F. 897002

Post-war plans are news. There is talk of housing schemes, employment for all, new industries, civil aviation, a revolutionary medical reform and social services hitherto unknown outside dreams of Utopia.

What are the personal post-war plans of W.A.A.F. 897002, a single unit in the British population, a relatively unimportant member of a large important community? Are these plans important and worth expressing and formulating? Yes, because in a democracy the individual is important.

My plans are simple and ordinary. My aim is a return to a sane and sweet normality in an England at peace in a world at peace.

Normality is my personal slogan.

When all the fighting is done and the enemy War is laid to rest, I want to return to a civilian status to lead a full, abundant, normal life.

I want to marry, for marriage is the aim, confessed or unconfessed, of the healthy normal girl. I aspire to being a good cook and housewife, one who makes a house a *home*, and can turn her hand to distempering and painting, dressmaking and clothes renovating, and who can tackle all the repair jobs that constantly crop up in a house.

Being in the W.A.A.F. has shown me the comradeship that can exist between men and women working together with one aim, so I want to be more than a housewife. I shall be a comrade and partner to my husband, a helpmate in the full sense of the word, sharing his work anxieties as well as sharing with him my domestic troubles; sharing his intellectual and political interests as well as his emotional life. We shall be lovers and, what is more, friends and co-workers.

Living a community life as a Waaf has taught me to be tolerant of other people's opinions and patient with other failings than my own. It has given me a deeper understanding of human nature and differing personalities. I want to carry this patience and understanding forward into my own marriage, and try to harmonize, with my husband's co-operation, our two temperaments, so that we shall truly be one in spirit.

I want children, because marriage without children is like a garden without flowers or fruit—a waste land. Scientists are complaining of the falling birthrate, and say that to preserve the balance of population there should be 3½ children from each couple. I shall do a little more than my duty and have four. I hope I shall have them early in my married life, when I can give them companionship and bring a younger outlook to bear on their youthful troubles.

I have definite views, too, on the upbringing and education of my children. I have never seen so many fine and bonny babies as now. So in post-war days I shall follow the advice given to war-time mothers, and shall also avail myself of the advice and practical help given by ante-natal and baby clinics.

But equally important with the building of my babies' bodies will be the training of their minds. As well as elementary training in cleanliness and good manners, I want to inculcate a sense of responsibility and teach them to make decisions for themselves, so that when they grow up they will be good citizens for a democracy. I shall do this by early giving them little responsibilities in the home, such as helping with the dusting and washing up. They will be allowed some choice in the matter of clothes to encourage in them a dress sense. They will have a reasonable amount of pocket money, but be expected to save and give to others. I shall provide them with a large library because carefully guided reading is a real education.

They will receive sex education from the beginning, because I intend never to answer a child's question with a lie or "story"; they must have confidence in me and a real respect for the truthful word. This is not a duty I shall leave to school teachers or to chance.

I never mean to use the word "Don't", but the positive creative word "*Do*". Rather than continuous nagging, forbidding them doing naughty things, I shall divert their natural energies into good channels by providing them with plenty of good things to *do*.

I want my children to be frank and easily conversational,

but courteous and considerate, well-informed but not priggish, free individuals with a sense of responsibility.

In all this I shall watch myself carefully that I do not become the repressive, dominating mother or the selfishly sentimental type. My children must be free. When they are young adolescents I hope I shall have earned their confidence so that they will come to me unabashed with the many problems of this time. They will be encouraged to bring home their friends of the opposite sex. I hope I shall never be so old that I forget my own youth.

I aim at being useful to my country as a good wife and mother, but as we shall be living in a new labour-saving house, and as each village and town will have its nursery school and kindergarten, there will be no reason why I should not also have a career.

I cannot aspire to greatness or fame, as I have no special talents, but I have had a commercial education, was a shorthand typist before volunteering, and in the W.A.A.F. have learned teleprinting. I have also learned that in a great organization like the R.A.F. even a humble job well done is important and that the smallest cog is necessary.

In civil life I shall fill a small niche somewhere in business as a part-time typist, teleprinter or secretary, but shall perform my task with the same sense of duty and with the same conscientiousness that in my Service days was expected of each member of the ranks. Having a field of interest outside the home, I should make a more interesting wife and a mother of broader understanding.

I hope I shall never lose the sense of citizenship I have felt while in the Service. Being a citizen of a democratic country carries with it responsibilities as well as privileges. I shall have a vote, and must take a lively interest in politics and topical affairs to know how to use it wisely.

I intend to take an interest in local government, because democracy is not only government *for* the people but *by* the people, and that involves me personally.

As a wife, mother and citizen, it is my duty to develop my intellect. My intelligence is something basic that I cannot alter, but on that I can develop my intellectual attainments. I intend to use the reference section of the County Libraries and hope to attend at least one class organized by the Workers' Educational Association, in a cultural subject like Musical Appreciation or Literature, or a social subject like Economics or Sociology.

But all work and no play makes a dull wife and a tired mother, so I shall continue to play. I shall cycle and hike, dance and skate with my husband, and later teach the children. We shall find time for the theatre and opera house. Thus I shall keep my youthful spirit, although my body shall of necessity age.

I intend to keep up the international friendships formed during war years, not only by correspondence but by visits abroad in holiday times, and by interchange of children when they reach student age. In these personal ways, international understanding will grow so that my children will realize that they are members not only of a country but of a larger group, *the world*, and that all people are brothers.

I never want to forget the sacrifice of the dead of this war, of the men I have known personally, who with a joke on their lips have courted sure death. To quote Rupert Brooke:

These laid the world away; poured out the red
Sweet wine of youth; gave up the years to be
Of work and joy; and that unhoped serene
That men call age: and those who would have been
Their sons, they gave, their immortality.

The dead have handed on their heritage and we have a responsibility so to live and speak, to act and teach, that peace will be, not an ideal to fight for, but an abiding reality.

I cannot make laws and pass reforms, but by living a normal, abundant life I can help in the general return to sanity, and peace and goodwill on earth.

which women share equally with men, so that it may be real and lasting.'

Yet *Woman's Own* had suggested earlier in the war that women should have the right to go on working. In July 1942, Rosita Forbes, after months lecturing to Servicewomen, wrote that:

'... few of them think that marriage alone will be sufficient occupation. All over the country I listen to girls saying "I'll have to go on working" or "I couldn't do without a job".'

And she went on to say that this attitude might lead to:

'... a new understanding between men and women in the future. Husbands will find it easier to understand when their wives demand jobs; the "I don't like to think of my wife working, when I'm quite able to support her" idea will probably disappear.'

And other magazines looked equally directly at the roles of men and women in the post-war world. In an excellent article in March 1944 *The Lady* asked four leading women *'What have women to look forward to? What jobs will there be for us after the war, what chances of security, what prospect of a settled home?'*. Dame Anne Loughlin, Vice-Chairman of the TUC, replied that:

'Men who have been replaced by women for the duration of the war should have their jobs back afterwards. But once that is done, I want to see all trades and professions open equally to men and women, at the same rate for the job. It's mainly because women were regarded as "cheap labour" that men used to resent their presence in industry.'

Mrs. V Laughton-Mathews, Director of the WRNS, agreed that:

'... jobs should not be labelled "man's (or woman's) work". The individual should be able to follow the line he or she is best fitted for ... There should be an end to the unnatural cleavage between the "career woman" and the home-maker.'

As the war approached its end the magazines seemed, on the whole, to believe that women deserved to have equality of opportunity but considered that many — perhaps most — women still looked upon being a housewife as their main purpose in life. Because of this they felt able to campaign for greater women's rights (including the provision of nursery schools, family allowances and so on) while at the same time encouraging those women who wished to opt for domesticity. Thus *Woman and Beauty*, for example, saw no contradiction in running a 'Post-war Career Planning Series' while at the same time printing the views of Margaret Lane who was convinced that *'the rebirth of home life is what 99 out of every 100 of us are living for'*. Her article, from November 1943, begins with the author overhearing a conversation between two ATS:

'... who were discussing their chances of jobs after the war. They were serious, intelligent and very worried. They evidently felt that they were part of

a vast horde which one day would be let loose upon the labour market to take part in a terrifying scramble. "It'll be bad enough for the men," said one of them, "but at least they'll have a better chance than us." Then, after some further gloomy discussion, she added, "of course the married women'll have to give up their jobs. It's only right."'

She went on to say that this conversation made her realise:

'... that there must be something radically wrong with our houses and all the things that go to make up home if after the war married women still prefer to work in other people's offices rather than in their own homes. The principle is wrong. Instead of married women being compelled to give up their jobs, home life must be made so attractive that they will want to get back to it just as fast as they can.'

In the rest of the article she suggests how life at home can be improved, since *'if it is a woman's place, it has got to be made really fit for the post-war woman'*. And she ends with a plan to be followed by *'every married woman who is looking forward to setting up house after the war'*.

In November 1944, Ella Thompson was asked by *Woman's Magazine* to write about 'My post-war aims'. The first of these was, *'a return to a sane and sweet normality in an England at peace in a world at peace. Normality is my personal slogan'*. This meant marriage, of course, *'for marriage is the aim, confessed or unconfessed, of the healthy, normal girl'*. But she will be an extra-special wife, since she aspires to be able to *'turn her hand to distempering and painting, dressmaking and clothes renovating, and ... tackle all the repair jobs that constantly crop up in a house'*.

Her life in the WAAF will have taught her the meaning of comradeship, allowing her to be a *'a comrade and partner'* to her husband, *'sharing his work anxieties as sharing with him my domestic worries'*. She will be able to do some work outside the home since they will be living *'in a new labour-saving house and ... each village and town will have its own nursery and kindergarten'*. She intends to *'fill a small niche somewhere in business as a part-time typist, teleprinter or secretary'*, and hopes that such a field of interest will make her, *'a more interesting wife and a mother of broader understanding'*.

As the article, reproduced on page 124, shows, her wartime experiences had equipped her to be a 'superwife'; the mixture as before, but bringing in extra cash, doing more jobs about the house and sympathising more with her husband's problems than did the average pre-war wife.

While Ella Thompson was serving in the WAAF, the distinguished writer Monica Dickens was working in a factory. In March 1944 she wrote in an article for *Woman's Journal* called 'Making the Most of Life', that whatever women intended to do after the war, at least they would have met new people and profited by new experiences. And some of these experiences would help them in their post-war life. To Service women she said that:

Making the MOST of LIFE

By Monica DICKENS

Perhaps the war has taught you how to mix with other people—how to enjoy tea at all hours—how to bicycle? Well, chalk it all up as experience

THERE are certain words which, to the end of my life, I shall never be able to see or hear without being instantly reminded of this war. "Potatoes" is one. "Waste" is another. You can't open a paper or walk down a street without being warned by some Ministry not to waste fuel, bread, paper, money, rubber, scrap iron or the railway companies' time. Waste has become our national sin.

The only thing which we may all squander to our hearts' content is opportunity. There are opportunities now which, if this is really the War to end wars, will never come again. You may be doing the right thing for your country by sitting in semi-darkness, eating cold potato cakes and trying to get clean in five inches of tepid bath water, but if you're wasting opportunity you're not doing right by yourself.

War is a waste of time when life is so short. But the war is with us whether we like it or not, and it's just because life is so short that it's important to use the war to your own advantage. I'm not talking about the Black Market; I simply mean not profiteering but profiting —profiting by experiences which we should never have had if we had lived out our lives in Peace.

Lives are revolutionized, careers nipped in the bud, families are separated, their members scattered across continents, you yourself, perhaps, have been whisked away from everything that stood for stability and security and are living in an environment both physically and mentally alien to your nature. Well, at least you've got out of a rut.

I don't want to sound smug, and I'm not sure that I practise what I preach, because I get as browned-off as anyone else. I live for weeks in a kind of suspended animation with one eye on the crawling clock and the other on the even slower crawling end of the war, which will enable me to get on with my own life again.

This is being thoroughly wasteful, and when I catch myself at it I try to remind myself of all the things I'm getting now which I should never have known if there had not been a war. Friendship is the chief of these; meeting an entirely new set of people and getting to know them with that intimacy that only comes from working side by side and getting tired together. Being in a factory is something that probably would never have happened to one in peace time. Chalk it up as experience, even if you intend to grab your hat and scramble the moment the bells ring for victory. At least you know what it feels like to punch a clock, to be a number and to queue up on Friday evenings for a pay packet with "GO TO IT" stamped on the outside.

You know the difference between a foreman, a charge hand and a section leader. You have penetrated some of the mysteries of Trade Unionism, you have savoured the atmosphere of noise, of free and easy Christian names and backchat, of the good honest hunger that makes you only too ready for tea at the peculiar hour of half past two.

I even have a glimmering of how an internal combustion engine works—a revelation, this. Many women have discovered a hitherto unsuspected bent for engineering and may go on with it after the war. I'm not one of these, but at least I've learned how to undo a tight nut and can change a fuse in the home and even do elementary plumbing repairs.

You're in one of the Services? Well, it's obvious what an experience that is : something to tell your grandchildren about, though I can't guarantee that they'll listen! Whatever your Service job, you've probably learned something that will stand you in good stead after the war : cooking, typing, mathematics, driving, catering, cobbling, engineering. You've learned how to take orders and how to give them—neither of them easy. You're learning how to handle people and how to take responsibility in a way that will equip you for a peace-time job that requires organizing ability. Another thing, which goes for everyone whose war job takes them out of doors—you're fitter than you ever were in your life. Hardly any of us got enough fresh air in the old days.

By the way, I've discovered the use of my legs. Before the war I never dreamed of walking if I could take a penny bus ride. I've discovered bicycling too, and the bicyclist's London, which is full of unsuspected hills and bumps in the road. I know the pillar boxes where the slot is placed so that you can post a letter without dismounting ; I know the interesting meteorological fact that no matter which way you go the wind is always against you.

The point about the experiences one has gained in this war is that one must be conscious of them while they are actually happening. This applies to peace time too, to life in general. To my mind, the secret of getting the most out of life is to be conscious of the present moment. Many people are so busy brooding nostalgically over things past or making plans for future events which may never even come off that they miss the third dimension of time completely and live their life almost entirely in retrospect and anticipation.

"I was happy when . . ." and "I shall be happy when . . ." are not the same as : "Now, at this moment, I am happy. I am enjoying this. This is interesting." Be aware of yourself doing a thing at the moment when you are doing it. See yourself in the picture if you like, dramatize yourself. I'm convinced that it's the way to get full measure from life.

In this war, nearly everyone has been faced, perhaps for the first time, with the

Married people will try to make intelligent homes for their children.

possibility of sudden death. Instead of being just a thing that happened to other people, accidents that you read about quite detachedly in the papers, it suddenly became a thing that could happen to you, personally. I think it's made us value life more. It's popularly supposed that when you think you are going to be killed, all the sins of your life flash by

Monica Dickens, writer, factory worker, nurse, great grand-daughter to Charles, appreciates the opportunities the war has brought her.

you. My own experience is that when the bomb that I thought had my name on it came warbling past my ear, I simply thought : "What a pity. All the things I wanted to do, and now I can't do them."

I think most people now have a heightened perception of the importance of putting a lot into and getting a lot out of life. There won't be so much frittering after the war.

Married people, having seen family life broken up and its whole survival threatened, are determined to put all they've got into making a united, intelligent home where children can grow into the kind of people who prevent wars instead of making them. People who have been away from home won't be heard complaining about the boredom of domesticity.

A lot of people, made geography-conscious for the first time by taking an intelligent interest in world news, are going to travel, and it looks as if travel facilities for everyone, instead of for the moneyed, leisured few, is one of the ideals which we are going to see made concrete. There are sure to be lectures and all kinds of public services for teaching us about other countries after the war—perhaps our women will develop a taste for acquiring knowledge and culture and become as fond of lectures as their American cousins !

Talking of the moneyed, leisured few, and always supposing that they have money after the war, will their women-folk, to many of whom war has brought their first job, want to return to leisure ? I doubt it. Since they've been working, many of them have discovered why they were not happy before. In spite of the blitz and war strain, there are far fewer nervous feminine disorders about.

The secret of happiness for a woman is to be creating something. That was what she was made for. If it's not babies, it must be something else—cooking perhaps, dressmaking, art, literature, engineering, gardening—she's bound to feel restless and unfulfilled unless she is creating. If her job is non-creative, then she must try to find for herself a hobby or outside interest in which her hands or her brain can create.

When I was first grown up I couldn't think what was wrong with me. I was restless, dissatisfied, impossible in the home, anti-social. I felt stale and old and dull ; I brooded over my appearance, was depressed by its defects and capable of being plunged into infectious gloom at a party if one side of my hair was not right !

Writing my first book was an agony, as witness how badly it was written. My brain, disused since I left school, was rusty, and it was a long time before it would tick over at all. Gradually, as things loosened up, as the pleasure in creating something, however trivial, began to take hold of me and as new interests crowded round my tentative steps into the world of books and authors and publishers, I began to feel properly alive for the first time for years.

I'm twenty-eight now and I feel eighteen, whereas at eighteen I felt more like forty. I've discovered the satisfaction of creative work.

Modesty is a virtue in women, but diffidence and lack of self-respect and of awareness of your own potentialities is a sin against yourself. The parable of the ten talents is one of the basic laws of life. You are put into the world as a personality, unique. There is only one "I" for everybody. It is your sacred duty to develop that personality, to have a proper and grateful pride in its talents and to see that they don't wither from disuse. No one else can do it for you although people may influence you and friendship and love may help you to justify your creation by making the most of life and of yourself.

'... you've probably learned something that will stand you in good stead after the war ... You've learned how to take orders and how to give them — neither of them easy. You're learning how to handle people and how to take responsibility in a way that will equip you for a peace-time job that requires organizing ability.'

And she believed that few women of the pre-war privileged class would want to return to a life of leisure. To many of these people the war brought their first job, and:

'... since they've been working, many of them have discovered why they were not happy before. In spite of the blitz and war-strain, there are far fewer nervous feminine disorders about.'

As for Monica Dickens herself, the war had given her things she could never have experienced otherwise — friendship, knowing what it is like to punch a time-clock, new skills, an insight into a different world. To all those many women in her position she said:

ENGLAND'S NEED

When this war is over
  England, then, will need
Men to plough her uplands,
  Men to sow her seed,
Men to guide her commerce,
  Men who will behave
Nobly for the England
  Their comrades died to save.

When this war is over—
  When broken every yoke—
England will need millions
  Of kind, home-loving folk,
Who, around the fireside,
  Will England's story tell,
And make their children eager
  To serve our England well.

When this war is over
  England will need most
Women led and governed
  By God the Holy Ghost;
Women strong of purpose,
  Women great of heart,
Who will help our England
  To play her queenly part:

Women for restating
  The truths which made her wise,
Women for rekindling
  The faith within her eyes,
Women for rebuilding
  Foundations all but lost,
Women who will sacrifice
  And never count the cost.

When this war is over—
  Lord! To England, then,
Give these joyous women!
  Give these mighty men!

FAY INCHFAWN

'Being in a factory is something that probably would never have happened to one in peace time. Chalk it up as experience, even if you intend to grab your hat and scramble the moment the bells ring for victory.'

And many women did intend to do just that, though we cannot be sure of the numbers. It is just not possible to establish with any degree of certainty how many women fought to keep their newly won independence after the war, how many gave it up with regret, and how many welcomed the chance to become dependent again. Certainly there were many women in each of these categories. And for every one who fought there may well have been another who gave in with relief. And this should come as no surprise. After all, for many women their wartime life had been tough, tiring and monotonous. Long days or nights in the factory, shopping for scarce foods at inconvenient times, children often farmed out to relatives or strangers. This sort of life was often abandoned with relief when the men came home.

We said earlier that women were uncertain what their future roles should be, and this uncertainty was reflected in the magazines. From the viewpoint of the 1980s it is possible to accuse the magazines of being too indecisive, of allowing space for too many, often conflicting views of what women should be aiming for. But that would be implying that they should have started off with firm convictions. This was just not possible, since none of the magazines — indeed no-one in Britain — could foresee in September 1939 just how much women would be involved in the war.

At the start of the war, it will be recalled, certain writers hoped that women would confine themselves to keeping things as normal as possible for their men away fighting. But this position had quickly to be abandoned as the war affected women in an increasingly direct way. And the magazines were hard pressed to do more than merely reflect such changes, while offering help and advice where possible.

By the summer of 1945 the nation in general, and women in particular, had been so affected that it was unthinkable that the clock could simply be turned back six years. There was little to show in the way of immediate changes. The women of 1918 had been rewarded for their war effort by being given the vote; the women of 1945 received nothing but the promises of a better life of brighter homes and consumer goods in the future. But for many women this was not enough. The freedom, independence and comradeship of the war years were considered to be obtainable in peacetime, too.

The magazines did little in the post-war period to encourage these aspirations. For the most part they contented themselves with advising women how to resume and make the most of a life of domesticity. But we must not belittle the contributions they made during the wartime years. For it was they — amid all the recipes for Victory puddings, the salvage slogans and make-up tips — who instilled in women a sense of pride in their ability to survive hardship and to undertake tasks of which, up till then, they had been judged incapable. And, as such, they have their place in the history of feminism in Britain.

ABOUT THE AUTHORS

JANE WALLER is a prolific writer of fashion books, short stories, poems and children's novels. She comes from a large family of artists and is herself a graduate of the Royal College of Art. She now divides her time equally between working as a potter and writing. This is her twelfth book, and the first she has written in association with her husband, Michael Vaughan-Rees.

MICHAEL VAUGHAN-REES's roots are in travel and communications. He has taught and lectured in most of Europe and in North Africa, and now designs specialized English language courses for overseas companies. This is his first book.

Jane and Michael have the largest private collection in Britain of women's magazines from the Second World War.